Y0-BXK-763

The Life Below the Ground

The Life

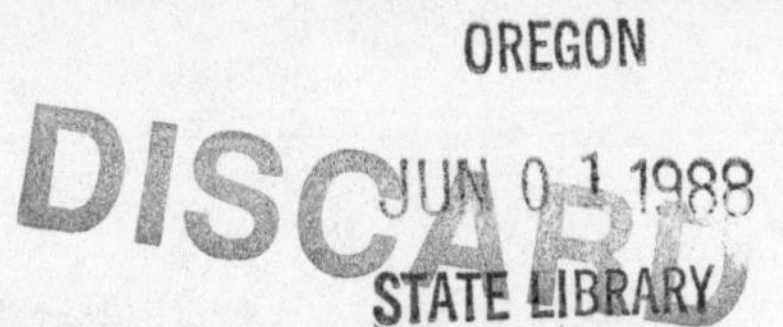

Below the Ground

A Study of the Subterranean in Literature and History

by Wendy Lesser

Faber and Faber Boston and London

For Nicholas

who shares my interest in tunnels,
subways, and holes in the ground

 Published in the United States by Faber & Faber Inc., 50 Cross Street, Winchester, Massachusetts 01890.

Library of Congress Cataloging-in-Publication Data

Lesser, Wendy.
The life below the ground.
1. Voyages to the otherworld in literature.
I. Title.
PN56.07L4 1987 809'.93372 87-9134
ISBN 0-571-12954-4

Printed in the USA.

Acknowledgments

I would like to thank the National Endowment for the Humanities, which gave me a fellowship for independent research in 1983, and the Rockefeller Foundation, which provided a luxurious month-long residency at the Bellagio Study Center in 1984. I very much appreciated and benefited from the "no strings attached" quality of both gifts.

Nobody but myself is to blame for the flaws in this book, but the following people have contributed to whatever merits it may have: John Anson, Gregory Farnham, Catherine Gallagher, Susan Gillman, Andrew Griffin, Thom Gunn, Douglas Hardy, Thomas Laqueur, Leslie Lass, Zachary Leader, Arthur Lubow, Katharine Ogden, Christopher Ricks, Timothy Seldes, Vikram Seth, and Mark Stevens. I thank them, variously, for their attentive readings, their diligent pursuit of underground materials, their astute (and sometimes severe) advice, and their help in getting the book published.

Finally, I want to thank my mother, Millicent Dillon, and my husband, Richard Rizzo, for their encouragement and friendship during the years it took me to complete this book. Without their interest in writing in general, and my writing in particular, this book would not have been written.

Contents

Introduction: Notes on the Underground

THERE ARE MANY DIFFERENT UNDERGROUNDS, AND THIS book can only be about a few of them. It is the kind of subject that tempts one to be either comprehensive or extremely specific—to produce either "The Underground in Myth and Reality" or "The Use of Underground Images in Nineteenth-Century German Prose Literature." This book is neither. Instead, it is an idiosyncratic meditation on the idea of the underground, the result of my having picked and chosen among the available undergrounds as they seemed pertinent and important.

Think for a moment simply about the underground as it manifests itself in our daily reality. There are the domestic undergrounds: cellars and basements, household plumbing, bomb shelters for those who became nervous in the 1950s. And then there are municipal undergrounds: sewage pipes and electrical systems and water mains and subway tunnels and excavations for new building construction and major foundations for skyscrapers. There are also aboveground functions that occasionally appear underground: shopping malls and convention centers and corridors that lead between buildings. And outside the city limits (sometimes even within them, though in garden-like settings) are the graveyards, where the dead are buried underground. Then, beneath the dead and the living, in older cities and other places of long settlement, are the dead civilizations: the layers of previous existence, of shard and bone and stonemasonry, which engage the archaeologist. And even beneath all these manmade undergrounds lies another subterranean world: the world of rocks, and minerals, and lava, and finally the core of the earth itself.

Some of these undergrounds—the shopping malls, the subways—are generally accessible and used all the time; others, such as the sewer pipes and water mains and graves and buried civilizations, are accessible under special circumstances to special people. But some are not accessible at all. No one has ever seen the core of the earth, or the bottom of the deepest ocean chasm, or the source of a volcano's lava. This is not to say that the barrier to accessibility remains firmly fixed. Preindustrial Europe could not have imagined the nineteenth-century coal-miners who were to burrow miles deep in the earth, nor could those miners have pictured the oil wells of the twentieth century. What this indeterminacy means is that the underground has always been situated oddly between the visible and the invisible—between that which one can see and touch in one's normal life, and that which one must accept on faith.

This may explain, in part, why the real underground I have been describing has given rise to so many fictional or imaginary undergrounds. There was, to begin with, Hades—that is, the imaginary underground is first of all the locus of death and rebirth, the place where dead souls go to be washed of their memories and returned to life on earth. In this sense, the underground is both place of origin and place of final rest. From this land of the shades developed the idea of the Christian hell—no longer the abode of the undifferentiated dead, but a place of eternal punishment for the damned alone. The notion of the underworld has always held something of mystery and terror for the living, but with Christianity the subterranean began to be equated with evil—a connotation which carries through to the present. The word "underground" is associated with poverty, with criminal activity, with the socially unacceptable. Even when a group purposely describes itself in this way (as do certain political or artistic movements), the choice signifies a rejection of the conventional notion of good, an adherence to the opposite of the accepted political code or aesthetic standard.

When I first began telling people that I was working on a book about the underground, the response was startlingly consistent and startlingly inappropriate. "Oh, you're writing about politics?" was the most frequent response, and "Oh, you're writing about pornography?" the second. It never occurred to the vast majority of my interlocutors that I might be writing about holes in the ground, and sewers, and basements, and so on.

Of course, if I were only writing about real holes in the ground, this would be a very different kind of book—a work of city planning or archaeology, possibly a book like David Macaulay's *Underground* (which, though written for children, is actually very informative for adults), or Benson Bobrick's *Labyrinths of Iron* (a wonderfully imaginative history of subways). And if I were writing about the Weather Underground or underground movies, it would be a book that didn't concern itself with tunnels or basements (except insofar as the revolutionaries hid there, or the movies were shown there). But my true interest in the underground is neither totally concrete nor totally figurative. I care about the points at which the real and the imaginary overlap—where places in the ground become hidden places in the individual or social mind, and vice versa. I am interested in the underground as a vital and responsive metaphor —not a pure figure of speech like the Weather Underground or the present-day Christian hell, but an active bringing together of two different degrees of reality.

This has partly to do with my own place in history, of course. I am too close to the Weather Underground to pay attention to it fairly, and too far away from the medieval notion of hell to "remember" its powerful connection with a geographical underworld. But I think the issue is more than just that of personal limitation. I don't think idiosyncrasy alone explains why the chapters in this book focus on a particular period of history lasting less than two centuries.

There was actually a time (we are beyond it now, and hence the inappropriateness of the usual response to my topic) when the underground had both a strongly physical and a strongly figurative meaning. I would date this period roughly from the 1790s to the 1950s—perhaps, if I were to be ridiculously specific, from the French Revolution in 1789 to the launching of the first manned space flight in 1958. Before that time, the two senses of the underground, the hole in the ground and the hidden aspect of existence, had not yet converged; after that, they became split apart, and the underground lost much of its mystical capacity to enchant. But during that period the idea of the underground was a powerful, terrifying, and entrancing one, in part because it was still developing in so many directions.

What I am talking about here, in a larger sense, is the way a metaphor exists in time. The underground is itself an excellent metaphor for metaphor. It is, on the one hand, a real place in the world, and on the other hand it is an idea or a feeling: the physical place seems inherently suggestive of the spiritual or literary connotations, and those connotations in turn enrich our experience of the material object. Like all good metaphors, the underground is simultaneously and inseparably a concrete thing and an abstract notion. But it is not always the *same* notion. What the underground "represents" (if I can use such a clumsy word for so delicate an operation) varies not only with the individual writer or reader, but with the time period in which the metaphor resides.

It should be clear by now that my idea of metaphor carries with it a certain belief about the relationship between the individual and history. I am reacting, I think, against two other, mutually opposed ideas about metaphor. One of these implies that the individual author is solely or largely responsible for the creation of metaphor. It is this sense which we draw on when we say that So-and-so writes very metaphorical prose whereas Whatsisname tends to be quite literal, or when we praise the richness of metaphor in a particular poet's work. From this point of view, Karl Marx, George Gissing, and Maxim Gorky would be directly responsible for the underground's significance as a metaphor for the lower class, Lewis Carroll and Sigmund Freud would have given it a connection to the unconscious, Ralph Ellison would have made it mean escape, and so on. This theory (which I am painting in its broadest and therefore least tenable form) posits the world as a bank of raw material out of which each author draws the images he needs, using them for his own purposes. Though it is a theory easily discredited by references to the social and linguistic context of literature, it is nonetheless a powerful theory that appeals to our ideas about how great writers work, and I do not wish to abandon it entirely.

The opposite theory, and one which I find in some ways more pernicious, suggests that metaphor is eternal and unchanging. This idea is inherent in the Jungian notion of archetypes, and it often takes its most persuasive form in the work of Jungian writers. Unlike critics who see each metaphor as newly invented by a single author, Jungians are interested in the continuity of metaphor over time, and are therefore, like myself, attracted to the repetition of a single image in various cultures and periods. The Jungian psychologist James Hillman has pursued this technique in *The Dream and the Underworld*, an exploration of the idea of death in dreams, in myth, and in the literature of psychology. For Hillman, there is only one meaning to the underworld metaphor, and that is death; all of the various shapes which this image takes are merely the shadowy signposts pointing toward that deepest reality. There is a stern Platonic rigidity to this conception, implying that we live in a world whose ambiguity and multiplicity are merely deceptive, and where our only task is to puzzle out the clues and find the single true meaning that lies behind each object or image. Nothing ever changes in this pre-established world of meaning, and since the material world we live in obviously *does* change over time, that world has to be rendered meaningless for this idea to work.

I would situate my idea about metaphor somewhere between these two extremes. If everything were up to the individual, Dante's rich and terrifying underworld would not be so firmly located between the pagan openness of Virgil's and the secularized emptiness of T.S. Eliot's. And the same example, which contradicts the "individualist" notion of metaphor, can also be used against the "eternal" definition: the three underworlds are clearly related to each other, but they are also quite different. That difference—the obvious change in the metaphor over time—is what first attracted me to my subject. For what I thought I noticed was a moment in history, now virtually past, when the underground became a particularly intense metaphor. The seeds for this transformation were already there in myth and literature, the materials Hillman draws on for his evidence. But they needed the catalyst of historical event to set them off.

When the Western world began to change toward the end of the eighteenth or the beginning of the nineteenth century, the significance of the underground also began to change. And I think the reason the metaphor grew more powerful was that the boundaries between fantasy and reality, between things in the mind and things in the world, became vague and blurred in regard to the subterranean. Old ideas which had been attached to fantastic tales now gained association with actual places one could touch and see—with mines, and subways, and tunnels, and excavations. And the pride that people felt in this technological downward progress mingled with the old fears held over from myth and religion to produce the distinctive lure of the underground, a feeling that was a mixture of horror and curiosity, attraction and repulsion.

I have been somewhat arbitrary in locating this transformation during the period 1789 to 1958; certainly the dates could easily waver at either end. But the last decade of the eighteenth century does seem to signal the start of a subterranean era. The French Revolution, for instance, is not the only "underground" event that took place in the 1790s. In 1793 a British amateur archaeologist published his account of several hundred barrows which he had excavated for historical rather than purely antiquarian reasons; in other words, he was looking for a key to the past as opposed to some nice ancient crockery. This was the beginning of modern archaeology. And in 1795 the Scottish scientist James Hutton, often referred to as the founder of modern geology, published the first full version of his ideas in his *Theory of the Earth*.

These developments influenced Western thought as a whole, but they seemed to take particularly strong hold in England (and later in the rest of the English-speaking world). For internal economic and social reasons as well, Britain became the focus of nineteenth-century concern with the underground. Thus industrial development and major metropolitan renovation led to political and social "subterranean" inquiries that matched and responded to the concern with the physical underground. The 1830s, for instance, were the period of Edwin Chadwick's nearly fanatical exploration of the sanitary conditions of London—an effort brought about by the lack of proper sewage facilities among the very poor, and the resulting prevalence of contagious disease in the closely packed urban population. The 1840s marked Friedrich Engels' analysis of the conditions of miners in England, along with other citizens classed in the "lower depths" of British society. In the 1850s, the newly founded Metropolitan Board of Works set out to modernize London's sewer and water system by installing a series of underground pipes. And in the 1860s Britain opened the world's first subway system, the London Underground. Meanwhile British writers began picking up the idea of the underground in their work. Novels like *Hard Times*, *North and South*, *The Nether World*, and *Demos* explicitly referred to the lower classes as subterranean creatures. From the realism of such novels the underground metaphor took off in different directions—to the children's fantasies of *Alice in Wonderland* and *The Princess and the Goblin* on the one hand, and to the science fiction worlds of H.G. Wells's *The Time Machine* and Bulwer Lytton's *The Coming Race* on the other.

Similar underground developments were occurring at about the same time in other Western countries. Jules Verne wrote *Journey to the Center of the Earth* in the 1860s, following decades of French geological debate. Eugène Sue and Victor Hugo wrote about poverty, criminality, and the Paris sewers in the closing decades of the nineteenth century. The Paris subway system, the *Metropolitain*, opened in 1900. The Americans also opened a subway—a small underground streetcar system in Boston—in 1897, and the New York subway system began operating in 1900. Before this there had been a different kind of "Underground Railroad" in America, the one used to bring escaping slaves to the free northern states. And soon after the turn of the century came the rapid development of "underground" political activity such as that advocated by Emma Goldman, John Reed, and other major figures of the American left.

The subterranean continued to be a factor in the early twentieth century—in European trench warfare of the First World War, in Freud's new idea of the unconscious, in the buried shelters in which British civilians hid from bombs during the Second World War, and in black

American writing from the 1940s. The underground also appeared in the developing popular arts of this century—in science fiction, in thriller fiction, and particularly in the movies. But at the same time the idea was starting to fade: its importance waned as the culture began to look outward rather than downward for its imaginative vehicles and its technological progress. The real death blow to the underground era came, I think, with the launching of Sputnik.

This is not to say that the importance of the underground ended equally for everyone, everywhere. To the inhabitants of cities like London and New York (and probably Paris, Rome, and Mexico City as well, though I know them less well), the underground continues to be an active metaphor. Thus Margaret Drabble can write a contemporary novel like *The Middle Ground*, about sewers, radical politics, and the things that bubble up from the unconscious; Iris Murdoch can make a similar use of the London subway in *A Word Child*; and Graham Swift, in his recent work *Shuttlecock*, can construct a fiction about a man who rides the Underground to his basement workplace, where he does confidential work for the Secret Service and eventually uncovers damning information about his father's undercover work during the war. For these British novelists, the connection between the figurative and the real underground is still alive: the metaphor is still vital and useful.

Far into this century, New York's subways have continued to exert both a mythic and a concrete influence over the people who use them. Randall Jarrell, in a letter to a German correspondent, wrote in 1949: "You would hardly believe how ugly, violent and overwhelming a big city like Detroit is; and in New York, looking at the crowds waiting in the subway stations, I've often thought, 'This *is* Hell. Hell must be exactly like this.' " In 1982, *The New Yorker* magazine picked up the same idea in one of its cartoons. In the first of five panels, a well-dressed man walks down some unidentified steps. As we progress through the panels, his appearance changes—he acquires hooves, then furry legs, finally a beard, horns, and a cape—and in the last panel a full-blown devil waits for a train in what is clearly a subway station. This is the subway station as hell, but it is also the New York citizen as unleashed id, for that transformed gentleman is Pan (in the midway panels) as well as Satan.

Some American cities, on the other hand, are too young to remember the underground era. Their present incarnations cannot hark back to that earlier period because they were never part of it; in fact, they arose under conditions that were diametrically opposed to it. This is particularly true, for instance, of a newly burgeoned city like Houston, now one of the largest metropolitan areas in the country. Situated in a hot, flat, featureless part of the Texas landscape, the city seems to have no geographical rationale: "Why should these crazy people have settled here," I can hear the archaeologists of the future wondering, "rather than anywhere else?" In older cities the stimulus for the city's existence lay on the surface—in major ports, or obvious trade routes, or sheltering mountains, or whatever—and the exploration of the underground came after the fact, after the city had already been settled. But Houston reverses this pattern. The reason for Houston's location lies underground, in the existence of oil, and thus the city grew backward, from underground exploration to surface settlement.

Moreover, Houston continues to have a reversed relationship to the underground even in its developed form. In older cities (and in fantasy and science fiction), the conventional, middle-class, "normal" people occupy the surface territory—the city's streets and sidewalks—while the poor, the criminal, the outlandish, and the demonic inhabit the lower depths. But in Houston the climate is so notoriously unbearable that the city-builders have connected all the downtown buildings with a maze of underground tunnels, through which office-workers and shoppers pass from bank to hotel to office building and back. Only the bums—only the "lower classes"—are out on the hot sidewalks and streets; everyone else is underground. This subterranean region is not the dank, dark, gloomy place of nineteenth-century imagination: it is wrapped in tweed wall coverings, and tiled floors, and indirect lighting, and well-regulated air-conditioning. The Houston underground has been reclaimed from the earth and turned into a shopping mall. And as if to signal that Houston is indeed the city without an underground past—the post-underground city—the National Aeronautic and Space Administration has for many years located its major launching facilities there.

For a literary example of some of these Houstonian reversals, one can turn to John Cheever's novel *The Wapshot Scandal*. Written from roughly 1959 to 1964, in the very earliest years of the space age, Cheever's novel is in part about a man who, as an employee of a Missile Research and Development program (the ancestor of the "Star Wars" defense), plays a small role in outer-space exploration. At one point the research site itself is described as "a population of twenty thousand, divided, like any society, whatever its aspirations, into first class, second class, third class and steerage. The large aristocracy was composed of physicists and engineers. Tradesmen made up the middle class, and there was a vast proletariat of mechanics, ground crewmen and gantry hands. Most of the aristocracy had been given underground shelters and while this fact had never been publicized it was well known that in the case of a cataclysm the proletariat would be left to scald." As in the Houston case, the older underground pattern has here been turned on its head. This new subterranean realm of the space age is no longer the haunt of the poor and the outcast, but on the contrary is now the refuge of the highest class, and safety rather than danger lies downward. The Peter Sellers mad-German-scientist figure in *Dr. Strangelove* makes a similar point in the closing minutes of that movie, which came out at about the same time as the Cheever book—that is, just *after* the end of what I have defined as the underground era.

My own relationship to this underground history is a peripheral one. I was born at the end of the era, only six years before the launching of the first manned Sputnik, and I grew up in the kind of middle-class surroundings against which the underground has always defined itself. Moreover, because these surroundings were in suburban California, they lacked any obvious relationship to an underground. There were no basements in my neighborhood, and no subway stations. There were no poor people to speak of in my town, and virtually no black people (they lived across the highway, in an unincorporated area of another county). There was no crime, and what underground politics there were (the origins of the New Left, the remnants of the Old) were so aboveground that they took place in foodstore parking lots and main-street bookstores. I don't even remember ever seeing an excavation for street or sewer repair; perhaps they did such work only at night, when the children were asleep. The whole notion of a physical underground simply did not accord with the way life was lived in California—which is partly what Edmund Wilson was getting at, I think, when he made the remark: "All visitors from the East know the strange spell of unreality which seems to make human experience on the Coast as hollow as the life of a trollnest where everything is out in the open instead of being underground."

So my own feeling about the underground came mostly through fantasy and fiction. From the age of twelve to the age of sixteen I read nothing but science fiction books, which are riddled with various undergrounds (still, in the space age); before that, I read children's books in which the underground often played a major role, and after that, when I was seventeen, I read John Reed's *Ten Days That Shook The*

World. For me the underground was first a place in the imagination, and second a place in history; it had nothing much to do with my own life in any public sense.

This began to change when I went to college in an East Coast city with an old subway system. As an undergraduate I took courses in geology and archaeology—desultorily, randomly, without connecting them. I was interested in city planning (I was interested in cities *period*, as a way of escaping the suburbs), and I looked into the archaeological history of cities, studying excavation reports on long-buried Near Eastern and Mayan civilizations. For several years Lewis Mumford's *The City in History*, with its sweeping glances at sanitation, transportation, and other underground developments, was my bible. And I began to look closely at the city around me, to ride the subway into and around Boston. During one of these trips it occurred to me that one could do a sociological study of the city's neighborhoods simply by riding the subways—by seeing who got in and who got out at various stations, until the car converted from all-white (at the Cambridge end of the line) to all-black (at the Roxbury end). Such observations will seem banal to anyone who grew up in cities, but to me they were news.

It didn't occur to me to write about the underground, however, until ten years after that thought about the subways, when I had just completed some research on nineteenth-century London. I was struck by the way the Victorians were both terrified and entranced by the underground. The idea of a citizenry which feared the gloomy, sunken alleys where its own underclass dwelt, and at the same time named one of its first subway engines "Cerberus," caught my fancy. In its manner of conquering the underground, through slum renovation and through technological advances in drainage and transportation, the Britain of the late nineteenth century also appeared to be conquering a much older fear of hell. Somehow the facts that the poor lived in basements, that rats scurried through the sewers, and that evil stemmed from below had all been brought together—not only in the novels of the period, which might be expected to take such imaginative liberties, but in the journalism and sociological reporting as well. This was the heart of my initial idea about the underground, a version of which now appears as the chapter called "The Nether World."

But the mixed attitude toward the underground, and the tendency to bring together various manifestations as if they were all part of the same fabric, came through in other cultures besides that of Victorian London. It stretched back to Virgil and Dante, and forward to the movies of the late twentieth century; it included Dostoyevsky and Kafka as well as Verne and Ellison. Though in writing this book I have kept mainly to the nineteenth and early twentieth centuries, I have not stayed strictly within the confines of my self-defined "underground era." When recent works seemed to bear directly on my topic—as do Thom Gunn's "Bringing to Light," Oliver Sacks's *Awakenings*, and Graham Greene's "Under the Garden"—I have not hesitated to include them, despite the fact that they were written in the 1960s and 1970s. Nor have I sliced the topic neatly into self-contained pieces, producing separate discussions of sewers, subways, basements, hells, and so forth. For the whole point, in my view, is to demonstrate how much all these things overlap—how the various downward explorations include all the other undergrounds as well as the one specifically being addressed. It is impossible, of course, to draw all the connections at once; my own limitations, as well as the size of the effort, prevent it. But when I bring archaeology sharply into conjunction with poetry, or science fiction with social novels, I hope to suggest the kinds of connections that do exist. By calling the metaphor of the underground to people's attention, I am trying to give it back some of its ebbing vitality—to make my readers perceive the way in which the underground functions in their own imaginations, in their own lives.

Why, then—if I am so interested in the physical aspects of the underground as well as its imagined side—have I chosen to focus so heavily on literature? I don't think this is really a book of literary criticism, as such. What I intended is that literature here be used as a kind of common experience: a vessel in which the underground metaphor is carried and preserved, ready to be excavated as needed. If instead I had based my discussion on interviews with sewer workers, or trips into caves, I would be stuck in my own late-twentieth-century period, and I suspect my "evidence" would be even more subjective than it is at present. With literature (and other accumulations of the written word), I can go back in time or across geographical barriers, and you can check me out at every step. Partly to enable you to do exactly that, I have relied mainly on readily available works of literature rather than obscure texts buried in specialized libraries; and I have assumed an English-speaking reader who, like myself, has no knowledge of Latin and only the slightest acquaintance with other languages.

As I suggested at the beginning of this chapter, I have been far from comprehensive, even in my selections within categories. I certainly do not cover every work of underground science fiction, nor every novel of Victorian social realism. This is partly a result of limited space and time, but it is also because I wanted this to be a personally written book—a book which stemmed from my own gradually brewing notions of the underground as well as from what other authors had to say. So, for instance, in my chapter on "The Child's Underground," I could have looked at many other books besides the few discussed there; but I particularly wanted to consider only books that *I* had read as a child, so that this reading would be an informed re-reading, imbued with the knowledge of the child I once was.

If I were to wait thirty years before completing this book, it would be a very different work, in many ways probably a better one. Not only would I have read more and learned more about the underground itself; I would also, I hope, have a fuller understanding of the terrors and entrancements of the underworld, a stronger sense of what birth and death mean, and a greater awareness of the unconscious. But I wanted to write this book now, to venture on my underground exploration just as I stand on the edge of that dark wood which, according to Dante, marks the middle of our life's journey, and the beginning of our descent into the underworld.

The Thriller Underworld

... for this is under ground, where old men scratch for knowledge, gold, and death.
—John le Carré, *The Naive and Sentimental Lover*

IN THE OPENING SCENE OF STEVEN SPIELBERG'S *INDIANA Jones and the Temple of Doom*, the dumb-blonde heroine, on being introduced to the swashbuckling eponymous hero, is surprised to learn that he is a famous archaeologist. "I thought archaeologists were little men who were always looking for their mommies," she sneers. "*Mummies*," Indiana Jones snarls under his breath.

Besides setting up the tug-of-war relationship that prevails between these two characters, this initial exchange also suggests the underground elements that are to surface later in the movie: the subterranean (and illegal) Temple of Kali, scene of the film's major criminal actions and source of the plot-motivating mystery; the even deeper mine worked by stolen children, whose labor fuels the Temple's operations; and the final hair-raising chase through the mine's underground tunnels. But in addition, the opening conversation about mommies and mummies introduces an important confusion that carries beyond the limits of the movie, defining the underground as alternately (perhaps even simultaneously?) womb and tomb.

If one wants to find the subterranean metaphor used imaginatively in the late twentieth century, it is to movies like *Indiana Jones*—or to the thriller novels which are its literary equivalent—that one must generally turn. Though what I am calling "the underground era" may have ended in 1958 or so, it still survives vestigially in the popular arts, where the subterranean retains not only its allure but its usefulness. Speeding subways, dank sewers, empty basements, and buried storerooms make ideal settings for chase scenes, break-ins, criminal hideaways, or the cornering of suspects. Moreover, such locations provide a physical analogue to the metaphor that informs most thrillers: the idea of a criminal "underworld." It makes a kind of poetic sense for the activities of such below-the-law characters to take place literally underground. And, finally, the thriller genre has an affinity with the subterranean because it is itself an "underground" activity: a form of literature that is considered "beneath" literature, a kind of film that is explicitly entertainment rather than art. While haughty genre distinctions are easy to deplore and ridicule, they can also be credited with backhandedly giving the thriller a special kind of freedom. For in excluding the spy story, the mystery, and the underworld movie from the realms of "high art," such attitudes have made it possible for writers like Eric Ambler, Graham Greene, John le Carré, Ross Macdonald, Maj Sjöwall, and Per Wahlöö—and for filmmakers like Carol Reed, Jean Melville, and Brian De Palma—to take liberties with the boundary between the ordinary and the extraordinary.

Secrecy is at the heart of the connection between the thriller and the underground. "Buried" material and hidden information form the basis of the thriller plot, which by definition is built around the unraveling of a secret. The "thrill" lies in the process of uncovering and its inherent dangers. In a thriller, the price of discovering the answer—for some of the characters, at least—is often death. The reader, too, experiences a kind of death in every mystery: that dying fall, the letdown at the end of every novel, where the suspense and anticipation finally exhaust themselves. The mystery's solution, however cleverly presented, can never equal the degree of anticipation its possibility arouses—in part because, as we devour a mystery, we are really wishing for answers beyond the ones that any author could provide, so that the writer's inevitable failure to feed this deeper hunger is always disappointing. In exploring a few underworlds, the thriller stirs up many others, leading us to expect revelations we'll never get about places in our own minds we hardly knew existed.

This psychological aspect of the thriller underworld comes across especially clearly in the work of Ross Macdonald. The author of novels with titles like *The Dark Tunnel* and *The Underground Man*, Macdonald makes no secret of his feeling that the mystery form lends itself to psychological detection of buried unconscious material. His detective, Lew Archer, is a kind of psychoanalyst/sleuth, an investigator whose cases deal mainly with disturbing family histories and their resulting traumas. As the idea of the "private dick" suggests, the Freudian element in detection is certainly not unique to Archer. But Macdonald emphasizes not only the sexual but also the subterranean nature of Archer's role: his tendency to "dig" for information, to uncover "buried" family secrets, to find the historical "roots" of a current problem, and so on.

The power of the revelations in Macdonald's novels has much to do with this psychoanalytic basis. His convoluted tales of mixed identity and incest and sexual substitution would be ludicrously repetitive and unbelievable if they did not strike at such powerful psychological material. (Any regular reader of Macdonald will have noticed these repetitions and overlappings. Once, for instance, I was finishing *The Dark Tunnel* in the same room as a friend who was starting *The Blue Hammer*; on about page forty he announced, "I know! This guy turns out to be a transvestite who is pretending to be his own sibling to escape his past crimes," to which I replied: "Not quite, but that *is* the plot of the one I'm reading.") All Macdonald novels are the same novel, but this extraordinary sameness is faithful to what may be a very ordinary truth: when you get down to a certain psychological depth, all of us have roughly the same story to tell. One might almost say that we read mysteries like Macdonald's not to be surprised, but to arrive at what we were unconsciously expecting all along. The intelligent mystery writer must, like Freud, make sure that his revelations are just the other side of obvious—on the tip of our minds, but slightly out of reach.

Of course, not all of the underground resonances in a thriller are Freudian or personal. There is a larger "memory" of the underworld as well—what might be viewed as a Jungian archetype, an aspect of the collective unconscious (if one credits the existence of such things). For a Jungian like James Hillman, for instance, the subterranean realm is by definition the land of death, and its function is to remind the living that death is the original and eternal condition. In a recent thriller called *The Mind-Murders*, Dutch author Janwillem van de Wetering picks up on this idea of the underworld when he describes the experience of an Amsterdam police "commissaris." The officer returns from an errand to find that his expensive new government-issue Citroen "was gone. His disappointment was mingled with fear. . . . The Citroen wasn't there and the ground on which it had rested wasn't there either. The commissaris, abruptly transformed from acting object into suffering subject, stared down into a gaping hole. The bright red bricks were replaced by a black aperture that sucked at his existence." As it turns out, there is a rational explanation; as the commissaris says, " 'There is always a superficial explanation . . . maybe the sewer burst, or a gas pipe. They suddenly had to dig a hole and my car happened to be in the way.' " Eventually he is able to retrieve his car from the place it was towed to. But what the commissaris can't retrieve is his faith in "the benevolence of the creation," his sense that the earth rests solidly beneath him. The experience has made him realize not only the transitory nature of property, but the ephemerality of life itself. As if to make the point more pointed, this little exemplary tale is embedded in a mystery story which considers how a murderer might hide a corpse in precisely the kind of hole that displaced the commissaris's car.

The suspenseful tale of danger and deceit often gets at other senses of the underworld as well. John le Carré pinpoints some of these meanings in a passage from *The Naive and Sentimental Lover* (ironically, and unfortunately, the least thriller-like of his novels). Here the main character is riding in a train through a tunnel: "The sounds are magnified in this long cave. History, geology, not to speak of countless set-texts from mediaeval faculties at Oxford, all deepen and intensify the underground experience. Minotaurs, hermits, martyrs, miners, incarcerated since the first constructions, howl and clank their chains, for this is under ground, where old men scratch for knowledge, gold, and death." And in the course of three sentences, a routine train ride has been converted into a lesson in mortality and immortality, a blending of mythic nightmares and practical terrors. Le Carré's joining of "gold" and "death"—a central pairing in the thriller genre—is here given a much older history, for those who have done their Oxford set-texts may well remember that Pluto, the Roman god of the dead, was also the Latin word for "riches."

John le Carré is, of course, the writer who has popularized the notion of a "mole," a secret counter-agent who risks his life by burrowing into the enemy camp and disguising himself as a friend. The physical reality of a mole's existence—the fact that he lives under the ground—is almost absent from le Carré's metaphor, where the word simply stands for a highly deceptive agent. This departure from concrete meaning is itself typical of le Carré's style, in which so many code words are used that one practically has to learn a new language to read the novels. The reader of a George Smiley book becomes a detective himself, digging into the alien terminology and sorting out the meaningful detail from the morass of meaninglessness. Yet the effort is never quite worth it—and this too is crucial to le Carré's method. As with Smiley's letdown at finally confronting his Soviet arch-enemy Karla, the "answer" to a le Carré novel is always inadequate to the quest. There is something fruitless in the very endeavor; all of le Carré's thrillers finally seem to be set in a Tantalus-hell "where old men scratch for knowledge, gold, and death."

Julian Rathbone, another British thriller-writer, is more explicit in his focus on the underground habits of the "mole." Such an agent is the main character of his 1982 novel *A Spy of the Old School*. Not only is Sir Richard Austen a Communist spy embedded in the British Secret Service; he is also, like Indiana Jones, an archaeologist—a man who is used to "digging things up" and "uncovering the truth." Furthermore, he becomes implicated in a murder in which the body has been left for many years in a basement, only coming to light when the bombed-out site is excavated for new building construction. And like Dostoyevsky's Underground Man, Rathbone's mole is subject to still another "underground" influence: the partially unconscious desire for self-exposure and punishment. Austen acknowledges this toward the end of this first-person novel, when he says: "Did I know what I was up to when I wrote *The Burning Matrix*? I half wanted to put in so much that any fool would guess at what had been left out, and yet half wanted to make a puzzle of it, wrap it up and mystify it, give them a run for their money." *The Burning Matrix* is Sir Richard's autobiography, but he could just as easily be describing the technique of a mystery writer who chronicles the exposure of a mole.

A thriller which plays on another sense of the word "mole"—emphasizing the animal's blindness to daylight existence rather than just his subterranean habits—is Ed McBain's 1958 detective novel *Killer's Choice*. McBain's novels tend to be filled with irrelevant information and throwaway characters who do nothing for the plot except to add "atmosphere." Here is one such atmospheric encounter between a New York City detective and an Ancient-Mariner-like elevator operator. The elevator man begins by saying to his captive audience: " 'This is a city of moles, you know that? I know people, they get off the subway, they walk underground to their office. . . . They eat their lunch in the arcade, underground. They go back to the subway underground when they leave the office at night. They never see the city. Me, I see two blocks of the city. How is it outside?' " And then, after eliciting two words of commentary from the close-lipped detective, he continues his urban plaint. " 'Up and down all day long,' the elevator operator said. 'Up and down, but I'm never going any place. I'm a vertical mole. I'd rather be a subway conductor. Then at least I'd be a horizontal mole . . .' "

In the process of making the interesting connection between subways and elevators (one I will pick up later in my discussion of De Palma), the McBain passage highlights an important characteristic of a certain brand of thriller: its link to a gritty urban setting. The darkness, futility, and anonymity of the standard New York existence are central to the atmosphere of Ed McBain's 87th Precinct novels. While one whole subgenre of mystery novels (beautifully delineated by W.H. Auden in "The Guilty Vicarage") deals with well-to-do country existence, there is another subgenre that necessarily takes place in the metropolis. In the latter novels, which might be viewed as the *films noirs* of mystery books, the underside of urban life is as much a theme as the particular crime around which the plot revolves.

The international masters of this form are Maj Sjöwall and Per Wahlöö, the Swedish husband-and-wife team who wrote the ten Martin Beck mysteries in the 1960s and 1970s. In these cop stories—which feature the investigative activities of Chief Inspector Beck and his various sidekicks, set against the background of a changing Stockholm—Sjöwall and Wahlöö spend as much effort on atmosphere as they do on the plots themselves; that is, the tendency evident in McBain's novels has been pushed even further in the same direction. Thus Stockholm's parks, streets, and major buildings, its redeveloped neighborhoods, its impersonal suburbs, and its public transportation system (which Beck uses far more than any American cop would) all form a crucial part of the novels. The crime, in each case, is not a trumped-up occasion for professional sleuthing, but a highly pertinent symbol of disaster or decay, representing events both internal (in Beck's life) and external (in Swedish society). *The Locked Room*, for example, in which Beck is faced with the old mystery cliché of a dead body minus weapon in a completely sealed room, also deals with Martin Beck's own post-divorce isolation as well as the more general issue of alienation and loneliness in Sweden's urban population. As Marxists who are nonetheless willing to examine the specific failures of their country's centralized economy, Sjöwall and Wahlöö have focused on social detail in a way that is more typical of Gissing or Dreiser than of most present-day "serious" fiction. It almost seems as if the subterranean material itself—the subways, the sewers, the world of "undercover" cops—has given their fiction an affinity with the works of the underground era.

There are several implicit undergrounds in the Martin Beck novels, including both the criminal underworld and the social underbelly of poverty. Occasionally the social and economic underclass gets linked with a physical underground—as, for instance, when Beck and his colleague Kollberg discuss the relative merits of buses and subways as refuges for the homeless: " 'The subway is warmer,' Kollberg objected. 'And there you can ride as long as you like, what's more, provided you don't pass through the gates but only change trains.' " The sense of warmth is relative, of course. In the early twentieth century, the London Underground put out a promotional poster which showed a brightly lit, red-and-green-upholstered carriage filled with well-dressed ladies and gentlemen; the poster caption said: "Underground: Always Warm and Bright." But this is a very different image of warmth from the fetid, depressing shelter Kollberg is invoking. Stockholm's subways are only a comparatively warm refuge—warmer than the streets or the buses. What's more important is their anonymity, the fact that one can ride endlessly, unsupervised, unharrassed by guards or drivers. Subways are a refuge for the homeless for very much the same reasons they are shunned by the upper and middle classes: officialdom doesn't pay much attention to what goes on down there.

The physical underground is also the locus for the criminal underworld in the Martin Beck novels—specifically in the final novel, *The Terrorists*. The plot, as the title suggests, involves a plan by foreign provocateurs to assassinate a visiting public figure by placing a bomb under the street over which the visitor's motorcade will drive. (The fact that the visitor represents a right-wing foreign government, and that Beck *et al.* do not relish the task of insuring security for his visit, is partly what differentiates the Sjöwall/Wahlöö book from any of the B-movie thrillers with similar plots.) Given this basis, it is inevitable that much of the planning and activity in this novel, on the part of both the bombers and the police, should take place in and about the underground.

A typical discussion is the one conducted among the cops when they try to figure out where the bomber will be most likely to strike. Beck asks each of his men to write down his own guess as to the probable location of a gas-main bomb, complete with explanation; he himself justifies his choice by writing: " 'At this particular place, there are plenty of underground tunnels and passages; first the internal communication system of the subway line presently under construction; secondly a complicated division of the drainage system. This area can also be reached by way of a number of street wells and other entrances by anyone familiar with the underground communication network of the city.' " Another cop (about whom the narrator comments that he "thought clearly, but wrote somewhat strangely") concludes: " 'Just where I pointed, there are a lot of already dug passages. . . . But we do not know if there are any bomb assassination terrorists down in the ground, but if there are, neither surface nor underground police can deal with them, but they might also swim through the sewers and then we will also need a sewer commando of frogmen.' " The awkward language, combined with the near-hysteria of that last image, makes this passage sound a great deal like a child describing a TV show. And in fact the underground bomb attack is a favorite plot of such TV adventures, because it creates the perfect recipe for suspense: an apparently calm surface countered by and intercut with scenes of frantic activity below ground. As the two descriptions quoted above imply, the underground bomber is by definition an even more terrifying creature than the routine bomber, precisely because his access points are multiple and generally invisible.

Like all the later Beck novels, *The Terrorists* contains a significant subplot, and this one has to do with a poor demented young woman who is essentially driven into criminal action by the failures of the courts and "social agencies." It is she, and not the foreign agents, who is finally responsible for the outbreak of violence during the official visit. Thus the terror in *The Terrorists* finally comes from within, from underneath the rest of society, in the form of one of its more oppressed souls. In the final Beck novel, our natural fear of the physical underground—of all those buried pipes and drains and tunnels, from which God knows what might emerge—is invoked only to be squelched; and it is another kind of subterranean power, the mazy workings of the society's governmental operations, that is shown to be the most dangerous. This danger, while less suspenseful than the underground commando bit, is more lasting and pervasive, for it involves a problem that underlies every aspect of daily Swedish (for which one can read "Western") existence. Thus the physical underground portrayed in *The Terrorists* itself turns out to be a metaphor for the authorities that installed it—those government agents and blocks of officialdom and elected figures and ignorant bureaucrats who control not only the sewers and subways and gas mains, but also the lives of the citizens who use these things. What is rotten in the Sjöwall/Wahlöö state of Sweden is not any particular Claudius, but the state itself.

The sense that society itself is "rotten at the core" is a frequent theme in the thrillers that use the underground. Such novels often seem to equate the pursuers and the pursued, the criminals and the detectives, by placing them both underground. If these plots were transferred to film, the activities of both sides (especially in the darkened setting) would look almost identical: the bombers creep through tunnels to set the bombs, the police creep through to dismantle them; the criminal rushes aboard a subway to escape, the cop rushes after him in pursuit.

Sometimes the pattern even gets reversed, and the "good guys" use the underground to escape from the criminals. This happens, for instance, in Eric Ambler's *A Coffin for Dimitrios*, first published in 1937. Charles Latimer, who is in many ways the typically naive amateur sleuth of Ambler's world, has been tracking the criminal Dimitrios through Turkey, Greece, Yugoslavia, and France, and has finally confronted him in Paris. After leaving the criminal, Latimer and his professional accomplice, Mr. Peters, are faced with the task of getting home without being followed by Dimitrios' men. Peters has the solution: " 'Return by Metro.' " He buys two Metro tickets at the nearest station and urges Latimer to stick close to him as they walk down the tunnel toward the trains. Ambler's description emphasizes the fact that "the tunnel split into two. One way was labelled : '*Direction* Pte. de Charenton,' the other: '*Direction* Balarde.' " Peters stops at this point and listens to the trains carefully—knowing what to listen for because " 'I spent half an hour here listening to them this morning.' " When Peters hears the rumble of the incoming train, he can tell which direction it's coming from and can therefore hustle Latimer into the right tunnel. The scene ends with a sense of overwhelming but carefully planned haste: "The train was by now almost in the station. The automatic door began to swing slowly across the entrance to the platform. As Latimer reached it and passed through with about three inches to spare, he heard, above the hiss and screech of the pneumatic brakes, the sound of running feet. He looked round. Although Mr. Peters' stomach had suffered some compression, he had squeezed himself through on to the platform. But the man in the grey raincoat had, in spite of his last-minute sprint, left it too late. He now stood, red in the face with anger, shaking his fists at them from the other side of the automatic gate."

The underground—elsewhere an *image* of escape (as in Alice's subterranean adventures or the slaves' Underground Railroad)—literally *becomes* the means of escape in this scene. And the features which enable it to perform this function are identical to the characteristics which might otherwise make it frightening: the speed with which the trains arrive and depart, the "automatic" regulation of passengers by heavy metal gates, the limited visual scope of the traveler (his "tunnel vision") and hence the increased significance of sound. In this passage, Ambler carefully plays off human sound against inhuman sound: Latimer's low talking while Peters listens for the trains, "the sound of running feet" against "the hiss and screech of pneumatic brakes." The escape is a matter of cooperation between the inhuman technology and the human intellect. It is the lack of human agency in the subway's operation, the absolute predictability of events, which Peters uses to insure the getaway. World traveler that he is, Ambler also focuses on the special features of the Paris Metro: in neither New York nor London do automatic gates prevent passengers from entering the platform, and in San Francisco an announcer actually states which direction the next train will come from. Thus Mr. Peters' mastery of this subterranean escape route has to do with acquired knowledge of a very specific underground, honed to perfection by recent practice ("'I spent half an hour here listening to them this morning'").

As you read the Ambler passage, it is almost impossible not to visualize the scene as if it were taking place in a movie. And indeed, as anyone who sees a lot of movies has undoubtedly noticed, the subway chase scene is a key element in a number of thriller films. In Jean-Jacques Beinix's *Diva*, for instance, the Paris Metro again becomes the hero's mode of escape from criminals, providing a particularly visual sequence in a film that aims consistently at visual allure. Fleeing the punk thugs who are chasing him, the young hero whizzes down the escalator on his Moped and, against all regulations, drives directly onto the subway car in time to escape his pursuers—a joke escape, but one that we gratefully accept. What makes this escape especially witty is the fact that Jules's subterranean flight saves him from two different kinds of "underground" pursuers: the corrupt producers of underground ("bootleg") recordings, and the equally corrupt drug-dealing criminals directed by the local police chief.

Another subway escape occurs in Brian De Palma's *Dressed to Kill*, where the prostitute-heroine thinks she has left her murderous pursuer behind in the station until he suddenly surprises her on the train. The De Palma use of the subway is rich with references to incidents and ideas that run through the rest of the movie. For example, the near-murder in the subway train parallels the original murder in the elevator (recall Ed McBain's link between the "horizontal mole" and the "vertical mole"), and both stress the danger inherent in New York's empty "public" places. The high technology of the subway's operation (the same aspect emphasized by the Ambler passage) mirrors the electronic interests of the teenage whiz-kid who saves the heroine and solves his mother's murder. The heroine's initial sense of having escaped her pursuer, and her subsequent shock of fear (her misperception being caused by the fact that one can't see into every subway car at once, while entrances and exits are possible from each), forecast the dream ending, in which false security is followed by threatened death. Her rush from car to car, emphasizing the tunnel-vision aspect of the train, replicates the murder victim's humorously frightening zoom through the long, narrow halls of the art museum. The movie's strong Freudian element (the murderer is himself a psychiatrist) lends added weight to, and derives additional material from, the implied threat of a long, thin, "buried" instrument (knife/penis/subway train). And even the homage to Hitchcock which pervades the movie may be surfacing subliminally here, in the notion of "strangers on a train."

While De Palma has used the image of the subway very specifically in this case, there are more general reasons for the frequency of underground escape scenes in thriller movies. What movies have that novels lack is, obviously, a visual dimension, and it is on that level that the underground chase becomes most effective. To begin with, the underground tunnel mirrors and exaggerates the unidirectional gaze of the camera, making a virtue out of the necessarily blinkered vision a film provides. In addition, film is particularly well-qualified to capture the fascinating discrepancy between surface "presence" and subterranean "absence": a movie can actually show a character disappearing into the underworld. Moreover, the existence of a vertical dimension increases the complexity and therefore the appeal of a chase scene; characters can move one below the other (sometimes at very close range and yet unknown to each other) rather than simply on a single plane. Finally, the fact that a subterranean technology already exists—that, as the cop in *The Terrorists* wrote, "there are a lot of already dug passages" down there—makes the underground a particularly rich source for the movies, which cannibalize our daily reality to produce exotic fictions.

The thriller film which, to my mind, most fully investigates the various meanings of the underground is Carol Reed's *The Third Man*. In part, this is because it builds on the work of a novelist, Graham Greene, who is interested in exploring various "depths": unconscious motives, deep spiritual convictions, hidden political and personal treacheries, "heart of darkness" settings, and so on. For Greene, the underground world of thrillers is barely differentiable from the everyday world of reality—which is perhaps why readers and critics have such difficulty telling his so-called "entertainments" from his serious novels.

In *The Other Man*, a book of interviews conducted by Marie-Françoise Allain, Greene refers to a passage in one of his books that condenses this idea—a passage which, significantly, takes place underground. He introduced it by remarking, "There are times in fact when I'm inclined to think that our entire planet gravitates inside a fog belt of melodrama. I've expressed the idea in *The Ministry of Fear*. The protagonist, Rowe, in an air-raid shelter during a raid over London, imagines a conversation with his mother and addresses her as follows (if you'll permit me to return to this passage)":

> *"This isn't real life anymore," he said. "Tea on the lawn, evensong, croquet, the old ladies calling, the gentle unmalicious gossip, the gardener trundling the wheelbarrow full of leaves and grass. People write about it as if it still went on; lady novelists describe it over and over again in books of the month, but it's not there any more.*
>
> *"I'm hiding underground, and up above the Germans are methodically smashing London to bits all around me. You remember St. Clement's—the bells of St. Clement's. They've smashed that—St. James's, Piccadilly, the Burlington Arcade, Garland's Hotel, where we stayed for the pantomime, Maple's and John Lewis. It sounds like a thriller, doesn't it, but the thrillers are like life—more like life than you are, this lawn, your sandwiches, that pine. You used to laugh at the books Miss Savage read—about spies, and murders, and violence, and wild motor-car chases, but dear, that's real life: It's what we've all made of the world since you died."*

The passage Greene quotes sets up an actual physical image of the idea he's conveying: a superficial existence of green lawns and shop-lined streets, under which a hidden world of air-raid shelters and thriller action bubbles and finally erupts, destroying that surface existence. And because this is an imaginary conversation between a son and his mother, the passage from *The Ministry of Fear* suggests a Freudian angle as well: Rowe, enclosed in an underground cavern, imaginatively returns to that other womb that generated him, and in speaking to his mother he thus attempts to cross the barriers of both birth (his own) and death (her past one, his impending one).

The Third Man is very pointedly a post-World-War-Two movie, set in the Vienna divided by that war; and this fact partially explains the importance of the underground in the film. The Second World War was the first war in which civilians were bombed from overhead. In place of soldier-filled trenches—the dominant subterranean image of the First World War—this later war gave us the civilian air-raid shelter.

This was an especially important image for the British; but even given his origins, Graham Greene seems remarkably obsessed with the bombings of London, which appear not only in the air-raid scene he quoted from *The Ministry of Fear*, but also in the central plot turn of *The End of the Affair*. For Greene, and possibly for Europeans in general, such bombings had a permanent effect on instinctive attitudes about underground and aboveground. The underground, formerly a frightening or dangerous place, became the only hope for safety and security (though it was a tenuous hope in the case of a "direct hit"), while the open streets and upper floors became the danger zone threatened by attacks from the sky. In French cinema (as in French life), this shift was evident in the change that took place in subterranean terminology: the criminal "underworld" gave way to the "underground" of the Resistance, as those who had to hide from the law changed from dangerous characters to sympathetic heroes. Such a shift is particularly noticeable in the work of Jean Melville, who made films about the criminal underworld before the war and about the Resistance just after it. But in Graham Greene's writing the connotation of the underground does not change completely: it is a shelter and a safety zone, but it also remains the location of the unconscious, of the criminal, and of death. Placing his hero/villain Harry Lime in an underground hiding place that recalls the refuges of the sympathetic characters from *The Ministry of Fear* and *The End of the Affair*, Greene asks us to condemn this man and at the same time identify with him; he asks us to accept Harry Lime as a manifestation of our own hidden cowardices and betrayals.

When you stop to think about it, it is startling how many of the revelations or transformations in Greene's work take place in womb-like hiding places: the whiskey priest in *The Power and the Glory* administering last rites to the dying American in a tiny, dark hut; Sarah crouched beneath a bed, simultaneously praying for and renouncing her lover in *The End of the Affair*; the little boy observing his father's arrest from under a counter in "I Spy" (a story which overtly links Freudian undertones with political-spy underworlds); and, most explicitly, the dying Wilditch's memory of his childhood underground adventure in "Under the Garden" (a story so rich in subterranean material that it earns close attention in the final chapter of this book). Yet Greene himself refuses to acknowledge the pertinence of this pattern as it applies to *The Third Man*. In her book of interviews, Marie-Françoise Allain says to him: "If your unconscious seems to be a reliable companion, you yourself sometimes give the impression of cheating him:

You introduce him into your novels and then pretend not to recognize him. You take pleasure in dropping your characters into symbolic molds. . . . *The Third Man* takes us into the sewers of Vienna . . ." To which Greene responds (completely justifying her accusation): "As for the Vienna sewers, there's nothing exemplary or symbolic about them: They were quite prosaically the sewers of Vienna."

But if Greene's remark to Allain is partly the sophisticated mock-ingenuousness of an author who refuses to read meanings into his works, it is also on some level the plain truth. The novella of *The Third Man*, which Greene wrote to prepare himself for the screenplay, is a far more prosaic work than the film that finally emerged. To a bare-bones story of intrigue in post-war Vienna, the director and the screenwriter jointly added most of the dimensions that make the movie a powerful exploration of the underground. What Carol Reed did, in collaboration with Greene himself, was to turn *The Third Man* into a full-blown movie equivalent of the richest Graham Greene novels. The author acknowledges as much when he remarks in the preface to the published novella: "The film in fact is better than the story because it is in this case the finished state of the story."

One of the key differences between the novella and the movie is the alteration in the central character, Holley Martins. Holley, played by Joseph Cotten, is the narrator of the movie's initial voice-over, the perceiver of its events; virtually no scene takes place in which he is not an actor or a witness. The novella, on the other hand, is narrated by Major Calloway, and the main character is named Rollo, not Holley. More importantly, the original Martins was an Englishman rather than an American. Greene explains most of these changes as a simple result of casting. "The choice of an American instead of an English star involved a number of alterations," he says in the preface. "For example, Mr. Joseph Cotten quite reasonably objected to the name Rollo. The name had to be an absurd one, and the name Holley occurred to me when I remembered that figure of fun, the American poet Thomas Holley Chivers."

This may indeed be how it happened, but it goes very little way toward explaining the perfection of the final choice. It is as impossible to imagine a British Holley Martins as it is to imagine a British Pyle in *The Quiet American*: both characters are the quintessential Greene figure of the innocent destroyer, the naive believer in goodness who, because he cannot comprehend evil, unwittingly becomes its instrument. Holley, pursuing truth and justice, leaves behind him a wake of death and destruction. He is so naive that he gives away his knowledge about "the third man" to precisely the wrong people—those who have already denied there was such a man—and in doing so seals the death warrant of his informant. Yet the character, played with the full force of Joseph Cotten's charm, is extremely appealing, making it possible for us to see why even the sophisticated, manipulative Harry Lime (masterfully played by Orson Welles) liked this ingenue, this believer in loyalty and decency. The name Holley itself is both ridiculous and sweet: "What a silly name," says Anna Schmidt at one point, and yet she confuses it with her beloved "Harry." Such confusions, as well as the many connotations of innocence inherent in the name (Christmas holly, the girl's name Holly, the word "holy"), would not have been possible with the original Rollo, though they now seem essential to the movie's plot. (The connotations of Lime, obviously, were part of Greene's original intentions: not only the mineral found in underground caves, but perhaps also something of the "slime" of sewers, as well as—in Greene's initial draft—the nationality of the "Limey" villain in this international episode. And maybe there is even a bit of authorial self-accusation in the notion of the color "lime green.")

The shift to Holley's view of the story represents a significant shift in the premise of the work. When Major Calloway narrates the novella, Harry Lime is a despicable though somewhat clever criminal and Martins, his ignorant defender, is a rather sleazy, weaselly man with a reputation for cruelty to women and a strong streak of vulgarity. But when Rollo-turned-Holley takes over the narration, it is Calloway who becomes the irritating character. Thus we are set up from the beginning to oppose the cops and side with the criminal; and though Holley eventually switches sides, this early allegiance sticks with us, making Lime's ultimate death far more disturbing than it is in the book. Like the other thrillers I've discussed in this chapter, the film of *The Third Man* encourages a certain confusion in regard to the relative roles of cop and criminal, pursuer and pursued, so that we are likely to find ourselves identifying with the "wrong" characters.

The camera does a great deal to assist in this confusion. In the famous sewer scene near the end of the movie, where Harry is finally cornered and killed, the camera itself intermittently takes on Harry's vision. At one point we see cops running down a tunnel toward us; at another, we see them facing us from above as Harry tries to climb out of the sewer. Earlier, we have been set up to identify with a fleeing man when Holley escapes from the villains backstage after his lecture. The spiral staircase that Martins runs up in that scene is almost a mirror image of the one that Harry runs down into the sewers, and seen from directly below (as the camera views it during the chase), Holley's staircase actually looks like a downward spiral into a pit.

But during the final chase scene the camera is fickle; it doesn't remain consistently on Harry's side, shifting away occasionally to view him from a distance. Just after he kills Sergeant Payne—his most unsympathetic onscreen action—Harry tries to crawl out of the sewers through a manhole, and we look from above as his fingers emerge from the grid like white maggots crawling out of the ground, colorless worms that prey on the dead. And our last vision of Harry alive, as his face expresses what could be either a prayer for preservation or a request for sudden death, is from Holley's viewpoint, just before Holley shoots him. This act is the final link in the chain that joins Holley and Harry, that equates innocence with evil; for in wiping out the evil, Holley too becomes a murderer.

The Third Man harps obsessively on notions of death, burial, depth, and descent. The first vision we have of the mysterious Harry Lime—or rather, the first vision we *think* we have of him—is of his coffin being lowered into the grave. Even before this, Holley arrives at Harry's flat to learn from the porter that his friend has already "gone": "Already in hell," says the porter, pointing upward, "or in heaven," pointing downward. That initial confusion between heaven and hell, up and down, reappears toward the end of the movie, when Harry and Holley sit suspended in a Ferris wheel carriage, swinging high above the ground. This bird's-eye view of reality is in fact Holley's private glimpse of hell—the people reduced to mere dots on the landscape and Harry boasting carelessly of his crimes, with the suggestion that he might be about to kill Martins as well. This scene is Harry at his most cynical: "They talk about the people and the proletariat," he says of the politicians, "I talk about the suckers and the mugs; it's the same thing." There's very much a "Better to reign in Hell, than serve in Heav'n" tone to his speech and indeed to this whole scene, despite the fact that Satan's lines were spoken from far below while Harry delivers his from on high.

The film contains repeated references to Holley's activity of "digging things up" or "getting to the bottom of things." From Major Calloway's point of view, this digging is harmful and even dangerous. To Holley's remark, "As soon as I get to the bottom of this, I'll catch the next plane," Calloway responds: "Death's at the bottom of this,

Mr. Martins; death's at the bottom of everything." (Holley's snappy reaction to that is: "Mind if I use that line in my next Western?") However, the digging metaphor appears to be contagious, for later in the film, after Holley has discovered that Harry Lime is still alive, Calloway says: "We should have dug deeper than the grave." He and his men then proceed, in fact, to dig up "Harry's" body and discover the body of Joseph Harbin instead. If the region beneath the earth represents death alone to Calloway, it represents both escape and death for Harry. In the course of the movie, this underworld black-marketeer vanishes underground four times: once, through deception, in the body of Harbin; once in the middle of a plaza, when Holley follows him from outside Anna's flat; again into the sewers, after Holley has lured him into the cafe; and finally into the grave.

Holley Martins' remark about using Calloway's line in his next Western invokes yet another kind of underground: the subterranean world of "trashy" literature. In *The Third Man*, literary status is presented as a class issue rather than merely a quality issue. The Cockney Sergeant Payne is a fan of Holley's novels, while the upper-class Englishman who runs the local literary society has never heard of him. It is this class distinction, among other things, that makes Baron Kurtz's fulsome praise of Holley's novels sound so ridiculous: one simply does not carry a lapdog under one arm and a trashy Western under the other. In Greene's novella, the confusion about Martins' literary status comes about through a case of mistaken identity (a famous writer with the same surname as Martins' pen-name was in fact expected by the literary society). The twist that leads to the confusion in the movie (the literary people are embarrassed to admit they haven't heard of Holley Martins, since they can't imagine a writer who is not their sort of high-class novelist) is both much simpler and more telling; it makes the pretentiousness of literary pigeon-holing all the more obvious. The deep social division between the two kinds of writing becomes most evident—and most humorous—when one member of the literary society begins to question Holley about the work of James Joyce. Holley may acknowledge the existence of genre distinctions but, like Graham Greene with his "entertainments," he is somewhat resentful of their implications. That this desire to separate genres stems from the same impulse that separates classes is clear not only in *The Third Man* but in other works by Greene as well. In that earlier quotation from *The Ministry of Fear*, for instance, the upper-class mother inhabits a world of croquet and tea on the lawn and "lady novelists," while the socially inferior Miss

Savage reads thrillers. But as Rowe points out to his imagined mother: "You used to laugh at the books Miss Savage read—about spies, and murders, and violence, and wild motor-car chases, but dear, that's real life."

Of course, what the Western or the thriller is to the novels of James Joyce, the thriller movie has traditionally been to the "serious" film—a connection Holley emphasizes when he says that his next book will be called *The Third Man*. By giving this projected piece of pulp the same title as their movie, Graham Greene and Carol Reed indicate that their allegiance is clearly on the side of the subterranean genre, and meanwhile force us to seek out semblances of ourselves in the high-minded audience that attends Holley's lecture. The very idea of a category called *film noir*—of which *The Third Man* is by now a classic example—is really a laughable perversion, a fancy French brand name imposed on a popular thriller form to assure us that this entertainment is really art. Reed and Greene are amused but also miffed that their film might be subjected to snobbish scrutiny. Their retort, voiced in Holley's remark about the title, is the equivalent of Raymond Chandler's defense of the detective story: "There are no vital and significant forms of art; there is only art, and precious little of that."

Just as literary class distinctions are more important in the movie of *The Third Man* than in the book, class in general is a more significant issue in the film. One aspect of this difference is the transformation of the key witness from a nondescript neighbor of Harry's to the porter of his building. When the novella's Rollo Martins becomes indirectly responsible for the neighbor's death, our distress is minimal because neither of these two characters is particularly sympathetic. But when Holley inadvertently causes the villains to murder the porter, the pathos of the situation is intensified not only by the appeal of both characters, but also by the fact that (as is often the case in Dickensian pathos) the victim is of a lower class than the man who brings about his death. This becomes a part of Holley's unintentional American arrogance: he brings destruction down on the heads of "little" people in his pursuit of a "larger" cause. (The author of *The Quiet American*, a prescient Vietnam novel, is fully aware of the wider implications of this pattern.) And this theme becomes especially pronounced in the movie because of the presence of an actual "little person": the murdered porter's son (again, a Dickens technique).

Yet the use of the child in *The Third Man* is far from sentimental. The most eerie scene in the film is the one in which the little boy, followed by a crowd of Viennese neighbors, chases Holley and Anna down the street yelling "Papa! Papa!" This child is no Dickensian waif. He is a primitively judgmental figure, a wizened little old man who has watched from below as the two adults yell at each other. He looks at things from "down there" with a distorted but piercing vision: when the camera takes his viewpoint (as it does during Holley's disagreement with the porter), the world takes on a dislocated and frightening intensity. And this boy is powerful beyond his size or even his awareness. With his cry of "Papa!" and his toddling pursuit of the American, he makes both Holley and the crowd feel that Holley is guilty of the murder. The child is a projection of many things: Holley's conscience, the neighbors' distrust of foreigners, the very strangeness and mystery of post-war Vienna. Even the camera, during the scene when the boy chases Holley, views him as a projection—a giant shadow thrown against a wall by the streetlights.

If the child is a shadow—is, in some form, death itself—he is also a version of Harry Lime. His shadow on the wall, and the sound of his little footsteps echoing down the street, are almost identical to the sights and sounds of Harry's flight from Holley several scenes later. The blown-up shadow could be a man's, and the child even resembles Orson Welles, with that round, smooth face and those big, staring eyes. Conversely, one might say that Harry Lime resembles a child, and Anna Schmidt does say it when she tells Holley that Harry is "a boy who never grew up." Of course, this phrase could describe Holley as well, and in a certain sense Harry Lime, Holley Martins, and the porter's nameless little boy are all versions of the same character. It is the figure of destructive innocence—of childhood as death—that marches through all of Graham Greene's works. The child in *The Third Man* brings us back to the equation of birth and death, of "mommies" and "mummies," with which this chapter began. It is as if only those who are still untouched by the surface world's existence—either because they are innocent like children, or callous like Harry—can embrace the possibility of death: the underworld is in some way their homeland, not an alien prospect colored by fear of the unknown.

The thrill of the thriller, its connection to death and the underworld, is one of the few forms in which adults of our period maintain contact with that dimension of existence. Serious literature still deals frequently with death; less frequently with poverty or crime; still less frequently with the notion of hell. But it rarely does so by placing these ideas in conjunction with a physical underworld. For such treatment of the underground, we must go back to the literature of the nineteenth and early twentieth centuries.

This journey backward can remind us, too, that the detective or thriller genre is itself a product of the "underground era"—notably of that master of the subterranean, Edgar Allan Poe, who published his work in the 1830s and 1840s. In stories like "The Pit and the Pendulum," "The Premature Burial," "The Cask of Amontillado," and "Descent Into the Maelstrom," and in his short novel *The Narrative of Arthur Gordon Pym*, Poe repeatedly considers the fearsomeness of the underground. D.H. Lawrence summarizes the pattern by remarking, "All this underground vault business in Poe only symbolizes that which takes place *beneath* the consciousness," and this is true enough as far as it goes. But one gets the sense that Poe's buried places represent more than just the individual unconscious. They are the manifestations of everything we cannot hope to understand or grasp fully—not only our own mental recesses, but death, and alien culture, and written language, and the irrational in man. In this sense Poe's detective stories are perhaps his *least* subterranean works, in that Dupin's method of detection relies heavily on rationality. Yet like his numerous private-eye descendants in twentieth-century fiction and film, Monsieur Dupin is also interested in "digging things up," in uncovering the buried truth—even when, as in "The Purloined Letter," that truth lies hidden right out in the open.

Poe's influence has been relatively indirect in America, and at this vantage point he emerges from the nineteenth century looking like a bit of an oddball. But his central concerns (the terrors of descent and burial, the thrill of the unknown, the obsessional vision of a crazed individual, and so forth) have permeated French literature of the later nineteenth and early twentieth centuries. One of the writers who seems to have drawn heavily on Poe—not only on his underground material, but also on his interest in the classical past, his fascination with exploration, and his curiosity about contemporary science—is Jules Verne. But in place of Poe's obsession with "galvanic batteries" and similar life-extending inventions, Verne substituted an interest in the much more mainstream science of geology. And this, in turn, makes his work an excellent example of the nineteenth-century overlaps between real and imaginary undergrounds.

Journeys Into the Underground: Science and Myth

Even at the end of the nineteenth century the earth's interior was the true terra incognita.

—Mott Greene, *Geology in the Nineteenth Century*

When Jules Verne published *Journey to the Center of the Earth* in 1864, he was building on a long-lived controversy. From Lucretius through Lyell, natural philosophers and scientists had expressed theories about what lay beneath the earth's surface. Yet by the time Verne's novel was written, when many of the principles of geology had been worked out and agreed upon, the nature of the earth's core was still in doubt. Thus *Journey to the Center of the Earth* was truly science fiction rather than pure fantasy: it played with possibilities that had not yet been eliminated, proposed scientific discoveries that had not been proved unscientific.

In fact, part of Verne's impulse in writing the book—and part of its popularity as fiction—probably stemmed from the currency of the ideas it dealt with. Geology was a science that preoccupied many literary minds of the period: Emerson, for instance, noted in his 1844 journal that "the use of geology has been to wont the mind to a new chronology. The little dame school measures by which we had gauged everything, we have learned to disuse, & break up our European & Mosaic & Ptolemaic schemes for the grand style of nature & fact." And Thomas Carlyle, in his 1836 *Sartor Resartus*, foreshadowed not only the geological concerns but even the specific setting of Verne's novel when he wrote: "In that strange island Iceland,—burst-up, the geologists say, by fire from the bottom of the sea; a wild land of barrenness and lava; swallowed many months of every year in black tempests, yet with a wild gleaming beauty in summer-time; towering up there, stern and grim, in the North Ocean; with its snow joluks, roaring geysers, sulphur-pools and horrid volcanic chasms, like the waste chaotic battle-field of Frost and Fire;—where of all places we least looked for Literature or written memorials, the record of these things was written down." Carlyle was here referring to the ancient "Scandinavian mythologies" which "have been preserved so well," but he might just as easily be describing Verne's Runic message from Arne Saknussemm.

I've given only two examples of the ways in which geology invaded the language and ideas of nineteenth-century writers, but many others can be found, in works ranging from the histories of Henry Adams to the novels of Henry James, from the poems of Wordsworth and Tennyson to the tracts of Ruskin and Morris. Nor did the influence run in one direction only, for geologists were themselves men of letters in the nineteenth century, and the British geological tradition grew directly out of the Scottish Enlightenment. In asking themselves what lay beneath the ground, these early geologists could not but be aware of the relationship between such questions and the concerns of myth and religion. Some of them were explicitly interested in religious issues—as when Hutton premised his theory of orderly geological development on the existence of an intelligent, efficient Supreme Being. But Christianity was not the only set of beliefs that informed nineteenth-century investigations into the nature of the earth. The classical underworld—that realm of burning lakes, massive creatures, and subterranean streams—was still a familiar presence to the Latin-speaking scholars of the last century. When Verne explored the underground in his *Journey to the Center of the Earth*, his imaginings owed as much to the mythic explorations of Virgil's Aeneas as to the factual controversies among the geologists of his own day.

This tension between myth and science, between "spiritual" and "rational" explanations of the underground, goes back at least to Virgil's own time. His near-contemporary Lucretius, writing about thirty years before the composition of the *Aeneid*, offers a theory of the underground that is directly at odds with the Virgilian portrait of Aeneas' visit to his dead father. Virgil allows his hero to descend to the underworld by means of a lake located in an extinct volcano, to witness the relative treatment accorded to the good, the evil, and the insufficiently well-buried, to converse with his father and other shades, and finally to return to the surface with renewed hope for the future. This underworld is the spiritual locus of the afterlife, but it is also a real place under the ground: one gets to it through a volcano crater, and it has its own geographical attributes (the river Styx that must be crossed at the entrance, the right-hand/left-hand division between eternal bliss and eternal punishment, the "bottomless pit" of hell, and so on).

Lucretius, on the other hand, denies the existence of all this fantastic material. For him, there is no afterlife and no hell. He argues that "death is nothing to us and no concern of ours, since our tenure of the mind is mortal. . . ." The corollary of his belief in a final death is a rejection of hell. "As for all those torments that are said to take place in the depths of Hell," he says, "they are actually present here and now, in our own lives. There is no wretched Tantalus, as the myth relates . . . There is no Tityos lying in Hell for ever probed by birds of prey. . . . As for Cerberus and the Furies and the pitchy darkness and the jaws of Hell belching abominable fumes, these are not and cannot be anywhere at all. But life is darkened by the fear of retribution for our misdeeds, a fear enormous in proportion to their enormity. . . . So at length the life of misguided mortals becomes a Hell on earth."

Whereas Lucretius' explicit intention is to raise these mythological elements in order to banish them, his invocations ironically have the opposite effect: of bringing them strongly to life, of making them seem historically real. Still, no twentieth-century psychologist could make a more sophisticated argument for projection as the source of hell's image, for guilt and unhappiness as the reasons people torture themselves with visions of eternal damnation. Lucretius' rejection of myth springs from apparently humanitarian motives; he makes his atheism into a vehicle for spiritual consolation, arguing for death as peace, eternity as projected fear.

Naturally this theory affects Lucretius' notion of what lies under the ground. In the first place, it is clearly *not* a spiritual underworld, as he emphasizes when discussing "Avernian" lakes (Avernus being the lake through which Aeneas entered the underworld). "All these phenomena occur in the course of nature," Lucretius stoutly asserts, "and the causes from which they spring are plain to see. There is no need to imagine that such places are gateways to Hell, or indulge in the further fantasy that by this route spirits are drawn into the Infernal Regions by the Powers Below, as lightfooted stags are commonly supposed to draw serpents from their lairs by the breath of their nostrils. How far this is from reality you may now learn, for I am setting out to give you the true explanation." This ringing note of confident empiricism is belied, however, by Lucretius' actual description of what lies underneath the ground. For, as the nineteenth-century geologists were obliged to acknowledge, one can't actually *see* into the center of the earth, so no amount of "plain seeing" can be adequate to its description. Instead one must rely on some kind of theory, some kind of imaginative vision.

For Lucretius, this vision naturally corresponded to what he posited throughout the rest of the universe: "First you must conceive that the earth, in its nether regions as in its upper ones, is everywhere full of windy caves, and bears in its bosom a multitude of meres and gulfs and beetling, precipitous crags. You must also picture that under the earth's back many buried rivers with torrential force roll their waters mingled with sunken rocks. For the plain facts demand that earth should be of the same nature throughout."

If this vision sounds to us more like science fiction than like scientific theory—sounds, in fact, remarkably similar to the windy caves and torrential waters Jules Verne inserted in his novel—we should recall that it nonetheless springs from a very acceptable scientific method. The principle of uniformitarianism, which Hutton introduced and Lyell propounded at the turn of the eighteenth and nineteenth centuries (and which has governed most of twentieth-century geology), is really a temporal version of Lucretius' spatial assertion that "earth should be of the same nature throughout." Empiricists both, great believers in what can be seen from their own vantage points, Lucretius and Lyell want to maintain that the scientific process is pretty much the continuous operation of existing and recognizable factors. They are both against any kind of "catastrophism," any argument that strange, unknowable processes (processes that have since disappeared) governed the formation of the world we live in. Thus Lyell argues for gradual buildups and declines as opposed to sudden movements of the earth, while Lucretius minimizes the "catastrophic" nature of volcano eruption by shrinking the phenomenon to human size: "You must remember that the universe is fathomless, and reflect how minute a part of the whole is one world—an infinitesimal fraction, less in proportion than one man compared to the whole earth. . . . Does anyone think it a miracle if somebody catches a fever that inflames his body, or is wracked throughout his frame by a painful disease?"

This strong tendency to minimize excitement, to prefer a calm and orderly science over an extreme and catastrophic one, seems to be a temperamental rather than a purely rational issue. To categorize one tendency as science and another as myth would be to throw stones from our own glass house, for (as Thomas Kuhn has shown) a shift in theory can leave one unexpectedly stranded on the side of the myth-makers. Indeed, it is perhaps more helpful to see these scientific theories as expressions of a deep desire for a certain kind of world—for an orderly world, say, as opposed to a revolutionary one. It makes sense that the nineteenth-century British geologists, coming from the only European country that did not experience a revolution in 1848, should stand apart from their Continental colleagues in believing in uniformitarianism as opposed to catastrophism. And it makes equal though slightly different sense for Lucretius to open his description of a rational, orderly science with a plea to Venus: "Meanwhile, grant that this brutal business of war by sea and land may everywhere be lulled to rest. For you alone have power to bestow on mortals the blessing of quiet peace."

As this quotation suggests, it won't do to distinguish Virgil and Lucretius in terms of allegiance to myth versus science, poetry as opposed to rational discourse. For despite the differences in their presentation of the underground, both draw on mythic or "subterranean" psychological and cultural forces to generate their tales. In particular, both *De Rerum Natura* and the *Aeneid* are long poems which celebrate the Latin language, and hence the culture of Italy, even as they go about their more descriptional duties. Moreover, Lucretius' book begins (uncharacteristically, given its rejection of myth) with an address to "Mother of Aeneas and his race, delight of men and gods, life-giving Venus"—to the same goddess, that is, whose machinations repeatedly influence the fate of her son in Virgil's epic.

But if the reference to Aeneas and his race of Italians links the two poems, the allusion to Venus points up their difference. For it is precisely in their treatment of love—especially married love, but also familial and friendly love—that Lucretius and Virgil differ most. *De Rerum Natura* does not avoid the issue; on the contrary, Lucretius devotes extensive space to the mutual pleasures of sex. But whereas Lucretius' theory of existence places pleasure at its core, Virgil's emphasizes consolation. The one experience that Lucretius' philosophy is not prepared to deal with is the experience of loss—or rather, he deals with it by embracing it as a given fact of the universe. To welcome the notion of a non-anthropomorphic universe in which events are basically the result of hyperactive atoms demonstrates either great courage or great fear. Perhaps the Epicurean Lucretius ignores the implications of love precisely because to attend to them would be too painful: a philosophy of pleasure cannot deal fully with love, for love entails pain and loss. Virgil needs his Underworld as a place where Aeneas can re-encounter Palinarus and Dido and Anchises; he needs the promise of an afterlife, and even of reincarnation, because the prospect of loss is otherwise too overwhelming. Yet Aeneas' encounters with the dead do not eliminate pain. On the contrary, his meetings with the dead Dido and, earlier, with his wife Creusa's ghost are extremely wrenching. Virgil is willing to accept this degree of pain in the universe because in exchange for the enduring pain he gets something valuable: the assurance that loved ones survive their deaths in some form. Lucretius' philosophy comes up with a solution that addresses one's fear of one's *own* death, by giving assurances that death is merely a peaceful and final end. But his denial of an afterlife, his argument against a Virgilian underworld, does not address the fear that one's loved ones will die.

It is Virgil rather than Lucretius who understands and responds to the pain of loss—the pain Proust describes in relation to Albertine's death, when he says in *Remembrance of Things Past*: "The idea that one will die is more painful than dying, but less painful than the idea that another person is dead, that, becoming once more a still, plane surface after having engulfed a person, a reality extends, without even a ripple at the point of disappearance, from which that person is excluded, in which there no longer exists any will, any knowledge, and from which it is as difficult to reascend to the idea that the person has lived as, from the still recent memory of his life, it is to think that he is comparable with the insubstantial images, the memories, left us by the characters in a novel we have been reading." For Proust, too, the deathward journey is a downward one, to somewhere beneath a "still, plane surface." Virgil seeks to resuscitate the dead, not by having them "reascend," but by letting the living Aeneas make a single, temporary visit. And the fact that this consolation comes through a myth or a fiction, in the form of stories about epic heroes, about "characters in a novel we have been reading," is precisely the paradox that Virgil and Proust enact. Art, like the underworld, exists to store and restore the images of the dead—to give us a sense that things do not end with death, but that some life-of-the-mind survives even that Lucretian finality, the mind's death.

If love is Aeneas' reason for entering the underworld, it is also a prime motive for Axel, the narrator/hero of *Journey to the Center of the Earth*. Though Axel's love for Grauben, the ward of his geologist/uncle, is an easily forgotten element of Verne's novel, it is actually central to the plot. At the book's beginning, when he is supposed to be helping his uncle to untangle the crucial document that will guide them underground, Axel is instead thinking about Grauben; "I love you very much, my dear little Grauben" is the exemplary sentence which springs to his mind when his uncle asks him, as part of the code-cracking, to " 'write down any sentence that comes into your head.' " When Axel hesitates to embark on the dangerous expedition, it is Grauben who pushes him into it, offering him the possibility of marriage on his return. Axel's first underground honor—his uncle's offer to name a subterranean bay after him—he cedes to his beloved, calling it Port Grauben; he takes for himself, at a later date, a mere island. And every time Axel fears that he will die underground, his emotions are dominated by the sense that he will never see Grauben again. Though Grauben is a forceful female by nineteenth-century standards, she is no Dido; perhaps it makes more sense to compare her to Venus, the intermittent guiding figure of Aeneas' journey. (Since Axel has no mother or father, his fiancée must do duty for the former, as his uncle does for the latter.)

As a matter of fact, Axel and Aeneas have a great deal more in common than the initial letter of their names. They both enter the underworld to seek knowledge: Aeneas of a historical and political kind, Axel in the service of geology. Their entrance is in each case a volcanic extrusion—Aeneas' Lake Avernus, Axel's extinct Sneffels. Each is accompanied in the underworld by an older, more knowledgeable male relative (Aeneas' dead father Anchises, Axel's uncle Otto Lidenbrock) and a local guide from the place of entrance (Sicily's Sibyl, Iceland's Hans). Underground, each crosses a body of water (the River Styx, the Lidenbrock Sea) and witnesses a similar range of subterranean marvels. For instance, Virgil's "twin sons of Aloeus, the gigantic creatures," his "breed of Titans," and his Tityos with "his body pegged out over a full nine acres" correspond to the giant sea-creatures and twelve-foot human figures of Verne's subterranean regions, while the hanging stalactites of Verne's caverns resemble the "black crag, . . . looking as if it were falling," that hangs over the damned souls in Virgil's hell. Like Aeneas, Axel encounters a "bottomless pit" in the heart of the earth. And like his predecessor among the shades, Axel makes discoveries about the history of his race—its past, in his case, rather than its future—when he finds underground the preserved bodies of long-dead humans. Finally, Axel and Aeneas both exit from the underground rapidly, unexpectedly, and by a different route from whence they entered. Virgil is so brief on this subject that Bulfinch rather takes him to task for the omission: "Aeneas and the Sibyl then took leave of Anchises, and returned by some short cut, which the poet does not explain, to the upper world." And Verne's erupting volcano, though more fully described, is hardly more satisfying to the practical reader, who even under the rules of science fiction can barely credit the safety with which the travelers ride hundreds of miles on the crest of a wave of lava. When Axel and his fellow-explorers do finally burst out to the surface, they find themselves in Sicily: that is, in the exact territory where Aeneas went into and came out of the underworld.

Lest we mistake these analogies for coincidence, Verne repeatedly alludes to Virgil throughout his own work. When Otto Lidenbrock presumes, early in the book, that the indecipherable message from Arne Saknussemm is written in a coded Latin, Axel "sat up with a jolt. My memories of Latin rose in revolt at the idea that this string of barbarous words could belong to the sweet language of Virgil." At the point when the adventure is actually about to begin—when the two scientists and their Icelandic guide are about to leave Reykjavik for the volcano—the author of the *Aeneid* again surfaces:

> *Then we mounted our horses, and with his final farewell Mr. Fridriksson called out to me a line of Virgil which seemed eminently applicable to the uncertain travelers that we were:*
> "Et quacumque viam dederit fortuna sequamur."

(This "eminently applicable" line translates roughly as "Let us follow whatever road fortune provides"—surely a sentiment that could have been expressed without Virgil's help, had the Virgilian reference not been the central point.) And as the three travelers are sliding down the interior of the crater, eventually to reach a depth of ten thousand feet below sea level, Axel comments about their slide: "This was Virgil's *facilis descensus Averni* with a vengeance"—a direct allusion to his and Aeneas' parallel modes of entering the underworld. In fact, that particular phrase from Virgil is the beginning of a passage which runs:

> *. . . The way to Avernus is easy;*
> *Night and day lie open the gates of death's dark kingdom;*
> *But to retrace your steps, to find your way back to*
> *daylight,*
> *That is the task, the hard thing.*

I would guess that we are expected to know this passage, and therefore to understand that Axel is making an ironic comment about the difficulty of getting back out. (Verne could not know that a mere century after he wrote the novel, people who knew absolutely no Virgil—in Latin or otherwise—would be reading his book. Or perhaps he *did* know it, and that was his version of an Arne Saknussem code, a secret message that would lead only the initiated down into the interior.)

What the classical quotations do is not only to invoke Aeneas as a previous explorer of the underground, but also to cement the kind of link I noted earlier between Lucretius and Virgil: that is, to connect the mythical with the scientific. Latin, for the mid-nineteenth-century scholar, was both the language of science and the language of classical myth. As the only common language among men of science, it represented an attempt to overcome the divisive effects of the Tower of Babel; thus Axel says of "Mr. Fridriksson, the natural science master at the Reykjavik school," that he "spoke only Icelandic and Latin; he came and offered me his services in the language of Horace, and I felt straight away that we were born to understand each other." But since this transcendence of barriers required moving backward in time (as the reference to Horace makes clear), the language clashed curiously with the modern, experimental approaches of the scientists who used it. In fact, the language itself forced the experimenter—at least, the experimenter with a temperament like Axel's—to see his scientific adventure in the light of classical myths, and to understand the new by linking it with the old.

Despite this obvious allegiance to the book's mythic ancestry, the scientific theories explored in *Journey to the Center of the Earth* were topical at the time of its publication. Side by side with Virgilian allusions are references to the central geological issues of the day: the argument over whether the earth was formed through slow, continuous processes (uniformitarianism) or sudden violent events (catastrophism); the conflict between "neptunic" theories of sea-origin and "plutonic" theories of fire-origin as ways of explaining the earth's major formations; and above all the raging controversy over the issue of internal heat. The disagreement between Axel and his uncle over the degree to which temperature will increase as they go downward is exactly the problem that obsessed French geologists of the nineteenth century. Thus we learn from Mott Greene's *Geology in the Nineteenth Century* that in the 1830s and 1840s the "most complicated line of contemporary research was the attempt by numerous observers to establish the earth's temperature gradient. It had been shown that the temperature increased with depth, but estimates of the rate of increase and the depth at which melting would consequently occur varied widely; calculations of the latter were further complicated by ignorance of the effects of pressure and temperature together on matter at various depths."

The argument about temperature gradient within the earth was connected to most of the other geological debates of the period, and the varying answers to this question were seen as providing basic evidence for one or another of the prevailing theories of the earth's origin. Thus geologists like Joseph Fourier and John Herschel repeatedly sought to solve the problem of "internal heat" as a means of getting at the processes by which mountain ranges, basaltic outcroppings, and other such features were formed. The uniformitarians, following Hutton and Lyell, believed in a notion of "gradual uplift" (note the overtones of salvation in the phrase itself) and corresponding subsidence, whereby igneous rocks would form under pressure in the earth's core and then be raised to the level of mountains. At least one camp of catastrophists, on the other hand, favored a concept of "secular cooling," whereby an initial planet of hot gases had gradually cooled from the surface inward, leaving a molten core and a wrinkled crust. Both parties acknowledged that the temperature below the surface would naturally rise as one went deeper. But the uniformitarians had to posit a temperature gradient sufficient to provide an ongoing, continual source of heat that would melt rocks and create volcanic pressure, whereas the catastrophists could presume that existing igneous formations were simply the result of *past* heat, implying nothing about the present state of the interior. Along with these two theories went corresponding notions of repetition versus progress: the uniformitarians held a cyclical, repetitive theory of the earth's history, whereas the catastrophists tended to believe that we were moving away from an initial state into some different phase. Given these distinctions, Verne's Otto Lidenbrock clearly falls into the catastrophist camp, for he says to Axel at one point: " 'Isn't it a fact that the number of volcanoes has greatly diminished since the beginning of the world, and may we not conclude that if there is heat in the center it is decreasing?' "

Even the scientific experiments Lidenbrock describes are drawn from actual methods of the period. Mentioning a visit paid to him by "the famous English chemist Humphry Davy," Lidenbrock outlines Davy's theory that the earth's surface was originally composed of metals " 'which have the peculiar property of igniting at the mere contact with air and water. These metals caught fire when the atmospheric vapours fell in the form of rain on the soil . . .' " Apparently Davy proved this theory to Lidenbrock by means of a little lab experiment: " 'He made a small ball largely composed of the metals I mentioned just now, and which was the perfect image of our globe; when he sprayed its surface with a fine rain, it blistered, became oxydized, and formed a miniature mountain; a crater formed at the mountain's summit, and an eruption took place making the whole ball so hot you couldn't hold it in your hand.' "

If this sounds like an incredible fictional device—the scientist as God, holding the earth in his hands—one need only go as far as contemporary science to find its real-life parallels. According to Greene, for instance, Fourier conducted a similar experiment in 1837, intended to prove his theory "that the earth's thermal gradient was just what would be expected if the earth was cooling from a hot state." Greene reports that "Fourier had heated globes of iron and measured the gradient of temperature within, which he found to be equivalent to one degree for every thirty meters when the scale was enlarged to the earth's radius." So the most science-fiction-like aspect of Verne's Humphry Davy experiment—the idea that the earth can be miniaturized for experimental purposes—is the very aspect drawn from reality.

Of course, Lidenbrock's scientific theory resembled no current theory of that time, since it posited a complete absence of heat at the earth's core. But in the mid-nineteenth century this was not as far-fetched an idea as it seems to us today. It was not until the 1880s—that is, nearly twenty years after the publication of *Journey*—that the "contraction theory" of the earth's formation was definitively proved false. As Greene points out, even towards the end of the century "nothing exact was known about the gradient of temperature or the distribution of densities within the earth, nor was the state of matter known. . . . From the time of Hutton till the twentieth century such experimental results were generally interpreted as suggestions of possibilities, and nothing more." Thus Lidenbrock's wild theorizing and willingness to disagree with prevailing authority are not out of keeping with the geology of the period. Moreover, his catastrophist stance is typical of Continental as opposed to British geology—that is, it resembles the sort of geological theory which would have influenced both the French Verne and his German creation, Lidenbrock. Whereas we have now come to accept Hutton's and Lyell's uniformitarian theories as the obvious and accepted forerunner of present-day geology, there was vast disagreement with these ideas among nineteenth-century Continental geologists. (In this sense, our history of science has itself become uniformitarian, recognizing in the past only those scientific ideas that substantiate present theories.) Surrounded by enormous mountain ranges, the French, Swiss, and German geologists had difficulty accepting the kind of gradualist theory which might logically explain the comparatively low hills of Britain. Rejecting Hutton's and Lyell's ideas,

Continental geologists instead traced their roots back to the Saxon mineralogist Abraham Gottlob Werner, a believer in the "neptunist" theory of the earth's formation. Even after neptunism itself was discredited, Werner was still viewed by many Continental geologists as the originator of modern geological methods.

Though Werner lived much earlier than Verne, dying in 1817 at the age of sixty-eight, his legend survived much longer (for instance, in an 1863 memoir—written a year before the publication of *Journey*—the mineralogist Henrik Steffens recalled an incident that had taken place in Werner's classroom); and one could safely hazard a guess that Verne's portrait of Otto Lidenbrock is based at least partially on the personality of Werner. For one thing, both men were Germans, in a science dominated by the French and the English during the nineteenth century (and the French Verne—who had to stretch a bit even to *create* a German character—never lets us forget Lidenbrock's nationality). According to legend, Werner had the ability to identify the specific type, and even the source-mine, of any mineral fragment displayed to him; Verne gives the same talent to Lidenbrock. Both men had short tempers and a tendency to stammer in moments of crisis. Both entertained numerous foreign visitors, and used these visits to keep abreast of geological developments in other countries. And both, above all, were adherents of neptunism.

According to Cuvier, who in 1819 delivered a talk about the recently deceased Werner to the French Academie des Sciences, the grand old man staunchly believed in the creation of geological strata through oceanic precipitation and a corresponding absence of internal heat in the earth's core. In *Journey to the Center of the Earth*, Lidenbrock uses the discovery of a vast subterranean sea to confirm a similarly neptunic theory:

> *"Well, Axel, there is a very simple answer to your objections, and that is that this soil is alluvial."*
>
> *"What! At this depth below the surface of the earth?"*
>
> *"Why, yes, and there is a geological explanation of the fact. At a certain period the earth consisted only of an elastic crust, which moved alternately upwards or downwards according to the laws of gravitation and attraction. Probably subsidences of the crust occurred and some of the alluvial soil was carried to the bottom of the abysses which suddenly opened up."*

Lidenbrock is not a complete Wernerian: he acknowledges, for example, the existence of igneous basalt and other lava formations. But it is only his evident belief in certain of Werner's key theories—in particular, his denial of the earth's store of internal heat—that enables him to make the journey at all, for any of the prevailing theories of Verne's own day would have held such a descent to be impossible on the grounds of temperature alone.

While the portrait of Werner-as-Lidenbrock gives the novel a real-life geological connection, it does not finally account for the credibility of Verne's *Journey* as a work of science fiction. What truly links Lidenbrock's theory with the living geology of his own day is not its neptunism, but its catastrophism. The notion that "at a certain period" the earth's crust had a different consistency, or that "the number of volcanoes has greatly diminished since the beginning of the world," represents a way of thinking that was very much alive in Verne's mid-century France. And once one credits a catastrophist explanation of geological history, one also credits the idea that the rules governing observable scientific fact may have changed over the centuries. This acknowledgment, in turn, gives rise to the possibility of myth's veracity. For if the past differed from the present, then many things become credible that do not seem so: maybe there *were* giants in the earth at an earlier time, and perhaps passages to the underworld *did* once exist. In other words, a catastrophist theory of geology is far more likely to locate geologic truth in outlandishly improbable stories of past events, while a uniformitarian theory presumes instead that "the present is the key to the past." Paradoxically, then, it is in part its scientific faithfulness to the prevailing tone of nineteenth-century Continental geology that allows Verne's story to suggest Virgil's myth. For in the realm of catastrophic geology, an earlier race of human beings might well have lived in a natural world that followed other laws than those governing ours, and visits to the underworld might therefore have been scientifically possible.

Seen in this light, Otto Lidenbrock's only mistake as a catastrophist is to presume that he lives in the world of the past, to believe that the fifteenth-century Arne Saknussemm can guide him underground in much the same way that the Sibyl guided Aeneas. This *would* have been his mistake as a real-life nineteenth-century scientist, that is. As a fictional character he makes no mistake and is, on the contrary, vindicated by the fictional work he inhabits. In this he resembles another believer in the patterns of the past, Don Quixote. Indeed, Cervantes' novel, like

Virgil's poem, is a powerful (if less obvious) ancestor of Verne's novel. The fact that Don Quixote is seen as a madman and Otto Lidenbrock as an eccentric genius may have more to do with cultural and sociological differences between the sixteenth and nineteenth centuries—especially changes in the status of the experimental, skeptical, anti-authoritarian scientist—than with any inherent differences in their respective approaches to fact. Don Quixote, refusing to capitulate to visible reality, was classed as a lunatic, while the nineteenth century was filled with scientific heroes (ranging from the French geologist Elie de Beaumont to the English naturalist Charles Darwin) whose theories could not be "proved" by simple reference to visible reality. The ability to dream up alternate worlds had become, by Verne's time, a necessary element of the scientific method.

This meant, of course, that the man of science was likely to partake of certain quixotic eccentricities. Verne seems to stress this fact by giving Lidenbrock a fair share of Don Quixote's characteristics. He is brave to the point of foolhardiness, and pigheaded enough to resist all contrary advice. Lidenbrock physically resembles our mental image of the Spanish knight, being a "tall, thin man," fifty years of age, with "big eyes . . . constantly rolling" and a "long, thin nose." At one point on the expedition he even rides a Rocinante-like horse, as Axel's reaction suggests: "I could not help smiling at seeing him, such a tall man, on his little horse, and, as his long legs almost touched the ground, he looked like a centaur with six legs." Axel, too, is clearly a Sancho Panza figure, constantly introducing practical concerns and realistic fears into his uncle's wild plans. Like Sancho in relation to the Don, he punctures his uncle's dreamy stories with wry bits of reality. " 'Do you remember a visit the famous English chemist Humphry Davy paid me in 1825?' " Lidenbrock asks, to which Axel replies: " 'No, I don't. For the very good reason that I wasn't born until nineteen years later.' " Like *Don Quixote*—and unlike most underground stories, from *The Aeneid* onward—*Journey to the Center of the Earth* is essentially comic in its mode, rather than tragic or epic. Its heroes get banged around a lot in the course of their escapades, but the wild antics of the subterranean forces finally have no more dangerous effect on them than Cervantes' blanket-tossers have on the knight and his squire.

But the most telling similarity between the two works goes beyond the wise/foolish nature of their heroes or the picaresque quality of their plots. *Journey to the Center of the Earth* ends up being like *Don Quixote* in that it is partially a book about itself. In Cervantes' work, Don Quixote is recognized throughout the second half of the novel by people who have apparently read the first half—the same first half we just finished reading ourselves. Similarly, at the close of Verne's story, Axel brings together the adventure he has been describing and the actual book we are holding in our hands: "In conclusion, I should add that this *Journey to the Center of the Earth* created a tremendous sensation all over the world. It was translated into every other language; and the leading newspapers competed with one another to publish the most interesting passages, which were commented on, discussed, attacked, and defended with equal conviction on the part of believers and skeptics. My uncle had the rare privilege of enjoying in his lifetime the fame he had deservedly won, and even received an offer from Mr. Barnum to 'exhibit' him in the United States."

Like Don Quixote, Otto Lidenbrock has become a legend in his own time by means of a written account which both creates and celebrates him. The barrier between fiction and reality becomes extremely tenuous here, and is made more so by the fact that the passage quoted above *does*, to a certain extent, reflect the real-world reaction. Verne's novel *was* "translated into every other language," and the pages I have just written are partial testimony to the way in which the most interesting passages have indeed been "commented on, discussed, attacked, and defended"—not only by contemporaries, but by critics writing over a century later. So the truth, and with it the impact, of this fictional passage depend on an external reality that Verne could not control: on the degree to which his novel was indeed to become famous. This gamble on one's own enduring literary success is like the one Cervantes engages in when he makes the second half of *Don Quixote* a commentary on the fame of the first half. By increasing our belief in the authors' abilities to foresee and perhaps even shape a reality beyond their fictional control, such comments also strengthen our (admittedly irrational) belief in their characters and their plots. For if they were telling the truth about the fame of their books, might they not also be telling the truth about chivalric adventures or downward journeys?

As in Cervantes' work, the plot of *Journey to the Center of the Earth* itself stresses the power of the written word. For just as Don Quixote chose his crazy profession after reading too many chivalric novels, Otto and Axel are led into the underground by a written document: Arne Saknussemm's coded message. There are actually two separate adventures of discovery in Verne's novel: the discovery of what Saknussemm's paper means, and the resulting discovery of the passage to the earth's center. The first thirty pages of the novel are taken up almost entirely with Axel's and his uncle's attempts to decode (and, in Axel's case, to suppress) the meaning of the written message. Like the earth itself, the message is something which hides the meaning at its core, shielding it from all but the luckiest and most persistent explorers. Lest we forget the parallel between these two events—the decoding of a message and the journey into the earth—Verne repeatedly reminds us of Saknussemm's role in the adventure by placing his signature at crucial points in the expedition. Thus Lidenbrock discovers Saknussemm's name "in Runic characters half worn away by time" on the volcano crater through which the travelers enter the earth; and he finds the initials A.S., again "half eaten away by time," next to the tunnel that leads from the underground sea to a deeper level of the interior.

In drawing this parallel between the interpretation of writing and the journey downward, Verne builds directly on ideas introduced in Edgar Allan Poe's 1838 work, *The Narrative of Arthur Gordon Pym*. The concluding "note" to that novella—which is, like Verne's novel, the tale of a fantastic trip to an unmapped place—explains that the mysterious "chasms" on the island of Tsalal could be read as gigantic written characters in Ethiopian, Arabic, or Egyptian script. The anonymous author of this note pedantically and unhelpfully remarks that the island's name itself "may be found, upon minute philological scrutiny, to betray either some alliance with the chasms themselves, or some reference to the Ethiopian characters so mysteriously written in their windings." Finally, the note (and therefore the novella) concludes with the quotation: " '*I have graven it within the hills, and my vengeance upon the dust within the rocks.*' " Poe's whole approach, in this afterword, wavers between explanation and obfuscation—as if to clear up a mystery in scientific, rational terms *were* to obscure its truth. Writing, he implies, exists to be partially misunderstood.

The fact that Saknussemm's signals are partially worn away, like the fact that they are written in Runic characters and in code as well, suggests that Verne is aware of the complex relation between verbal description and the journey into the earth. A sense of the inexpressible pervades the whole enterprise, from Axel's initial feeling that "Runic letters struck me as something invented by scholars to mystify the unfortunate world," to his eventual amazement at the gigantic cavern enclosing the underground sea: "I gazed at these marvels in silence, unable to find words to express my feelings. . . . New words were required for such sensations, and my imagination failed to supply them."

The Runic script is appropriately mystifying, for it leads the scientists to mysteries which are themselves beyond the realm of speech. Language, or writing, is the key to the abyss, but it is also inadequate to that nether world. Only a language which encompasses the possibility of the impenetrable—which seeks depth rather than absolute clarity, operates through allusion rather than explicit statement—can therefore describe the journey to the interior. The elaborate scientific theories of Verne's own day were insufficient to cover such ground; for this kind of writing the novelist had to hark back to Virgil. For it is only the evasive language of poetry or fiction, with its dependence on metaphor and its willingness to remain in doubt, that can approach the mysteries at the center of the earth. That hidden world will only reveal itself to those who, like Virgil, Poe, and Verne, are willing to straddle the abyss that divides the imagined from the real.

Digging for the Past: Poets and Archaeologists

Setting to work 5,000 years ago in the lower Tigris and Euphrates Valleys of what is now Iraq, the Sumerians applied their reedy writing instruments to countless tablets of moist clay, created the world's first written language, wrote the first history books, the first epics, the first medical prescriptions, the first receipts—and the first tales of creation. Indeed, among the few words in English derived from Sumerian are "abyss," the primordial sea that the Sumerians called the Abzu, and "Eden," the lost paradise.

—*New York Times*, April 18, 1984

IF THE NOVEL IS ABLY EQUIPPED TO EXPLORE THE UNDERground through language and metaphor, the poem is even more so. In part this is because metaphor is itself central to the technique of poetry. Poets are in the habit of bringing together unlike things to create an evocative image, as in Ezra Pound's two-line "In the Station of the Metro":

The apparition of these faces in a crowd;
Petals on a wet, black bough.

Here the actual becomes ghostly (an "apparition") as it shimmers and gives way to the imagined organic metaphor. To join the imagined and the visible—to *make* the visible into the imagined—is one of the poet's chief tasks; and the underground metaphor, with its variety of significances and its long history of use, easily lends itself to such conversion. Moreover, many of the subjects which dominate the idea of the underground—death, the unconscious, the roots of language, the past—are also those which inform poetry.

In an interview published in *American Poetry Review*, the Australian poet Les Murray agrees when his interviewer remarks on the frequency of "underworld" locations in his poems. "That's the one place I have in common with Heaney," he says. "Heaney and I both like it down there, under the surface of the earth, but he likes it wetter than me; he knows about wet soils." Murray's reference to the Irish poet Seamus Heaney instantly generalizes the underground tendency beyond his own poetry, or even his own continent (though later in the interview he is to remark that "disappearing into the landscape is very Australian"). He gives the image a still broader significance, while at the same time making it more personal, when he begins to talk about Jungian archetypes, mentioning a series of dreams "where I encountered my grandfather in various ways. When I was young he used to have in these dreams an extra wing on his house that had a library in it. Now my old grandfather never read a book, to my knowledge. His culture was entirely cattle-droving, drinking, reciting Bobbie Burns, and writing checks for his ne'er-do-well friends. . . . Anyhow, in my dreams he had this extra library with wonderful books in it; the last time I ever saw him in one of those dreams was in an undecorated cave under the ground where he and a whole lot of other chaps were sitting naked. I've always been conscious of caves and underground. It's something that came to me archetypally before I struck it in books." He then adds, a bit too offhandedly: "I suppose it might be connected, if we got Jungian about it, with the fact that my mother died when I was twelve, and she went underground."

I would call that getting Freudian as much as getting Jungian, but we need not quibble about psychological terminology here. What mainly interests me about Murray's remarks are the way they strongly echo John le Carré's description of the underground, as a place "where old men scratch for knowledge, gold, and death." Murray's old man is his grandfather, his "knowledge" is that library in the extra room, the "gold" is the grandfather's checks, and the death is his mother's. The dream, or Murray's telling of it, even equates literary knowledge with the underground by having the "extra library" of the early dreams give way to the "undecorated cave" of the last one—an important equation for the dreamer, who has turned out, unlike his grandfather, to be a literary man. Murray's dream also duplicates to a surprising degree the pattern in Graham Greene's "Under the Garden," which is about a young boy visiting an earthy old man who lives underground, possesses secret knowledge and great wealth, and has lost a daughter. The nakedness of Murray's grandfather, in particular, seems to have an affinity with the bodily coarseness, the intense focus on physical existence, that characterizes Greene's underground old man (and that signifies, perhaps, the "undecorated" id—or that mad creature whom Shakespeare described as "unaccommodated man . . . a poor, bare, forked animal"). The fact that le Carré, Greene, and Murray have independently come up with the same image argues for the underground experience as something beyond the merely personal, though in each case the experience is described in highly personal and idiosyncratic terms.

So perhaps Murray's selection of the underworld as an emblem for his work says as much about poetry in general as it does about his specific poems. As the image of Orpheus suggests, to journey downward is an inherent part of the poet's role. A singer armed with melodious lyre, able to charm all living things, Orpheus represented the power of poetry in the classical world. But he also represented the limits of poetry, for he could not bring back his beloved Eurydice from the dead. The story of Orpheus has seemed important and emblematic to poets ranging from Ovid (who made him a central figure in the *Metamorphoses*) to Bob Dylan ("she's an artist—she don't look back"). Robert Duncan, in his unfinished *H.D. Book*, points out the significance of Orpheus in the poet's conception of himself: "It is like a dream but not a dream, this going out into the world of the poem, inspired by the directions of an other self. It has a kinship too with the seance of the shaman, and in this light we recognize the country of the poem as being like the shaman's land of the dead or the theosophical medium's astral plane. In the story of Orpheus there is a hint of how close the shaman and the poet may be, the singer and the seer." Like the shaman, the poet can visit the underworld and speak with the dead; but Orpheus' story shows that the dead are nonetheless irretrievable, that they cannot be brought back to the surface.

A poet who has contemplated this fact deeply and interestingly is Rainer Maria Rilke, one of whose books was in fact titled *The Sonnets to Orpheus*. Here I want to look at another of his Orphic poems, the one which actually tells the story of Eurydice's final disappearance. "Orpheus. Eurydice. Hermes" begins (in Stephen Mitchell's translation) with the line: "That was the deep uncanny mine of souls," and goes on to describe the souls themselves as "veins of silver ore." Though it invokes an industrial image of Hades (in the fashion, for instance, of nineteenth-century social novelists), this description of the underworld does not have any of the hellish overtones one finds in other mining analogies. On the contrary, Rilke's underworld is soft and gentle. There are no burning hellfires: the only red is the blood which wells up "among the roots, on its way to the world of men." There are no screams of tortured souls: instead, the dead move "silently." The fearsome depths are mediated by "bridges/spanning the void," and *down* is virtually equated with *up* as Rilke describes

that great gray blind lake
which hung above its distant bottom
like the sky on a rainy day above a landscape.

The scenery consists of "gentle, unresisting meadows," a pastoral landscape through which "one pale path unrolled like a strip of cotton." This is an underworld which has already been accepted and welcomed, made domestic and appealing, at the same time as it retains the "uncanny" quality of a dream.

"Down this path they were coming"—they consisting of the three figures named in the poem's title. They are not named anywhere else in the poem: we know them instead through their attributes, such as Orpheus' "delicate lyre" or Hermes' "little wings fluttering at his ankles." Eurydice is no more than, and no less than, the italicized pronoun *she*. It is as if Rilke's underworld were a world without proper names, where only essences endure and human labels have ceased to matter.

Though the early part of the poem comes to us through Orpheus' sensibility ("He said to himself, they had to be behind him. . . . If only he could/turn around, just once . . ."), the center of the poem resides in Eurydice. It is she who personifies the transformative nature of death, who accords completely with this serene vision of the underworld:

But now she walked beside the graceful god
her steps constricted by the trailing graveclothes,
uncertain, gentle, and without impatience.
She was deep within herself, like a woman heavy
with child, and did not see the man in front
or the path ascending steeply into life.
Deep within herself. Being dead
filled her beyond fulfillment.

Weight and depth are here given their most positive meanings, so that the downward pull of "heavy with child" and "deep within herself" is made to seem satisfying—"beyond fulfillment"—rather than imprisoning. (This is partly due to Mitchell's translation; Edward Snow's more literal translation from the German renders that line "She was within herself, like a woman rich with child," with an exact repetition—"She was within herself"—three lines later.) This is the woman Orpheus loves—"A woman so loved that from one lyre there came/more lament than from all lamenting women"—but she has also ceased to be that woman: "She was no longer that woman with blue eyes . . ."

She was already loosened like long hair,
poured out like fallen rain,
shared like a limitless supply.

She was already root.

Eurydice has become, in death, impersonal. But if the earlier images suggest a disembodiment, a flowing outward, the final image of the root conveys a sense of condensation and embeddedness. She has become a thing that grows downward, that seeks its nourishment in the underworld rather than in the world of light. And she is all potential: able to give rise to something else ("like a woman heavy/with child") but still entirely self-contained. Eurydice is so immersed in her own death that she is oblivious to her restoration to life, her "salvation" by Orpheus:

And when, abruptly,
the god put out his hand to stop her, saying,
with sorrow in his voice: He has turned around—,
she could not understand, and softly answered
Who?

The poem ends with Eurydice walking back down that pale path, the eternity of her state reflected in the echoing last lines:

her steps constricted by the trailing graveclothes
uncertain, gentle, and without impatience.

Her sense of herself is so timeless, so contextless, that the walk up the steep path "into life" can be described with the same language as the walk back down into Hades—just as the idea of pregnancy, of unborn life, can be used to convey Eurydice's sense of her own death. Life, in this vision, is just a brief and easily forgotten interlude between the state of not-having-been-born and the state of having-died.

Of course, this is Rilke's Eurydice, and Rilke was more than half in love with death himself. But what he gets at here is the irreversible nature of death, the degree to which loss is permanent—which is really what the myth of Orpheus is about. Orpheus, being human, *had* to look back. To "look back" is to remember the past—and if we do not remember what we have lost, we have no motive to try to retrieve it. So Orpheus' quest was doomed from the beginning, for the backward-looking tendency which made him still desire Eurydice was also what made him lose her.

As Robert Duncan has suggested, the poet is the figure who bridges the underworld and the surface world. For Rilke, it is the underworld which matters more: the poet succeeds to the extent that he can immerse himself in that world, convey its essence, become like the dead. For Thom Gunn, on the other hand, it is the world of the surface which finally matters. He too is willing, like Orpheus or Rilke, to venture downward and explore what lies underground, but he does so always from the standpoint of the living. It is the life aboveground which gives meaning to that below, and not vice versa.

This comes through most clearly in his poem about Proserpine —a figure analogous to Eurydice, but different in that she is regularly allowed to return to the surface. Proserpine's return is limited but eternal; it is a compromise between the powers of her husband (death) and her mother (the fertile earth). Gunn's poem is called "The Goddess," and I quote it here in full:

When eyeless fish meet her on
her way upward, they gently
turn together in the dark
brooks. But naked and searching
as a wind, she will allow
no hindrance, none, and bursts up

through potholes and narrow flues
seeking an outlet. Unslowed
by fire, rock, water, or clay,
she after a time reaches
the soft abundant soil, which
still does not dissipate her

force—for look! sinewy thyme
reeking in the sunlight; rats
breeding, breeding, in their nests;
and the soldier by a park
bench with his greatcoat collar
up, waiting all evening for

a woman, any woman
her dress tight across her ass
as bark in moonlight. Goddess,
Proserpina: it is we,
vulnerable, quivering,
who stay you to abundance.

This is the mythical made mundane, a Hades which is literally under the ground, so that Proserpine must move upward through subterranean streams, "through potholes and narrow flues," through geological strata of "fire, rock, water, or clay" and "soft abundant soil," past "rats breeding," until finally she emerges in a city park. And in the process this goddess of spring is transformed from a force "naked and searching/ as a wind" to the imagined equivalent of "a woman, any woman/her dress tight across her ass." Just as the man-made clothes make that woman's body sexier and more beautiful ("as bark in moonlight") than that of the "naked" goddess, so human desires and human imaginings give Proserpine her earthly function. Especially in the stanza describing her emergence into the light, the poem's language is purposely "earthy," purposely crude: the thyme reeks rather than smells, the rats breed incessantly, and the soldier (as if in imitation of the rats) lusts for "any woman." But this vulgarity is itself a sign of vitality, an emblem of the sensuous physicality which Proserpine has missed during her long winter underground. Where Rilke's Eurydice is "filled beyond fulfillment" by death, Gunn's Proserpine is "stayed to abundance" by mortal life. It is we—"vulnerable, quivering"—who give to memory, and language, and the past, and the unconscious, and death, and the whole world that lies beneath the surface, their power over our existence—though it is a power that we cannot possess if we do *not* so give it.

"The Goddess" is connected, I think, to another Thom Gunn poem called "Bringing to Light." This poem is about memory and about excavation—about the hidden layers of cities and the lost cellars of the mind that are unearthed by chance digging. Gunn's poem builds on the same metaphor that Proust uses when he has Marcel say: "Words do not change their meanings as much in centuries as names do for us in the space of a few years. Our memories and our hearts are not large enough to be able to remain faithful. We have not room enough, in our present mental field, to keep the dead there as well as the living. We are obliged to build on top of what has gone before and is brought to light only by a chance excavation . . ." All the types of burial that concern Proust—of the dead in their graves, of lost cities in the earth, of meanings in words, and of emotions in the memory—are part of Gunn's poem as well; Proust even uses the same phrase, "brought to light," to describe the process of excavation. But whereas Proust's passage, indeed his whole extended novel, echoes with deeply felt personal nostalgia, with obsessive concern for the individual's past, the feeling behind Gunn's poem is one of profound impersonality, as if the self's memory were truly being excavated from the outside by a professional archaeologist or construction contractor.

The 71-line poem begins—abruptly, fragmentedly—with a stanza that explicitly links urban reconstruction to archaeological exploration:

powder, chunks of road, twisted
skeletal metal, clay
I think
of ancient cities of bringing to light
foundations under the foundations

According to Gunn, the poem was set off by the digging-up of Market Street in San Francisco, in preparation for construction of the BART subway. While this provides an interesting connection to another type of Underground (that is, the London subway which Thom Gunn rode as a child), it is not necessary information; for the poem's purposes, the catalyzing event could be any kind of urban digging. The city's age is important, though: San Francisco is *not* Athens or Rome, and hence the "ancient cities" are functions of the poet's imagination rather than real forebears buried beneath the current metropolis. There is an irony here, in the fact that the poet "brings to light" an ancient past which the city is too young to have; the classical past resides in language and human memory rather than (in this case) solid objects. This classical background comes through more strongly several stanzas later, where the poet recalls Homer's characters:

Achilles and Achelous the river god
he fought unite in person

and in name as the earlier
Achelous who precedes both

If classical poetry is what stimulated archaeologists to seek out Troy and Mycenae and Minos, modern urban excavations now have the reverse effect, sending this poet back to the classical poetry—as if archaeologists, by uncovering the lost cities, have made excavation itself a process reminiscent of the classics. The merging of past with present takes place through language: Achilles becomes Achelous through their similar sound, and both become "the earlier Achelous who precedes both." This poem is partly about the way words themselves, like human memory or buried cities, contain and preserve the past.

The second stanza introduces the word "cellars" ("bringing a raft of tiny/cellars to light of day"), which is to become central to the poem's structure. And in fact cellars turn immediately into structure, into "craters/like a honeycomb bared." The image contains both sweetness and threat—not so much the threat of a bee's sting as of its regimented, organized, memory-less life. This is the first hint of the impersonality that will color the poem, the first note suggesting the involuntary and finally inhuman aspects of unconscious memory.

The regimentation of the honeycomb gives rise, in the third stanza, to an image of imprisonment:

In one cellar, a certain manikin
terribly confined
in his sweat and beard
went crazy as Bothwell.
In another, his jailer lived,
here are his shelves for
cup and smock. He was a jailer
so knew he was free.

It is too crude, in a poem of this complexity, to say that the prisoner represents unconscious memory and the jailer the ego, but something of that sort is perhaps being suggested here. The self considers itself in control of its mind because something else is less in control, but it ignores the degree to which the general condition of imprisonment affects it as well. The image also calls up a realistic picture of a high-security prison, which, "like a honeycomb bared," has row on row of lighted rooms ("the luminous tiers" of the following stanza) placed around a central hollow.

The suppressed word in the prison stanza is "cell," and it finally appears a couple of stanzas later. The poet has told us of a childhood non-memory, an event known by pictures alone, a picnic which "still takes place, but in/a cellar I cannot locate." This cellar then, like a cell, divides:

There is a cellar, a cell, a cellular
room where a handsome spirit
of wilfulness picnics with me
all day limber imaginary brother

So that by the time the word "cell" itself appears, it contains the meanings not only of prison cell and brain cell, but also the buried sense of "cellar," which has done duty for it thus far. This memory, then, is hidden somewhere down below, waiting permanently for excavation but never finally accessible to the mind that contains it. The poet has imposed on this absent memory the feelings of a later time—the adult awareness of homosexual desires ("dandling me between his feet/kissing my eyes and mouth/and genitals making me/all his own all day/as he is mine"), the nostalgia for an idyllic "picnic on a hill/in Kent," the feeling of pleasure that the grown man presumes but can't actually recall. The sense of possession is a tenuous one: to be "his own all day/as he is mine" is not necessarily as strong as it sounds, if such inaccessibility can characterize "my" memory, "my" past. (One thinks again of the jailed jailer, whose ownership of his freedom is equally tenuous.) And if someone's own mind is so largely hidden from him, how fully can others possess him, or he them? The motion toward love is also a motion toward division: Achilles and Achelous, becoming one and stemming from one, are at the same time fighting each other.

Now the poem turns explicitly to language and memory:

But beneath the superior cellars
others reach downward
floor under
floor Babel reversed

The image of "Babel reversed" is hardworking and overdetermined, and the fact that it works so perfectly here would seem to substantiate Gunn's feeling about the deep connection between language and holes in the earth. On the one hand, the excavated site is literally a Tower of Babel turned upside down, a descending series of narrowing "luminous tiers," each circle slightly smaller than the one above it. And on the other hand, the movement of the poem is precisely toward "Babel reversed," back to the common roots of all language (in infancy, in the unconscious, in the origins of civilization). This second meaning comes out a few lines later:

joining each other in their origins

separate words return to their roots
lover and mother melt into
one figure that covers its face
nameless and inescapable

The points at which "lover and mother melt into/one figure" are at the origins of each person's being (the fetus in the womb, the nursing infant) and at the origins of Western writing (Oedipus in Sophocles' play). Again, excavation has brought the poet back to classical sources, as if somehow that first period of great literature were before Babel, as if the Greek language were our unifying "mother" tongue. The image of the words returning to their *roots* (the term used here in both its linguistic and its botanical, earth-seeking senses) is followed by the two stanzas about Achilles fighting and merging with Achelous, which in turn end with the lines

toward their common root
in the lowest the last the
first cavern, dark and moist
of which
the foundations
are merely the Earth.

This "first cavern" is too large and deep and complex to be *merely* the "dark and moist" place from which each of us was born, but it is that too—as well as the primordial sea, the "abyss" of the Sumerians, the warm, fertile ocean out of which the first life came. (And think, too, of Les Murray's remarks about the "dark and moist" underground, which run from "Heaney and I both like it down there, under the surface of the earth, but he likes it wetter than me . . ." to "I suppose it might be connected, if we got Jungian about it, to the fact that my mother died when I was twelve, and she went underground." Thom Gunn's mother also died when he was young, as he tells us in the essay "My Life Up To Now.")

The poem's last stanza evokes the beginning of all life even as it goes back over the other images—of love and division, of imprisonment and freedom, of the irretrievable memory and the determining past—which have dominated the poem:

nothing
but a faint
smell, mushroomy, thin
as if something
even here
were separating from its dam

a separating
of cells

Here we are back once more at the literal hole in the ground, with the "mushroomy" smell of old earth unearthed, but we are also miles away from the human race, viewing all human processes—love, memory, writing, civilization—as purely "a separating of cells." The "mother" of the earlier stanza has been reduced here to an animal's "dam." The poem's final tone conveys a sense of vast distance: the distance between ourselves and our inaccessible memories, between our world and the ancient civilizations, between language and meaning. It is as if only the most unsatisfying levels of knowledge—the factual knowledge, for instance, that all human existence is reducible to "a separation of cells"—can finally be brought to light.

At one public reading of "Bringing to Light," Thom Gunn introduced the poem by saying: "You should picture something like Bruegel's *Tower of Babel* turned upside down—or, really, Dante's Inferno, I guess that would be." The "Babel reversed" image is of course part of the poem, but the comparison to the Inferno adds a new dimension not only to Gunn's poem but also to Dante's. For it was not clear to me, until Thom Gunn said this, that Dante's hell *is* a kind of upside-down Tower of Babel—physically, of course, but also in its relationship to language, God, and human pride. Like the building of the Tower of Babel, the *Inferno* is in part an act of rebellion against God even as it is simultaneously a religious act; and, like a "Babel reversed," Dante's poem achieves its aim through linguistic unity and coherence.

One of the odd things about the *Inferno* is the way it mixes literature with history, merging what we might think of as "poetry" or "fiction" with what we think of as "real life." Thus the inhabitants of Dante's hell range from mythological figures like Orpheus and Antaeus, to characters who are known to us almost exclusively through literature (like Homer's Ulysses, or Virgil's Dido), to characters who, though historical in origin, take on literary importance through Dante's sympathetic attention to them (Paolo and Francesca, Count Ugolino); and finally to a host of Italians with no other claim to literary fame than the fact that they *were* real historical figures whom Dante knew or knew of. Similarly, the poem itself is at once scrupulously realistic and bizarrely fantastic. It is difficult to take the idea of a journey through hell as anything other than purely allegorical, and yet Dante takes pains to have all the details work out accurately, so that every move on the part of the two travelers can be accounted for, temporally and spatially, in terms of real-world laws of motion. Dante and Virgil never simply disappear from one circle or level and reappear elsewhere. They climb, or take a ferry, or fly on a monster's back, or get lifted by a giant—that is, they inevitably rely on some solid (if incredible) form of transportation.

Furthermore, the poet and his guide themselves straddle the worlds of the fictional and the real. Had Dante wanted to make his poem fictionally seamless, he could have made his mortal a version of Everyman and chosen Aeneas as the knowledgeable guide. One can assert, after all, that Aeneas has visited the underworld in a way that one cannot, with equal certainty, make the same assertion about Virgil. But Dante is not after such a neat division between the fictional (or the allegorical) and the real. By naming the traveler after himself and the guide after Virgil, he sets up a purposely confusing relationship between authors and the fictional worlds they create. One the one hand, his act of naming is an effort to lend credibility to the tale of the journey: since Dante and Virgil were real people rather than literary creations (this line of reasoning runs), their journey to hell must also have been real. But, on the other hand, this gesture has an effect similar to what happens when Proust lets fall that the narrator of *Remembrance of Things Past* is named Marcel. When authors become characters in their own fictions, they lose some of their reality as authors and become partially converted into fictional characters. Thus Marcel Proust survives for us mainly as the narrator/author of his novel, while Dante is primarily the narrator/author of his epic poem; each has been subsumed into his own creation, sucked down into the hole he dug himself.

How one is ultimately known by readers is not an irrelevant detail in the *Inferno*, but a central aspect of its meaning. As Dante tours through the underworld, we repeatedly hear about his future fame—for instance, when his old teacher Brunetto says to him:

> "*Follow your star, for if in all*
> *of the sweet life I saw one truth shine clearly,*
> *you cannot miss your glorious arrival.*
>
> *And had I lived to do what I meant to do,*
> *I would have cheered and seconded your work,*
> *observing Heaven so well disposed toward you. . . .*
>
> *It is written in your stars, and will come to pass,*
> *that your honours shall make both sides hunger for you:*
> *but the goat shall never reach to crop that grass.*"

(I have used John Ciardi's rhyming translation here because, though it's not always literal, it gives a pleasingly idiomatic and relatively accurate sense of the way the poem works as verse.)

One *can* take Brunetto's prophecy as a statement that Dante will eventually make it to Paradise, leaving aside the issue of his fame as a writer. But it is not clear how the older scholar and statesman, had he lived, could have helped Dante on his road to heaven; he seems more likely to be referring to worldly success, and in particular to Dante's fame as a poet. This is certainly how Dante appears to take it, for as he moves through hell he uses this prophecy to pry names and stories out of the less forthcoming of his native informants.

> "*So may the memory of your names and actions*
> *not die forever from the minds of men*
> *in that first world, but live for many suns,*
>
> *tell me who you are and of what city;*
> *do not be shamed by your nauseous punishment*
> *into concealing your identity,*"

Dante says to the alchemists Griffolino and Capocchio; and Virgil similarly encourages Antaeus to speak to Dante by urging:

> ". . . *this man can give you what is longed for here:*
> *therefore do not refuse him, but bend down.*

For he can still make new your memory:
he lives, and awaits long life, unless Grace call him
before his time to his felicity."

What the dead souls in hell "long for" is apparently fame aboveground—or, more accurately, remembrance among the still-living. That Dante sees himself as fulfilling this aim is part of what I mean by calling the *Inferno* an act of rebellion against God. If we were still in Virgil's universe, where the underworld was peopled with the saved as well as the damned, such a favor by a visiting poet might seem in line with Olympian intentions; but for Dante to promote the reputations of the sinners in a Catholic hell seems to be rather going against God's wishes—especially if that is precisely what the sinners most desire. Nor can Dante be justified on the grounds that he is a religious version of the Victorian social observer, an Edwin Chadwick of the spiritual sewers, for he is not content merely to document the general conditions underground; on the contrary, he is always quite anxious to get specific names, even when (as in the cases just cited) the damned are not eager to give them. And once he has these names, he does not trumpet them abroad purely to embarrass the sinners, as a Puritan minister might do. Instead he is often surprisingly sympathetic, as well as unusually scrupulous about recording the motives and conditions that gave rise to the sins. Thus most readers are left pitying rather than condemning Paolo and Francesca, or even the Count Ugolino, whose piteous tale about his sons starving to death before his eyes is one of the most distressing moments in the poem. For once, the levels of damnation seem not to matter: Ugolino, a traitor consigned to the Ninth Circle, earns as much sympathy as the tragic lovers in the Second. Similarly, the portrait of Brunetto Latini, Dante's former teacher, is so powerful and moving that it causes one to wonder whether God really ought to send people to hell for sodomy, which is apparently Brunetto's only sin.

For Dante to write poetry that keeps alive the names of the damned is, in its way, as audacious an act as for him to journey through hell itself. And the two acts—of speech and of travel—are actually connected at one point in the poem, when Dante and Virgil climb laboriously over the ruined bridge between the sixth and seventh "bolgias" (literally, "pits") of the Eighth Circle:

My lungs were pumping as if they could not stop;
I thought I could not go on, and I sat exhausted
the instant I had clambered to the top.

"Up on your feet! This is no time to tire!"
my Master cried. "The man who lies asleep
will never waken fame, and his desire

and all his life drift past him like a dream,
and the traces of his memory fade from time
like smoke in air, or ripples on a stream.

Now, therefore, rise. Control your breath, and call
upon the strength of soul that wins all battles
unless it sink in the gross body's fall.

There is a longer ladder yet to climb:
this much is not enough. If you understand me,
show that you mean to profit from your time."

I rose and made my breath appear more steady
than it really was, and I replied: "Lead on
as it pleases you to go: I am strong and ready."

What links speaking to journeying is breath, the motivating force behind both acts. Dante's closing speech to Virgil is made possible by and is meant to demonstrate (even exaggerate) his possession of breath. Its lack is what causes him to sit down, and he is told to vanquish that lack with strength of "soul" (which, in the form of "spirit," is another version of breath—or would be for Virgil, whose native tongue is Latin). As breathing is what enables Dante to move and to speak, it is also what gives him the power to sing his tale—not only because writing too is an act of speech, but also because his role as a living soul, the only "breathing" man in hell, is what will qualify him to write the story upon his return home. The aim of all this expenditure of breath is, explicitly, fame; and without that fame, Virgil says, mortals are as evanescent as breath itself, "like smoke in air, or ripples on a stream." Surely this is quite a profane thought: that fame earned by one's own breath, and not salvation by God, is what makes one immortal. Such faith in one's own body, one's own achievements, is in line with Dante's climb down through hell and (eventually) up to heaven. That climb is itself an act of self-assertion: like the builders of the Tower of Babel, Dante is literally climbing toward God.

The Tower of Babel makes an appearance in Dante's hell in the person of the giant Nimrod, the builder of the Tower, " 'through whose evil [according to Virgil] mankind no longer speaks a common tongue.' " Nimrod is confined in the lowest level of the Inferno, and he himself manifests the punishment of Babel by speaking only nonsense: " 'Raphel may amech zabi almi,' " he cries when Dante first sees him. Though Virgil abruptly tells him to shut up (" 'Babbling fool,/stick to your horn and vent yourself with it' "), I think we are intended to be moved by this piteous attempt at speech. It sounds as if it *almost* means something important: "Raphel" could refer to the angel, "amech" is very close to the Italian word for friend, and "almi" is one letter off from the Spanish word for soul. And for a reader of Dante in translation, the speech has the added poignance of being the only line of the poem which is identical in English and Italian. Nimrod's nonsense, in other words, is the only pre-Babel speech, the only words that mean the same thing to everyone—a fact that Virgil almost suggests when he says witheringly: " 'every language is to him as his is to others, which is known to none.' " (In this one instance, ironically, I've had to use John Sinclair's literal prose translation to render exactly the sense of the Italian.)

Before we accept Virgil's condemnation of Nimrod—during which Dante noticeably says not a word—it might be useful to consider what meaning this incident could have for the author of the *Inferno*. As I've already suggested, he too is engaged in building a tower that extends from the depths of hell to the heights of heaven —only his is constructed of words rather than bricks. (The lines of Dante's poem even bear a marked resemblance to stairs, with each stanza of the *terza rima* building on the rhyme scheme of the previous stanza: ABA, BCB, CDC, and so on.) Moreover, like Nimrod, Dante is responsible for the fact that the world of literature "no longer speaks a common tongue." At a time when literary writing was habitually done in Latin—the language of his guide Virgil—Dante wilfully chose instead to write in the Tuscan dialect, thereby increasing the variety of tongues that could be considered literary. He thus exaggerated the consequences of Babel, introducing yet one more language which could only be understood by a limited region (though for his countrymen he was doing the opposite: shifting the domain of literature from the "nonsense" of Latin to the terrain of everyday speech, where anyone could understand it).

Virgil mocks Nimrod for his inability to make language function adequately: " 'Waste no words on him,' " he admonishes Dante; " 'it would be foolish.' " But for Dante the inadequacy of language to the world he is trying to describe is one of the crucial facts of his poem. Just after leaving Nimrod and the other giants, he introduces Canto 32 by saying:

If I had rhymes as harsh and horrible
as the hard facts of that final dismal hole
which bears the weight of all the steeps of Hell,

I might more fully press the sap and substance
from my conception; but since I must do
without them, I begin with some reluctance.

For it is no easy undertaking, I say,
to describe the bottom of the Universe;
nor is it for tongues that only babble child's play.

The Italian at this point reads "lingua che chiami mamma o babbo"—or, in Sinclair's translation, "a tongue that cries *mamma* and *babbo*." Here again are nonsense words like Nimrod's—but they are nonsense words that appear in similar form in many languages, that do have a meaning, and that mark the earliest speech of most children. Thus Dante is doing precisely what seems impossible: describing hell in the same "tongue" he learned to speak as an infant. He acknowledges the audacity of his enterprise and then proceeds to go ahead with it, as if to say that his fear of language's limitations (like the Babel-builders' fear of God) will not be enough to stop him. Earlier in the poem he has allied himself with the babblers and the speechless when he says at the beginning of Canto 28:

Who could describe, even in words set free
of metric and rhyme and a thousand times retold,
the blood and wounds that were now shown to me!

At grief so deep the tongue must wag in vain;
the language of our sense and memory
lacks the vocabulary of such pain.

But this *caveat* is also a boast. For, not content with the limitations of ordinary "free" speech, Dante has burdened himself with the rigid requirements of his elaborate rhyme scheme—a pattern which is so powerful and so noticeable that one can never forget the presence of the transmitting language in this poem. While Christian apologists might suggest that the patterning of the *Inferno*'s poetry, like the complex structure of its hell, is evidence of God's grand sense of order, Dante's remarks suggest otherwise. In both the passages quoted above, he implies that he alone faces this impossible task (for to suggest that God would find such work impossible or even difficult would be openly blasphemous). And when Dante does call on divine assistance in his writing, he calls not to the Christian God but to the classical Muses:

O Muses! O High Genius! Be my aid!
O Memory, recorder of the vision,
here shall your true nobility be displayed!

Like the construction of the Tower of Babel, this poem is a tribute to human abilities rather than to divine power. And like the Tower, it has resulted in an exclusiveness of language, for Dante's masterful and constant use of rhyme has made it impossible for the poem to find an accurate equivalent in any tongue other than Italian; as Ciardi's evocative but far from literal version shows, one cannot do a rhymed translation of the *Divine Comedy* while retaining complete faithfulness to Dante's exact meaning.

Translation plays an odd role in the *Inferno* itself. Though Virgil was a Latin poet, his shade seems to have no trouble speaking with Dante in Italian—a sign, perhaps, that the world after death is one of pre-Babel linguistic unity. Yet Dante contradicts this impression when he introduces the shades of Ulysses and Diomed. Here Virgil must act as translator or at least intermediary, for " 'they perhaps/might scorn your manner of speaking, since they were Greek.' " Dante (or his God) has imprisoned these Greek heroes in a two-horned flame in the Eighth Circle of hell, quite near the bottom—and yet the poet shows more eagerness to speak to these shades than to any others in hell:

"Master," I cried, "I pray you and repray
till my prayer becomes a thousand—if these souls
can still speak from the fire, oh let me stay

until the flame draws near! Do not deny me:
You see how fervently I long for it!"

Dante's desire for knowledge of Ulysses—at the expense of, and in contradiction to, his religious piety—resembles the passionate questing of Ulysses himself, whose search for knowledge led him to die far from home. It is at this point in the *Inferno* that Dante's religious and literary/historical feelings most sharply conflict with each other. What has been an ostensible search for religious knowledge, a spiritual journey, becomes instead a quest for information about epic events, a version of "digging for the past."

If poetry resembles the archaeological exercise of digging downward into the classical past, the reverse is no less true: the early phases of archaeology were themselves often built on the inspiration of poetry. The Homeric participants in the Trojan War—the very figures who most strongly sparked Dante's historical curiosity—were also the prime movers behind one of the major archaeological digs of the nineteenth century, Heinrich Schliemann's excavation of Troy. Schliemann, one of the first noteworthy archaeologists (though not one of the most careful or accurate), apparently developed his interest in archaeology as a result of early exposure to Homer's tales. "Though my father was neither a scholar nor an archaeologist," wrote this German businessman-turned-archaeologist, "he had a passion for ancient history. He . . . related to me with admiration the great deeds of the Homeric heroes and the events of the Trojan war, always finding in me a warm defender of the Trojan cause. With great grief I heard from him that Troy had been so completely destroyed, that it had disappeared without leaving any traces of its existence." Like Dante's Virgil, Schliemann's father guided him through the underworld of the classical past—and like Virgil, this guide had access to the Homeric past only through Latin ("My father did not know Greek, but he knew Latin, and availed himself of every spare moment to teach it me"). Thus it was through language—Dante's medium of underworld exploration—that Schliemann was first introduced to the past that lay underground.

Literature, and especially classical literature, continued throughout his life to inform Schliemann's pursuit of knowledge. Thus he taught himself French in six months by memorizing "the whole of Fenelon's *Aventures de Telemaque*," and similarly learned Russian through "an old grammar, a lexicon, and a bad translation of *Les Aventures de Telemaque*." (Eventually acquiring over twenty languages in like manner, Schliemann himself became a veritable Tower of Babel.) For Schliemann as for Dante, the borderline between myth and history, between literature and reality, was not firmly fixed. "The Trojan war has for a long time past been regarded by many eminent scholars as a myth," Schliemann commented. "But in all antiquity the siege and conquest of Ilium by the Greek army under Agamemnon was considered as an undoubted historical fact. . . . For my part, I have always firmly believed in the Trojan war; my full faith in Homer and in the tradition has never been shaken by modern criticism, and to this faith I am indebted for the discovery of Troy and its Treasure." Like the author of the *Inferno*, Schliemann seemed to discern a mutual influence between the literary/historical past and his own work: the past would inform him (as the shades in hell communicated with Dante), and he in turn would preserve this record for posterity. Thus his own fame was seen as both a result of, and an aid to, the fame of the Trojan War. Like Dante, he ventured down into the world of myth and came up with a first-person testament to its reality.

Even the physical nature of Schliemann's dig resembled Dante's Inferno, for, according to his assistant Rudolph Virchow, "now that the last year's excavations have almost completely laid bare the boundaries of the old city, the vast pit should present the aspect of a funnel, at the bottom of which the ruins of Ilium lie within a pretty small compass." And when Schliemann completed his excavations in 1873, he had succeeded in unearthing not one but *nine* levels of Troy—that is, exactly the number of circles in Dante's hell. Though twentieth-century archaeologists have suggested that the Homeric Troy is actually the sixth or seventh from the bottom, Schliemann wrongly identified the bottom level as the "real" Troy—undoubtedly in much the same spirit with which Dante referred to the smallest, lowest circle of hell as "the bottom of the Universe."

But part of the reason Schliemann interpreted the lowest level of his dig as the Homeric Troy went beyond Dante's use of depth. It had to do, in addition, with Schliemann's equation of depth and value. In finding his so-called Priam's Treasure of gold—and, more importantly, his long-lost, treasured city of Troy—at the base of his funnel, the archaeologist was reversing the sense of the underground that one finds not only in Dante but in much of the writing contemporary with Schliemann. For Dante, the downward spiral corresponded to an increasing degree of sin, increasingly horrific punishments, and an overall sense of deepening fearfulness. In much of the literary and social science writing of the nineteenth century, the underground was similarly a place of evil: a dark, suffocating, threatening world peopled by demons, radicals, criminals, and the unwashed poor (often seen as overlapping categories). But for Schliemann the underground was a source of enlightenment, wealth, satisfaction, and fame—as if he had managed to scratch for the first two elements of le Carré's "knowledge, gold, and death" without ever running into the third.

Perhaps Schliemann's 1850 visit to gold-rush California, where he made a fortune almost accidentally while ostensibly clearing up his dead brother's estate, gave him an unusual sense of subterranean possibilities. Like the Texas oil barons of a century later, he saw the resource-yielding underground as a useful rather than a fearful place. But in other ways as well Schliemann signified, to a remarkably coincidental degree, an opposition to the general nineteenth-century interpretation of the underground. In 1871—the very year of the Paris Commune—he was unearthing the successive layers of Troy, establishing the orderly relationship of the past to the present: Schliemann was exposing the hierarchical nature of history (each layer resting neatly above the preceding one) and discovering a king's long-hidden wealth, while meanwhile the Communards were engaged in radical "underground" politics designed to disrupt forever such hierarchies and such wealth. Perhaps even more amusingly (though no less coincidentally), Schliemann lived and worked in St. Petersburg as a wealthy self-made businessman in the early 1860s—the period during which Dostoyevsky wrote *Notes From Underground*. So Heinrich Schliemann, the man who considered the underground a source of treasure and fame, might easily have been a model for one of the supercilious, bustling figures who jostled and ignored the mousey Underground Man on the Nevsky Prospect.

I have focused on Heinrich Schliemann because he offers an apt and colorful embodiment of the early archaeological impulse, but nineteenth-century archaeology in general was something of a Dantean (or infernal) enterprise. Beginning in the late eighteenth century with the excavation of some Wiltshire barrows, archaeology *per se* (as opposed to mere antiquarian collecting, or digging for buried treasure) did not approach its modern form until the middle of the nineteenth century; in fact, its emergence as a science coincided almost exactly with the 1859 publication of Darwin's *Origin of Species*. This is because, like Darwin's theories, the modern form of archaeology directly contradicted the older, Christian-imposed theory of the earth's history—in particular the assertion, voiced by Archbishop Ussher, that the world had been created in completed form in 4004 B.C. As Grahame Clark says in *Archaeology and Society*: "It was possible under the old dispensation for archaeology to develop from antiquarianism, and even for the outlines of secondary prehistory to take shape in parts of Europe—after all, Thomsen's Three Ages could fit into the span of Archbishop Ussher's chronology with several thousand years to spare—but quite definitely there was no place for Paleolithic man. It needed a revolution in men's conception of the nature and antiquity of man as an organism before the bare notion of primary prehistory could take birth." Like history, archaeology is by definition a science which, in Clark's phrase, is "involved . . . deeply in the flow of time." And yet, unlike most history, it must rely on downward explorations into unwritten realms in order to establish the passage of time. In this, as in other ways, the science of archaeology is akin to Dante's literary work, and to other poetic works as well.

Like Dante's project in hell, nineteenth-century archaeology operated through the disturbance of the dead—through the excavation of dead civilizations and even of entombed bodies, often frozen or preserved in twisted shapes that resembled those of Dante's sinners. Like Dante's writing, archaeology was both a radical and a conservative act: radical in that, digging downward to the "roots" of things, it defied religious rules about the unknowable, seeking like Ulysses to know everything; conservative in the way it observed the importance of hierarchical order, and in its reverence for the past. (What I say here about Victorian archaeology is apt in many ways to the twentieth-century profession—particularly in Britain, where archaeology is carried on very much as a nineteenth-century gentlemanly pursuit even to this day. Conversely, though many of my archaeological quotations are drawn from twentieth-century British writers, their import and even their tone have a remarkably Victorian feel.)

The fearfulness of the archaeological adventure, and the Dantean courage of its heroes, are illustrated in a story Glyn Daniels tells (in *The Idea of Prehistory*) about Cuvier, the founder of vertebrate paleontology, "the pope of bones." According to Daniel, Cuvier's "reputation was enormous as a naturalist, and enhanced by tales like the famous one of his visit from the Devil—only it was not the Devil but one of his students dressed up with horns on his head and shoes shaped like cloven hooves. This frightening apparition burst into Cuvier's bedroom when he was fast asleep and declaimed: 'Wake up thou man of catastrophes. I am the Devil. I have come to devour you!' Cuvier studied the apparition carefully and critically and said, 'I doubt whether you can. You have horns and hooves. You eat only plants.' " The seriousness that makes the joke funny—Cuvier's apparent belief that the Devil himself could be examined and described, could be submitted to his own penchant for categorization—stems from a form of selflessness combined with deep professional pride, much like the combination that impelled Dante. In Cuvier's case, the profession is that of paleontologist; in Dante's, epic poet. Dante's daring in describing Satan, in essentially reducing him to orderly *terza rima*, is the kind of blasphemous act that is only possible for a believer.

The relationship between descriptive language and events that are beyond words, a conflict central to Dante's poem, is also an issue in archaeology. In fact, a major subcategory of the science, often confused with archaeology itself, is the subject of "prehistory": literally, the period of human history that took place before the written record. If Dante's experiences defy linguistic representation because they horrifyingly exceed language's capabilities, prehistory is set in opposition to writing because it predates it. Glyn Daniel, for instance, remarks: "The material which the prehistorian uses . . . is the unwritten remains of the early past of man, the mute, silent witness of the origins and early development of prehistory. . . ." Grahame Clark goes further, suggesting that "as a general proposition it must be accepted that the value of archaeological evidence as a source of information about human history varies inversely with the extent and nature of documentary sources." And Mortimer Wheeler, in *Archaeology From the Earth*, cements the dichotomy between writing and archaeology even as he attempts to unify the two: "Not for an instant, of course, is it pretended that the spade is mightier than the pen; they are twin instruments; but, in this matter of digging. . . ."

For Dante, of course, the pen *was* the spade with which he dug down through layer after layer of hell. Even as he purported to find the infernal scenes indescribable, he proceeded to describe them. And Wheeler, too, finally comes round to an equation between digger and writer (or reader), when he remarks that "the successive accumulations of construction and debris on a buried occupation-site have much the same validity as the successive pages of a book, and, to be understood, must be comprehended in their proper sequence, like the pages of a book." In the same way, Glyn Daniel's compliment to Heinrich Schliemann's archaeology takes the form of a praise of authorship: "he had, by digging in the ground, made Homer come alive in the dusty hillside of the Troad and later at Mycenae. He had created a fresh chapter in the human past, had himself written prehistory, and demonstrated with overwhelming effectiveness that we must not give it up, that the speechless past could speak, that lost is not lost, that gone is not gone forever."

To give voice to a dead and silent past is seen as a primary intention behind both Dante's effort and that of the archaeologists I have quoted here. Speak to me, Dante repeatedly urges the otherwise mute shades, and I will convey your story to the world of the living.

Render up your history, the archaeologists say to the physical detritus that constitutes the "silent witness" of prehistory, and we will make the past live again. Viewed from this angle, the past is both valuable and visible; it belongs to mortal man, and it is his responsibility to preserve it.

The future, on the other hand, is a touchy topic for both Dante and the excavators. In the *Inferno*, prophets and seers like Tiresias are condemned to the Eighth Circle and doomed to a physical deformity that prevents their ever looking ahead. And archaeologists seem similarly nervous about prediction: whenever the possibility of a future is mentioned in archaeological writing, it is generally at the expense of the present. For whereas the past confirms our present values, offering only that side of itself we care to accept, the future is just as likely to contradict them. We are the subjects of our past, but we become mere objects to the future. Glyn Daniel humorously points this out when he says: "Each week—or if we are fortunate, twice a week—we see our domestic refuse being carted off and dumped in municipal refuse dumps—a stratified accumulation of gin bottles and tin cans, broken teacups and rotting cabbage stalks for the archaeologists of the future to study." (Perhaps it is no coincidence that the rise of archaeology, at least in England, came at the same time as an increased attention to the whereabouts of domestic refuse—witness Dickens' "Golden Dustman.") The archaeologist as garbage-scavenger is a conception which reduces not only the excavator himself, but also the culture which he excavates. The metaphor, however accurate, feels ludicrous and backward, like Dante's image of the future-tellers in hell, who were "distorted so that the tears that burst from their eyes/ran down the cleft of their buttocks." To uncover and recover the past makes poets and archaeologists feel godlike, but to attempt to look at the future reminds them of their mere mortality.

There is one respect in which archaeologists resemble, not Dante, but Orpheus. Like a passionately singleminded Schliemann, Orpheus went down into the underworld to rectify a loss, to reverse the passage of time by retrieving his dead beloved; and though he almost succeeded in bringing her up again, he lost her forever by looking back at her. It was his own act, in other words—his own desire to *see*, to *know*—that led to this final loss.

If Dante seemed to have faith in a largely retrievable past, archaeologists have been forced to believe otherwise. Mortimer Wheeler sums up the problem by saying: "At its best, excavation is destruction;

and destruction unmitigated by all the resources of contemporary knowledge and accumulated experience cannot be too rigorously impugned." The type of archaeology he criticizes was exemplified by Schliemann's approach, as described in this twentieth-century account: "Schliemann, bubbling over with the desire to unearth Troy, and untrained in scientific archaeological methods, went smashing down through layer after layer with ruthless abandon. He was not interested in the clutter of later cities that overlay his precious Troy. He hacked his way down through them, demolishing and destroying without bothering to photograph and record." But of course, as Wheeler suggests, even careful archaeology still destroys its object: a photograph or record, though it provides knowledge about a thing as it once was, is not the thing itself.

Destruction aside, there is a further loss acknowledged in the practice of archaeology: archaeologists recognize that their science cannot retrieve individuals, but only societies or cultures. Dante, on the other hand, appeared to believe that he could preserve in poetry the individual names of the dead and thereby assure their immortality. But most of those names are now meaningless to us—not because we can't be told their significance (indeed, there are copious notes on the subject in every translation of the *Inferno*), but because we have lost the immediacy of acquaintance that was second nature to Dante. When he put Ciacco in the circle of gluttons, or Buoso degli Abati in the thieves' circle, he was elaborating very specific ideas about specific people; but for us these names represent no more than a generic glutton or a generic thief. To the extent that Dante has merely recorded names (and not recreated whole characters, as he does with Brunetto or Ugolino), he has allowed his poem to become a kind of prehistorical dig, in which objects gain importance not through any inherent meaning but purely through what Daniels calls "their situation in undisturbed strata." Ciacco and Buoso are significant because of where we find them in Dante—in the Third and Eighth Circles—and not because of any personal characteristics they may have had in real-life Florence. Like archaeology, which (according to Grahame Clark) deals "not with individuals or with the relations of individuals to one another and to society in general, but with societies, including their internal stratification and their local organization," the *Inferno* is in this sense a social study rather than a personality-preserving narrative. It takes a different kind of poetry—a more Orphic poetry—to establish the importance of the personal over the social. The Orphic poet moves people out of history into the realm of story, saving them from the passage of time as Orpheus attempted to save Eurydice. Such a poet makes character transcend context—makes character itself into a work of art.

In an essay appropriately entitled "Digging Up the Past," the archaeologist Sir Leonard Woolley makes exactly this distinction between inherent (or artistic) meaning and contextual (or historic) meaning. "Supposing," he says, "that a peasant somewhere or other unearths a marble statue or a gold ornament; he sells it, and it passes from hand to hand until from a dealer's shop it makes its way into a museum or a private collection. By this time nobody knows where it was found or how, it has been torn from its context and can be judged only as a thing in itself; its quality as a work of art does not suffer, but how about its historical value?" Leaving aside Sir Leonard's knightly assumptions about the ignorance of peasants, one can still glean from this passage a strong sense of the difference between aesthetic appreciation and archaeological knowledge. It is to Sir Leonard's credit that he is willing to admit the former can exist without or aside from the latter. (In contrast, an archaeologist with whom I took a course at college proudly announced that if he ever found a "unique" pottery shard—an utterly unusual object that fit into no context—he would discard it, for it would have no archaeological value. I gasped at the imagined loss, and henceforth abandoned my intentions to study archaeology.)

It has become fashionable in recent literary criticism to doubt the existence of inherent value, to assert that *all* meaning is contextual. Granted the obvious and trivial level at which this is valid—granted the fact that what we call "true" or "beautiful" is dependent on our place in the world and in history—still, it is important for us to assume and believe that some things are true and beautiful (that some things are "art") while others are not. Those who refuse to do this, I think, can neither evaluate nor appreciate good poetry. For the consolations of poetry have largely to do with the distinctions it both makes and refuses to make between the eternal terrain it claims for itself and that "real world" which is our daily context. And whether he leans toward eternity, as Rilke does, or, like Thom Gunn, toward mortality, the poet bridges these two worlds by imitating Orpheus: by descending into the underworld and returning, with his Hades-inspired song, to the surface.

The Nether World: Class and Technology

Watching coal miners at work, you realize momentarily what different universes different people inhabit. Down there where coal is dug it is a sort of world apart which one can easily go through life without ever hearing about. Probably a majority of people would even prefer not to hear about it. Yet it is the absolutely necessary counterpart of our world above.

—George Orwell, *The Road to Wigan Pier*

WHAT MARKS THE USE OF THE UNDERGROUND METAPHOR in the works discussed in the two previous chapters is, to a certain extent, its universality. Geology and archaeology are sciences that describe everybody's earth: we all walk on the layers of soil and rock and lava that extend beneath our visible world; we are all descended from the prehistorical figures whose lives are transmitted through the "silent witness" of their buried debris. Not everyone visits the underground and returns, the way Orpheus, Proserpine, Aeneas, and the *Inferno*'s "Dante" do: but everybody, sooner or later, dies; everybody risks the death of loved ones; everybody faces the darkness of that eventual descent into the underworld.

For the nineteenth-century social observers and social novelists, however—particularly in Britain—the underground represented the habitat of an alien population: the "lower classes," the people of "the lower depths," the "nether world." The idea of a class-stratified society had been introduced by Edmund Burke as recently as 1792, but by the middle of the nineteenth century it had already become a linguistic commonplace. Moreover, it was an idea with biological as well as social connotations: the *lower* class was seen as farther down the evolutionary scale, in some sense *sub*human. (Note how language repeatedly reinforced the notion of height and depth.)

From the point of view of a middle-class Victorian, the working classes were practically another species, physically as well as socially, intellectually, and morally. And this was not an opinion shared only by the more conservative of society's members; if anything, it held greatest sway among the social observers who actively deplored the condition of the poor. For instance, in *The People of the Abyss*, his account of a 1902 visit to the East End, the ostensibly sympathetic Jack London says: "The streets were filled with a new and different race of people, short of stature, and of wretched or beer-sodden appearance." (London, being an American, uses "race" where a British writer might instead have alluded to animal "species.") A couple of decades earlier, in 1889, the English novelist George Gissing, drawing on the same widely held image of the subhuman poor, wrote in *The Nether World* about an outing at the Crystal Palace, "a great review of the People." "See how worn-out the poor girls are becoming," he writes, "how they gape, what listless eyes most of them have! The stoop in the shoulders so universal among them merely means over-toil in the workroom. . . . Observe the middle-aged women; it would be small surprise that their good looks had vanished, but whence comes it that they are animal, repulsive, absolutely vicious in ugliness?" Gissing would seem to be constructing a sympathetic argument—for instance, in his statement that the "stoop" is "merely" the result of overwork (rather than, say, an indicator of a more simian genetic makeup). But the grammar of that final sentence virtually equates vice with bestial ugliness, so that "vicious" suggests both evil (in the human sense) and untamed (in the animal sense).

As the titles of Gissing's and London's works imply, this bestial population is associated with the underworld even when it actually lives aboveground. But the "alien species" attitude becomes still more pronounced when the people it refers to are literal denizens of the underground. Friedrich Engels, writing in 1845 about the male and female English miners, noted that "nearly all miners are physically stunted," though "the muscles of the arms, legs, back, shoulders and chest are overdeveloped because they take the strain." The subhuman quality suggested by this gorilla-like physique is reinforced in Engels' remarks about the miners' morals. "There are more illegitimate children in the mining districts than elsewhere," noted this famous antagonist of bourgeois morality, "and this in itself is sufficient evidence of what those half savage creatures are doing when they get below ground."

In the course of Engels' remarks, the underground seems to become the source of dark sexuality as well as the locus of the particular group being discussed. In such passages, part of what comes across as a Victorian fear of the working class may in fact be attributable to a fear of the underground itself. The image, that is, was not an empty and transparent one that gained all its power from the thing it symbolized. On the contrary, by the mid-nineteenth century there were almost as many fearsome associations inherent in the idea of an "underworld" as there were in the idea of the laboring masses. The confusion and the intensity that infused the Victorian use of the metaphor arose from the way in which these two kinds of fear became linked and intermingled, just as the figurative notions of the underground merged with and colored the nineteenth-century sense of the real constructions that lay beneath the ground.

Perhaps the most frightening of the imaginary undergrounds, as Dante demonstrated, was the idea of hell—which, in its original form, was the idea of death. Myths such as those of Orpheus and Proserpine (which, through *Bulfinch's Mythology*, became accessible to every English-speaking reader) suggested the difficulty of escaping from death's palace once one had entered the doors; the River Styx was notoriously difficult to cross from the side of the dead to the side of the living. And this classical fear of the underworld as death was reinforced, perhaps in part even caused, by the custom of burying dead bodies underground. (Think of the terror associated with the graveyard, for instance, in scenes from Dickens' *Our Mutual Friend*, *Great Expectations*, and *Bleak House*.) Bulwer Lytton makes the point about burial explicit in his 1871 novel *The Coming Race*, where the eponymous subterranean culture (which one would expect to have *no* fear of the underground, because it lives there all the time) disposes of its dead by cremation, meanwhile looking upon death as a welcome rather than frightening event. When informed of the surface world's method of interment in graves, a representative of this coming race remarks that " 'to me your custom is horrible and repulsive, and it would serve to invest death with gloomy and hideous associations' "—suggesting that even this hypothetical underworld population innately fears the idea of the dead remaining underground.

If death alone was frightening, imagine how much more so was the Christian hell, the repository of eternally damned spirits. Hell may now exist mainly as a part of a Christian's moral geography, but it was once designated specifically as a place under the ground. And though nineteenth-century science, especially in the fields of geology and archaeology, somewhat weakened the idea of a physical hell that lay beneath the earth's surface, the image itself nonetheless survived. Even among twentieth-century agnostics, if they be literate agnostics, there remains a sense of the underground that is tinged by Dantean visions of hell. Thus George Orwell, writing in the 1930s, remarked of a coal-mine: "The time to go there is when the machines are roaring and the air is black with coal dust, and when you can actually see what the miners have to do. At those times the place is like hell, or at any rate like my own mental picture of hell. Most of the things one imagines in hell are there—heat, noise, confusion, darkness, foul air, and, above all, unbearably cramped space."

Miners were not the only people in nineteenth-century Britain to be exposed to the "hellish" underground. Following the construction of railway tunnels and the early branches of the Underground, all classes of British society began to venture below ground, with the subway companies offering first, second, and third class fares and attempting to provide corresponding degrees of comfort. (There were, however, special rush-hour subways specifically designated "Workmen's Trains"; and Gustave Doré's famous engraving of one such train—a picture in which the embarking London workers are portrayed in the unlikely garb of miners—shows the extent to which miners and the subterranean working class remained firmly linked in the middle-class imagination.) Oscar Wilde's son Vyvyan Holland, writing about a ride he took through a Continental railway tunnel in 1896, did not explicitly refer to hell, but he used all the same images that characterized Orwell's "own mental image of hell." "The smoke gradually filtered through the edges of the windows into our compartment until we could hardly see it," says Holland; "the solitary oil-lamp in the roof grew dimmer and dimmer, and the temperature kept on rising. To add to our discomfort, the noise of puffing and clanking was deafening. Presently, above all the din, some children in the next compartment got into a panic and started screaming."

It was the fear of rides such as this which prompted *The Times* to remark in 1862, the year before the opening of the first underground railway line in London: "A subterranean railway under London was awfully suggestive of dark, noisome tunnels, buried many fathoms deep beneath the reach of light or life. . . . It seemed an insult to common sense to suppose that people who could travel as cheaply to the city on the outside of a Paddington 'bus would ever prefer, as a merely quicker medium, to be driven amid palpable darkness through the foul subsoil of London." The phrases "beyond the reach of light or life" and "amid palpable darkness," suggesting as they do the opposition of God's light and Satan's darkness, manage to reinforce the physical sense of danger with religious or moral overtones. Though the underground railway companies responded to such fears by taking extreme precautionary measures to insure safety (there were *no* fatal accidents to passengers during the entire twenty-five-year period of steam operation), they did amuse themselves by playing on the mythical notion of the "underworld" in the naming of the steam-engines: the first locomotives came from the Vulcan Foundry, and some of the early engines were given classical names like Pluto, Dido, and Cerberus. Such names suggest a strange combination of fear and attraction, of "old" superstition and "new" pride in technology. It would seem to be the sense that they were vanquishing the underworld—making it accessible and traversible, and thereby defeating its pre-industrial power to frighten them—that gave the Victorians a special pleasure in their sewers, subways, and other underground achievements.

This victory, which involved tearing up and urban-renewing a number of London neighborhoods, was seen as a simultaneous conquest of the "foul subsoil" of an imaginary hell and the depths of the terrifying lower classes. The two kinds of depth are explicitly brought together in a section of Gissing's *The Nether World*, where he shows a pathetic waif called Pennyloaf (a Cockney abbreviation of Penelope—another classical allusion, used with ironic effect) returning home to her slum neighborhood in search of her husband. This slum, Shooter's Gardens, has earlier been described as "a picturesque locality which demolition and rebuilding have of late transformed," and is remarkable mainly for its obscurity and its sunken position ("To enter from the obscurer end, you descended a flight of steps, under a low archway, in a court itself not easily discoverable"). The infernal quality of the Gardens and its adjoining alley, the Court, is strongly conveyed in the nightmarish scene of Pennyloaf's return: "In this blind alley there stood throughout the day a row of baked-potato ovens. . . . At seven o'clock of an evening fires were wont to be lighted under each of these baking-machines, preparatory to their being wheeled away, each to its accustomed street-corner. Now the lighting of these fires entails the creation of smoke, and whilst these ten or twelve ovens were getting ready to bake potatoes the Court was in a condition not easily described. A single lamp existed for the purpose of giving light to the alley, and at no time did this serve much more than to make darkness visible; at present the blind man would have fared as well in that retreat as he who had eyes, and the marvel was how those who lived there escaped suffocation. In the Gardens themselves . . . the air had a stifling smell and a bitter taste." As if this hint of sulfur were not strong enough, Gissing then introduces the words of a street-corner lunatic named Mad Jack, who screeches that the poor of this slum are being punished for their wickedness in a previous life: " 'This life you are now leading is that of the damned; this place to which you are confined is Hell! There is no escape for you. From poor you shall become poorer; the older you grow the lower shall you sink in want or misery; at the end there is waiting for you, one and all, a death in abandonment and despair. This is Hell—Hell—Hell!' "

I am not suggesting that Mad Jack's opinions are exactly Gissing's. But I think it's clear that Gissing is using the physical description of the slum (evocative of a Dantean or Miltonic hell in its "darkness visible," its "stifling smell," its "bitter taste," and its burning fires), combined with the madman's prophecy, to play on his audience's probable attitude toward the poor. The more *laissez-faire*-minded among Gissing's readers were already primed to think of slum-dwellers as the damned, brought to their condition through faults of their own. Mad Jack's taunt—" 'You . . . were once rich people, with every blessing the world can bestow. . . . Because you made an ill-use of your wealth . . . therefore after death you received the reward of your wickedness" —is a crazy, inverted version of a Samuel-Smiles-like claim that anyone, with enough effort, could become a self-made rich man. (It is also, of course, a parody of the "appropriate" punishments visited on the sinners in Dante's hell.) In his horrific description, Gissing is both using and mocking a prevailing ethic which made the poor responsible for their own damnation. Because Gissing himself was so ambivalent about the "mob," it is not absolutely clear how he intended the parody to work, but at the very least it creates a sense of discomfort and distress in the reader. In the passages quoted above, you are led into making your own associations between the slums and hell, and a madman's rantings are then held up as the mirror to your thoughts.

As Gissing's description of the Court implies, it was natural for the upper classes to associate the lower classes with the subterranean, since many of the poor literally lived and worked in dark, cave-like, buried rooms. Arriving in London from a northern industrial town, the heroine of Elizabeth Gaskell's 1855 novel *North and South* notices: "There might be toilers and moilers there in London, but she never saw them; the very servants lived in an underground world of their own, of which she knew neither the hopes nor the fears; they only seemed to start into existence when some want or whim of their master and mistress needed them." As Gaskell suggests, the kitchens of even the grandest houses in Victorian London were always located in the basement, and this was the territory to which all servants were consigned. Even the butler and the head housekeeper took their meals "belowstairs"; it was a sign of rank—such as that of a governess—to be permitted to eat in one's own room upstairs.

Other poor people besides servants lived underground as well—and the poorer they were, the more likely they were to live there. Thus in *The Nether World* the working-class John Hewett, having lost his job, sinks down in the world and inhabits an appropriately low dwelling: "The cellar in which John Hewett and his family were housed was underneath a milk-shop; Amy led the way down stone steps from the pavement of the street into an area, where more than two people would have had difficulty in standing together. . . . To poor homes Sidney Kirkwood was no stranger, but a poorer than this now disclosed to him he had never seen." Even the word "disclosed" here suggests the unearthing of something hidden away from the light of day. This cave-like dwelling was both a dungeon and a tomb: John Hewett's face "was like that of some prisoner, whom the long torture of a foul dungeon has brought to madness," and when his wife dies, he raves: " 'Do you remember what hopes I used to have when we were first married? See the end of 'em—look at this underground hole—look at this bed as she lays on!' " This is an extreme case; but earlier in the same novel Gissing has referred to the Clerkenwell alleys, with their small industries and dwellings, as "grimy burrows," "recesses of dim byways, where sunshine and free air are forgotten things." Twenty years later, Jack London confirmed this subterranean vision of the East End when he described his visit to the home of one of its better-off citizens. "This dining room, on the same floor as the kitchen, was about four feet below the level of the ground and so dark (it was midday) that I had to wait a space for my eyes to adjust themselves to the gloom," London says. "Dirty light filtered in through a window, the top of which was on a level with the sidewalk, and in this light I found that I was able to read newspaper print." Whereas writers like Dante, Poe, and Verne create a link between writing and the underground, London sets them in opposition: the chief characteristic of this basement dwelling is that it is almost too dark for reading.

For the most part, Victorian writers and observers associated underground dwellings and workplaces with all the terrifying sides of working-class life: poverty, squalor, darkness, foul air, imprisonment, death. But occasionally the lower regions would simply be equated with class, without the more common negative overtones. In *The Nether World*, for instance, there is a description of subterranean work that defines class through both clothing and location: "Bob wore a collar. In the die-sinking establishment which employed him there were, it is true, two men who belonged to the collarless; but their business was down in the basement of the building, where they kept up a furnace, worked huge stamping-machines, and so on. Bob's workshop was upstairs, and the companions with whom he sat, without exception, had something white and stiff round their necks." This might have been an opportunity for Gissing to stress the heat and discomfort of the lower regions, but, on the contrary, he uses it to comment on the "stiff" atmosphere of the slightly higher environment. If this is a remark on the inevitability of class distinctions, it is also a mockery of the airs which those who snobbishly make such distinctions are likely to give themselves, and a corresponding praise of the relative ease, power, and straightforwardness it assigned to "the collarless . . . down in the basement."

An even more telling example occurs in Gissing's *Demos*. Among the central characters of this novel are the members of the Mutimer family, initially a stable, happy, responsible, clean-living example of working-class existence. Our first vision of them is in their basement kitchen: "The kitchen was small, and everywhere reflected from some bright surface either the glow of the open grate or the yellow lustre of the gas-jet; red curtains drawn across the window added warmth and homely comfort to the room. It was not the kitchen of pinched or slovenly working-folk; the air had a scent of cleanliness, of freshly scrubbed boards and polished metal, and the furniture was superabundant." The same elements that elsewhere signify a hellish environment—fire, heat, enclosure, the color red—are here used to represent a cozy retreat from the outside elements (as they are, in a similar way, in the turn-of-the-century Underground poster I mentioned in an earlier chapter, the one captioned "Underground: Always Warm and Bright"). This vision of domestic coziness and warmth becomes the lost paradise against which Gissing charts the swift economic rise and moral fall of the Mutimers. Mrs. Mutimer, the mother responsible for all this domesticity, is the only family member who opposes the new prosperity; when her son Richard moves her to a better house, she resists sitting in the upstairs parlor and instead prefers to spend her time in the basement kitchen—a habit that her son counters by hiring a servant to occupy that domain. Though this plot element reeks slightly of the buy-them-bathtubs-and-they'll-store-coal-in-them school of thought, Gissing is somewhat more sophisticated than that. Instead, he seriously presents the underground kitchen as the heart of working-class domesticity, the symbol of what can be lost when one moves up the social ladder—much in the manner of the more simpleminded yet nonetheless moving parts of Dickens.

But both Gissing and Dickens had far from simple attitudes toward the underground: they each stretched, tested, and reshaped the metaphor to suit their various novelistic purposes. Especially when they turned their attention to the evils of northern industrialism, both novelists altered somewhat the relation between the "upper" world and the "lower." Thus in *Demos* and *Hard Times* the workplace itself—including its masters as well as its men—becomes associated with hell, whether it be an underground mining industry or an above-ground textile mill. In other words, the hierarchical separation of classes, which in London takes a physical upstairs-downstairs form, becomes much more figurative in "Belwick" or "Coketown," where the industrial workers are relegated to hell not because they are underground, but purely by virtue of the kind of work they do. And whereas the wealthy of London remain safely removed even from the hellish quarters of their own domiciles, the industrial capitalists of the north essentially take on the role of Satan, functioning as taskmasters of the lower regions.

The physical descriptions of these northern factories, like those of the London underworld, still invoke the image of a hot, smoky hell—but this time it is one that has erupted out of its place under the earth and has sprung up onto the surface. Thus Gissing says of the industrial district described at the beginning of *Demos*: "The good abbots, who were wont to come out in the summer time to Wanley, would be at a loss to recognize their consecrated home in those sooty relics. Belwick, with its hundred and fifty fire-vomiting blast-furnaces, would to their eyes more nearly resemble a certain igneous realm of which they thought much in their sojourn upon earth." And Dickens' Coketown, though not as explicitly compared to hell, nonetheless has all the attributes that one associates with that domain: "It was a town of red brick, or of brick that would have been red if the smoke and ashes had allowed it; but as matters stood it was a town of unnatural red and black like the painted face of a savage. It was a town of machinery and tall chimneys, out of which interminable serpents of smoke trailed themselves for ever and ever, and never got uncoiled. It had a black canal in it, and a river that ran purple with ill-smelling dye, and vast piles of buildings full of windows where there was a rattling and a trembling all day long, and where the piston of the steam-engine worked monotonously up and down, like the head of an elephant in a state of melancholy madness."

Here the usual Dickens tendency to adopt biblical rhythms serves a special purpose: the weighty sound of the sentences joins forces with phrases like "interminable serpents" and "forever and ever" to suggest the solemn eternity of hell. The colors, too, are a hellish red and black—fire and smoke, blood and burnt flesh—and even the "black canal" and the "river that ran purple" call to mind the other-worldly hues of the River Styx. The constant "rattling and trembling" evokes the din that other writers have attributed to hell; it might also suggest an atmosphere of ghoulish fear, in the form of the rattling and trembling of animated bones. Finally, that repetitious, seemingly pointless gesture of the steam-engine—"monotonously up and down, like the head of an elephant in a state of melancholy madness"—mirrors all of the pointless repetitions that hell's damned souls are doomed to enact forever.

Within this infernal world of Coketown, this subterranean region coughed up to the surface of northern England, the figure representing the working class is Stephen Blackpool (whose name itself evokes ideas of depth and obscurity). Stephen is a sympathetic character, but he is also one of those ritual Dickensian victims who—like Little Nell, Jo, Smike, or Betty Higden—always seem less human than the central victim/survivors of the novels (Little Dorrit, Oliver Twist, Lizzie Hexam). In *Hard Times*, Stephen belongs to a separate species from the schoolmaster Gradgrind, the industrialist Bounderby, and the intended reader: he speaks in a heavy dialect (more so than his female social equivalents, Rachael and the old Mrs. Bounderby); he has no expectations for happiness in life, but nonetheless keeps on working faithfully for no discernible reason; and he is able to withstand with remarkable resignation and goodwill his complete exclusion from the society of his unionized co-workers. This could be the description of a saint, but it might also be a beast or a robot. When Dickens first introduces Stephen, even the language seems to stress his subhuman quality: "In the hardest working part of Coketown; in the innermost fortifications of that ugly citadel, where nature was as strongly bricked out as killing airs and gases were bricked in; at the heart of the labyrinth of narrow courts upon courts, which had come into existence piecemeal, every piece in a violent hurry for some one man's purpose, and the whole an unnatural family, shouldering, and trampling, and pressing one another to death; in the last close nook of this great exhausted receiver, where the chimneys, for want of air to make a draft, were built in an immense variety of stunted and crooked shapes, as though every house put out a sign of the kind of people who might be expected to be born in it; among the multitude of Coketown, generically called 'the Hands,'—a race who would have found more favour with some people, if Providence had seen fit to make them only hands, or like the lower creatures of the seashore, only hands and stomachs—lived a certain Stephen Blackpool, forty years of age."

I find it hard to reproduce this passage without commenting on Dickens' brilliance as a stylist—on the way the single long, add-on sentence reproduces, in its form, the "piecemeal," "crooked" structures that lead us inward to "the heart of the labyrinth" which is Stephen himself. And—as in much other Dickens—one can't help but feel that the "shouldering," "trampling" buildings are more lively than the people who occupy them. But my real interest, for the moment, lies in the apparent reference to evolution. Though this novel was published five years before *The Origin of Species*, that interjection about "the Hands"—along with the Lamarckian "stunted and crooked" houses that determine their inhabitants' shapes—strongly suggests that the Victorians would have had to invent Darwin if he hadn't existed already.

Evolution, as a general theory, appealed to the Victorian mind in a way that went far beyond its scientific validity. Not only did it reinforce all the desired notions of a flexible hierarchy, a careful ordering of rank up which one could climb according to a combination of personal and hereditary merit. It also suited the aesthetic of "form following function" espoused most clearly by Ruskin, but also displayed in the great mid-Victorian railway terminals, the Crystal Palace, and the major new factories of the north. And because they were so anxious to find a direct connection between form and function, or between physical and moral worth, the Victorian believers in the self-made man were likely to tend toward Spencerian or Lamarckian rather than strictly Darwinian theories. For an age that believed in progress, teleological evolution was an enormously attractive idea: it was much easier to believe that biology was moving toward a grandly planned affirmation of human superiority than to acknowledge that it was merely responding (as Darwin theorized) to random environmental influences. And Lamarck's "inheritance of acquired characteristics" notion had a similar appeal: not only did it speed up the evolutionary process ("improving" it, in that respect, as the speeded-up factory technology improved industry), but it also seemed to place biological development more completely under human control. This argument was a theoretical asset to proponents of both sides of the social question. Lamarckian evolutionary theory allowed factory-owners to blame the poor for their own situation (since it only took one generation, after all, to "acquire" success), while it also enabled social reformers to blame the industrialists for reducing workers to physically useful organisms, turning them into mindless Hands. Dickens, as always, complicates the argument: in the passage I just quoted from *Hard Times*, he seems to be taking the latter position, but he does so by ironically referring to "Providence" and "signs." These were big words in the *laissez-faire* vocabulary, but they were also extremely unscientific words; so Dickens appears to be erecting an "evolutionary" theory on an extremely faulty foundation, perhaps intending thereby to bring the whole structure down.

If in life he is the example of the well-behaved "good" Hand, in death Stephen Blackpool becomes something a bit more disruptive. Pursued unjustly by Bounderby's law-enforcers for a crime actually committed by Tom Gradgrind, Stephen attempts to return to Coketown to clear himself, but during his nighttime journey falls down an abandoned mine shaft. It is here, after several days, that Rachael and Sissy find him—in a notorious hole aptly known as "the Old Hell Shaft." In the climactic scene where Stephen, half-dead already, is brought up to the surface, Dickens merges together the ideas of hell, death, working-class labor, and the physical underground. The pit, like Edgar Allan Poe's, becomes a grave for the living dead: Sissy Jupe, running for help, feels that "it seemed hours and hours now since she had left the lost man lying in the grave where he had been buried alive." The deadly evils of hell are invoked in the line: "The Old Hell Shaft, the pitman said, with a curse upon it, was worthy of its bad name to the last; for though Stephen could speak now, he believed it would soon be found to have mangled the life out of him." And a melodramatic impression of hell-fires burning in the background is created through a description of the observers' faces: "The sun was setting now; and the red light of the evening sky touched every face there, and caused it to be distinctly seen in all its rapt suspense."

What Stephen finally says, when he is lifted up into this circle of observers, constitutes the novel's most powerful argument against contemporary labor conditions. Stephen's words to Rachael invoke "the pit" as an image of death, mining, and hell all at once: " 'I ha' fell into th' pit, my dear, as have cost wi'in the knowledge o' old fok now livin', hundreds and hundreds o' men's lives—fathers, sons, brothers, dear to thousands and thousands, an' keepin' 'em fro' want and hunger. I ha' fell into a pit that ha' been wi' th' Fire-damp crueller than battle. I ha' read on 't in the public petition, as onny one may read, fro' the men that works in pits, in which they ha' pray'n and pray'n the lawmakers for Christ's sake not to let their work be murder to 'em, but to spare 'em for the wives and children that they loves as well as gentlefok loves theirs. When it were in work, it killed wi'out need; when 'tis let alone, it kills wi'out need. See how we die an' no need, one way an' another—in a muddle—every day!' " This is the individual tale lying behind Engels' statement that "in no industry in the United Kingdom are there so many fatal accidents as in mining." With his reference to the "petitions," Dickens seems to be granting to the miners—the true underground workers, the lowest of the low—a right that he hesitates to give to factory laborers: that is, the right to combine in an effort to improve their working conditions. The fearsome idea of "the Union," represented elsewhere in the novel by the unscrupulous Slackbridge, is here given some validity, some compelling need to which it might seem the answer. Yet even here Dickens won't go so far as to suggest a political solution: his business with Stephen is mainly to arouse pity and hence guilt on the part of middle-class readers, not to suggest a process for the laboring classes to resort to.

And even that sense of pity must finally, for Dickens, be premised on a sense of alienation. Stephen Blackpool is clearly an "other," a being dissimilar to the novel's intended readers. In the passage quoted above, the distance is made clear in Stephen's language, a dialect that even seems to involve *unnecessary* orthographical changes. (What, for instance, is the difference in pronunciation between "folk" and "fok"?) By making Stephen's words difficult to read, Dickens introduces a subliminal level of resentment along with the pathos: we groan a bit, internally, when we see a long paragraph of Stephen's speech to be got through, since we know it will involve some effort at translation. Thus, at the very moment that he is making his most impassioned plea for the working class, Dickens is most strongly presenting it as an alien population. In this scene about underground labor and underground death, he is emphasizing rather than smoothing over the issue of class difference. It is this aspect of Dickens which sometimes leads people to classify him as a "bourgeois" writer, but it is also this aspect which makes him frighteningly honest, and which therefore gives his novels their strange and enduring power. We who can read (who, so to speak, are not prevented from reading by the darkness of our basement dwellings) *are* afraid of the poor, the illiterate, the unwashed, the "lower class." If I shy away—my revulsion tinged with guilt—from the homeless poor sleeping in New York's tunnels, or the matted-haired madmen of Berkeley's streetcorners, I certainly cannot claim any superiority to the "middle-class" side of Dickens.

A much more detached vision of the social underground appears in Henry James's most Dickensian novel, *The Princess Casamassima*. With greater detachment comes greater sympathy, and James is clearly fond of his working-class hero, bizarrely named Hyacinth Robinson. As his fairy-tale name suggests, it is Hyacinth who is in some ways the "princess" of the title; and, as such, he plays the ingenue role enacted by women characters—Isabel Archer, Milly Theale, Maggie Verver, etc.—in James's other novels. For Hyacinth, radical politics are an attraction, an illusion, and finally a curse. But so, in a very similar way, is his acquaintance with the Princess Casamassima herself: like the promise of political action, she exerts on Hyacinth a stronger power than her real person alone warrants. Thus the novel brings together, as seeming moral equivalents, the aristocratic, "high" tastes of a princess and the subterranean world of underground politics (underground in the root sense of "radical," as well as in the strategic fact that they are hidden from surface view). The aesthetics and the politics are both compelling, both illusory; and this link between them is strengthened by the fact that the princess herself becomes fascinated with the idea of revolution.

James's working class isn't presented as the alien set of beings it is in Engels, Gissing, and Dickens (though, to be fair to Dickens, I should point out that *all* his characters are "alien" in one way or another; in that sense, he's no harder on the working class than on humanity in general). Hyacinth Robinson and his political mentor, Paul Muniment, are the two most solid creations in James's novel; it is, rather, the princess herself, and aristocratic characters like Lady Aurora Langrish or Hyacinth's absent father, who have a mythical or grotesque quality ("grotesque" in the Dickensian sense of being always the same, incapable of developing out of their own stereotypes). Perhaps the fact that James was American rather than British made him feel somewhat less daunted by the idea of crossing class boundaries—or made him inclined to see special individuals as separate from, rather than representative of, their class. Neither Hyacinth nor Paul is intended as emblematic of the entire working class—Hyacinth because his refined aesthetic tastes set him apart, Paul because he is unusually intelligent and independent. Yet, whatever the qualifications, these characters come closer to being working-class heroes than those created by any English novelist prior to D.H. Lawrence (and he too, it must be pointed out, made Paul Morel a special case).

In *The Princess Casamassima*, images of a physical and even a geological underground are repeatedly invoked to describe working-class radical politics. This underworld is at various times seen as oppressed or powerful, heavily weighted down or imminently threatening to explode, and the metaphors vary accordingly. In almost all cases, the references to the underground are connected to the idea of secrecy—usually but not always involving plans for a political revolution. Thus a conversation between Hyacinth and Rose Muniment about her brother Paul's activities runs:

> *"What my brother really cares for—well, one of these days, when you know, you'll tell me."*
>
> *Hyacinth stared. "But isn't he tremendously deep in—" He hesitated.*
>
> *"Deep in what?"*
>
> *"Well, in what's going on, beneath the surface."*

Here the adjective "deep" applies both to Paul's politics and to his character: he is immersed in radical activity, and also obscure even to his closest relative. The very evasiveness of Hyacinth's references—his pause after the preposition in "deep in," the vagueness of "what's going on, beneath the surface"—mirrors the secrecy that surrounds radical politics. There is already more than a tinge of romanticism in Hyacinth's phrasing, and that element becomes dominant a few pages later when we learn that he "had had a happy impression that Muniment perceived in him a possible associate, of a high type, in a subterranean crusade against the existing order of things." The irony of the contrast between "*high* type" and "*subterranean* crusade" is surely intentional; and indeed it is Hyacinth's aristocratic imagination, rather than his low social position, which attracts him to radical politics in the same romantic way the Princess herself is attracted (though he stands to lose a great deal more by the attraction). Hyacinth's failure to make as much of an impression on the Princess as Paul does comes in part from the fact that he is too "high" a type, represents too little of the "subterranean" world—even on a psychological level, where his relative ingenuousness corresponds to Paul's deepness.

(In this context of subterranean terminology, I should point out that James himself, in his personal letters as well as his published writing, is often drawn to the language of "the abyss." Sometimes he specifically gives the underworld a positive connotation, as when he writes to a fellow author, Mrs. Everard Coates: "we are both very conscious that a work of art must make some small effort to *be* one; must sacrifice somehow and somewhere to the exquisite, or be an asininity altogether. So we open the door to the Devil himself—who is nothing but the sense of beauty, of mystery, of relations, of appearances, of abysses of the whole. . . ." And even when he purports to be deploring the downward journey, some element of its lure nonetheless enters in, as when he writes about a recent illness to his beloved Hendrik Andersen: "So I've pulled through—and am out—and surprisingly soon—of a very deep dark hole. *In* my deep hole, how I thought yearningly, helplessly, dearest Boy, of you"—a passage in which the "underground" nature of his homosexual love perhaps unconsciously determines his choice of words. For James, the abyss represents both pain and profit, both suffering and redemption—a combination that appears in a particularly mundane form when he writes humorously to Edmund Gosse of his "appalling experience of American transcendent *Dentistry*—a deep dark abyss, a trap of anguish and expense, into which I sank unwarily (though, I now begin to see, to my great profit in the short human hereafter)." The devilish nature of the underworld, its association with Faustian pacts, is never very far from James's imagination—but they are often pacts he is willing to engage in himself.)

As in the other social novels I've discussed in this chapter, the underground in *The Princess Casamassima* is used partly as a figure of speech to describe the oppressed, victimized side of working-class life. The princess, for instance, alludes at one point to "those who are underneath every one, every thing, and have the whole social mass crushing them"; and Hyacinth draws on the same metaphor when he contemplates the misery of the London poor during a difficult winter: we learn, as if from his perspective, that "the season was terribly hard; and as in that lower world one walked with one's ear nearer the ground, the deep perpetual groan of London misery seemed to swell and swell and form the whole undertone of life." Here the "groan" of the lost souls suggests the standard Victorian image of the nether world as hell. But this passage also contains another sort of image in the words "swell and swell," which—though explicitly used to describe a swelling sound, an "undertone"—also seem to refer to a physical, geological type of expansion. It is this aspect of the underground metaphor which dominates the novel: the idea of a potential eruption of powerful forces housed beneath the surface of the earth. Thus the princess comments to her friend Madame Grandoni: " 'I am convinced that we are living in a fool's paradise, that the ground is heaving under our feet' "—a mixed metaphor which manages to suggest both earthquakes and hell (this time seen positively, as the opposite of the "fool's paradise"). And later in the same conversation she urges: " 'Are we on the eve of great changes, or are we not? Is everything that is gathering force, underground, in the dark, in the night, in little hidden rooms, out of sight of governments and policemen and idiotic "statesmen"—heaven save them!—is all this going to burst forth some fine morning and set the world on fire?' " The heaven/hell metaphor remains vestigially (explicit in the disdainful phrase "heaven save them!"), but the image has largely been transformed into a geological one.

James's volcanic metaphor for class uprising is interestingly close to the language used by Karl Marx thirty years earlier, in an 1856 speech given in London: "The so-called revolutions of 1848 were but poor incidents, small fractures and fissures in the dry crust of European society. But they denounced the abyss. Beneath the apparently solid surface, they betrayed oceans of liquid matter, only needing expansion to rend into fragments continents of hard rock." Elsewhere, in the *Communist Manifesto*, Marx reverts to a less scientific vision of the underground when he compares modern bourgeois society to "the sorcerer who is no longer able to control the powers of the underworld that he has called up by his spells." But whether the image is Faustian or geological, Marx's point remains the same: the real though hidden power of industrial society lies within the "lower" class.

What is unusual about *The Princess Casamassima* is that James has chosen to adopt this metaphor of a powerful underground without either adopting or rejecting the politics from which it stems. His is one of the few Victorian novels that seriously envision the possibility of the "underground" coming to dominate the "surface"; yet unlike the other novels of the period, which tend to view the mob with horror, James's hazards this possibility without expressing any significant degree of fear. Nor does James achieve this coolness by ironically reducing the political activists—as, say, Conrad does in *The Secret Agent*, a novel which, like *The Princess Casamassima*, literally embodies the explosive power of terrorism in a destroyed individual. In Conrad's work, however, that exploded character is a feebleminded boy, and the novel's proponents of radical politics are all demented, corrupt, or simply lazy. Paul Muniment and Eustache Poupin, on the contrary, are morally powerful, psychologically unified, relatively persuasive advocates of revolutionary politics.

But James evades the terrifying side of the political possibilities he raises by ultimately removing the important stakes from politics altogether. In the end, the realizations that matter in *The Princess Casamassima* are personal rather than political; the psychological depths are the ones that crucially interest James; and it is Hyacinth, not British society, that finally self-destructs. Unlike the princess, whose rank and foreign nationality safely remove her from the issues she toys with, Hyacinth is at least half buried in the underground himself: he is half British and half lower-class by birth, brought up in poverty but with a "high type" of sensibility. And it is this inner conflict—this inability to annihilate or safely defuse either side of his personality—that finally brings about his suicide. He is both the assassin and the assassinated.

While James's deepest interest is psychological, his "moral lesson" (if he can be said to preach such a Victorian item) is not unrelated to the concerns voiced by the other writers I've discussed. What makes the underground so frightening and yet so compelling—not only to the Victorians, but to their twentieth-century inheritors—is that it is at once alien and essential: the middle classes cannot afford to divest themselves of it, and yet they can never feel comfortable about its presence. George Orwell summarizes the situation best when he remarks in *The Road to Wigan Pier*: "You could quite easily drive a car right across the north of England and never once remember that hundreds of feet below the road you are on the miners are hacking at the coal. Yet in a sense it is the miners who are driving your car forward. Their lamp-lit world down there is as necessary to the daylight world above as the root is to the flower. . . . More than anyone else, perhaps, the miner can stand as the type of the manual worker, not only because his work is so exaggeratedly awful, but also because it is so vitally necessary and yet so remote from our experience, so invisible, as it were, that we are capable of forgetting it as we forget the blood in our veins." Throughout this passage, Orwell constantly reinforces with images and turns of phrase the idea that those who work for our civilization's comfort are "so vitally necessary and yet so remote." The distance comes through not only in explicit statements—"hundreds of feet below," "lamp-lit world down there"—but also in the distinct separation of pronouns: "you" or "we" for those above-ground, "they" and "he" for those below. (Like Dickens, Orwell is obviously writing for the middle-class reader.) Yet the essential tie between the two worlds is made clear in the organic similes—a flower and its root, a human body and the blood in its veins. The result of this contradictory set of images is to create exactly the kind of psychological effect that troubled Hyacinth Robinson: the sense that we contain, within our own bodies, an alien being whose fate, however separate from ours, is so intimately linked with it that he can only be destroyed if we destroy ourselves.

The realization that one might be inextricably wed to a subterranean Other, to a version of oneself that is both less evident and more powerful than one's surface self, appears strongly and explicitly in Edward Bulwer Lytton's *The Coming Race*. A science fiction novel first published in 1871, *The Coming Race* initially seems to contradict all the usual Victorian attitudes toward the underground. The first-person narrator, exploring the depths of a mine, wanders accidentally into a subterranean realm populated by a different "race" of beings. (Again, the emphasis on race may be peculiarly American, for though the author of this work was English, the narrator describes himself as a native of the United States of America.) But far from being the degraded creatures of the social novelists' imaginings, these underground beings—the "Vril-ya"—are far superior to the human race in every obvious respect except one: they are unable to produce art of any significance. Bulwer Lytton links this single disadvantage to the utopian perfection of their existence when he has one of the Vril-ya tell the narrator: " 'We find, by referring to the great masterpieces . . ., that they consist in the portraiture of passions which we no longer experience—ambition, vengeance, unhallowed love, the thirst for warlike renown, and such like.' " Aside from this one drawback (which enables Bulwer Lytton to indulge in the standard anti-utopian musings about the need for suffering), the Vril-ya live a seemingly perfect life. Their society has no violence, no poverty, no ignorance, no overcrowding; they have learned how to fly, with beautifully graceful artificial wings; and they are such an advanced and peaceful people that they don't even eat meat.

As one progresses through the novel, it becomes clear that this vision bears a powerful if inverted relationship to the more typical image of the inferior subterranean class. Like Lewis Carroll in *Through the Looking Glass*, Bulwer Lytton has relied on the technique of reversing everything. Thus the society of the Vril-ya is one in which children labor until they grow up, and then spend their adulthood in leisure; in which nobody wants the burden of riches or power, and people will only accept such responsibilities unwillingly (Lord Lytton himself, it should be noted, was a well-off politician); in which death is a state to be looked forward to rather than one to be feared; and so on. Bulwer Lytton has simply turned his own society on its head, and it is therefore natural that the underground, which represents ugliness, crime, and ignorance in the social novels of his period, should instead stand for beauty, peace, and knowledge.

Yet even the positive aspects of *The Coming Race*'s underworld are finally presented as terrifying, and this is largely because of one major reversal. In the realm of the Vril-ya, the women are the superior sex. Taller, stronger, more intelligent and more powerful than their masculine counterparts, they have greater inherent control over the energy-giving "vril" (a sort of proto-nuclear power that both sustains and destroys life). And what the narrator finds even more terrifying is that these women woo their prospective mates rather than waiting quietly to be asked. Despite the fact that one of these Amazonian goddesses saves our hero from certain death and returns him to the upper world, he finds himself unable to feel anything but a slight revulsion for this powerful and admittedly beautiful creature. Indeed, her strength is the *cause* of his distaste, for as he says at one point: "Is it that, among the race I belong to, man's pride so far influences his passions that woman loses to him her special charm of woman if he feels her to be in all things eminently superior to himself?" And even the men of the Vril-ya, accustomed as they are to superior women, seem to share some of this fear, for the society has adopted various rules to protect men and assure their happiness—most pointedly, the rule that women must give up their wings upon marriage, whereas men retain a lifelong ability to fly. Nor does wing-envy appear to be a noticeable problem in this happy state, for the women seem content to give up all power in order to secure the objects of their affection.

Because of this particular reversal, the threat of a takeover by this "coming race" is closely linked to the threat of a takeover by women. This is indeed the intimate Other, the frightening enemy brought into the domestic camp. Though they are presented as superior beings, the narrator nonetheless views the Vril-ya as dangerous and destructive to the interests of aboveground humanity. He ends the novel by remarking that "the more I think of a people calmly developing, in regions excluded from our sight and deemed uninhabitable by our sages, powers surpassing our most disciplined modes of force, and virtues to which our life, social and political, becomes antagonistic in proportion as our civilization advances,—the more devoutly I pray that ages may yet elapse before there emerge into sunlight our inevitable destroyers." Bulwer Lytton is being both serious and ironic here—mocking the superiority complex of the nineteenth-century British and American males, and at the same time pleading for the value of the society they've created. In the end he is also relying on the same emotion that fuels the other Victorian works about the underground: the sense that whatever population emerges from below, whether it be bestial or angelic, will in any case bear a demonic relationship to humanity.

The fear of the intimate enemy, the sense of dependence mixed with terror that colors *The Coming Race*, takes an even more intense form in H.G. Wells's 1895 novel *The Time Machine*. To a certain extent, *The Time Machine* follows the standard path of the utopian novel. A nameless guide (called the Time Traveller by Wells's narrator) describes to the narrator and several other gentlemen a world he has discovered hundreds of centuries in the future. Aside from the small bits of frame story at the beginning and end, the entire novel is taken up with the Traveller's tale. Because his machine carries him through time but not through space, it is clear that this newly discovered world is supposed to be the England of the future. (Potential audience skepticism on this point is anticipated in the reaction of the gentlemen-listeners, none of whom really believes the story.) The basic characteristics of this future society—as the Traveller slowly realizes—is that the human race has been subdivided into two distinct species: the Eloi, a group of beautiful but useless hedonists; and the Morlocks, a collection of ugly but powerful figures who live beneath the ground and feed off the Eloi as if they were cattle. (The latter image has been repeatedly exploited in the science fiction that followed Wells—most recently, to the best of my knowledge, in the movie *Escape From New York*.)

The reason it takes the Time Traveller so long to figure out the true power relations in this society is that he automatically assumes the underground group is a "lower" (hence less powerful) class. In other words, the Traveller mentally transmutes the figurative language of his own period into an actual equation between the underground and the social "lower depths." That he is able to draw on physical evidence from his own period of history to support this equation is part of what makes his mistake credible. He describes his initial theory as follows: "There is a tendency to use underground space for the less ornamental purposes of civilization; there is the Metropolitan Railway in London, for instance, there are new electric railways, there are subways, there are underground workrooms and restaurants, and they increase and multiply. Evidently, I thought, this tendency had increased till Industry had gradually lost its birthright in the sky. I mean that it had gone deeper and deeper into larger and ever larger underground factories, spending a still-increasing amount of its time therein, till, in the end—! Even now, does not an East-end worker live in such artificial conditions as practically to be cut off from the natural surface of the earth?"

What Wells has done here is to emphasize the technological side of the nineteenth-century underground: the subways, the subterranean businesses, and so on. There is much evidence to show that these facilities, particularly the subway, were *not* exclusively used by the working poor, but were instead the province of the middle classes; "sewer-rats," for instance, was the slang term applied to City businessmen who regularly commuted to work by subway in the 1880s. But Wells chooses to emphasize the link between the physical underground and the "under" class. He carries the subterranean metaphor of the social novelists to an extreme—not only by stressing the technological and *literally* below-ground developments that led to the social division he describes, but also by invoking evolutionary theory to create a whole new underworld species. "And this same widening gulf," the Traveller hypothesizes, ". . . will make that exchange between class and class, that promotion by intermarriage which at present retards the splitting of our species along lines of social stratification, less and less frequent. So, in the end, above ground you must have the Haves, pursuing pleasure and comfort and beauty, and below ground the Have-nots; the Workers getting continually adapted to the conditions of their labor." And even when he discovers that these "Haves" are really bovine victims, possessing no stronger claim on the intellectual heritage of nineteenth-century humans than do their underground masters, the Time Traveller still falls back on Darwinian theory: "There is no intelligence where there is no change and no need of change. . . . So, as I see it, the upper-world man had drifted toward his feeble prettiness, and the under-world man to mere mechanical industry. But that perfect state had lacked one thing even for mechanical perfection—absolute permanency. Apparently as time went on, the feeding of the underworld, however it was effected, had become disjointed. Mother Necessity, who had been staved off for a few thousand years, came back again, and she began below. The under-world being in contact with machinery, which, however perfect, still needs some little thought outside habit, had probably retained perforce rather more initiative, if less of every other human character, than the upper. And when other meat failed them, they turned to what old habit had hitherto forbidden." So it is the "machinery," and the ability to control it, which in the end allows one group to retain some mental agility, however feeble. As if to reinforce the warning, Wells's own tentative grasp on the mechanical processes of his time is conveyed by the phrase "being in contact with machinery"—suggesting through its very vagueness the degree to which his more refined class has already lost such contact.

While Wells may have given his Morlocks some of the mental initiative of his ancestors, he certainly withheld from them any physical inheritance of value. This was partly a strategic move in the construction of his fiction: by making the Eloi look like super-humans and the Morlocks resemble furry beasts, he could strengthen the shock of the realization that the Eloi were merely cattle for their underworld masters. But in dividing the physiques in this way, Wells was also building on the appearances and beliefs of his own period—those attitudes toward the "bestial" working class that I've noted in other nineteenth-century authors. Even the specific fear of being devoured by those beasts can be found in the Victorian writers who preceded Wells—specifically in Elizabeth Gaskell's *North and South*, where the image of cannibalism is applied to a threatening mob of striking workers. "As soon as they saw Mr. Thornton," Gaskell writes, "they set up a yell,—to call it not human is nothing,—it was as the demoniac desire of some terrible wild beast for the food that is withheld from his ravening." It is almost as if the existing power relation were being unconsciously turned upside down: because the laborers were what enabled the middle classes to eat, the middle classes feared being eaten *by* them.

Engels converts this metaphorically expressed fear into a more general political prophecy when he says in his chapter on miners: "If the capitalist class is as mad as all that, and if they are so blinded by temporary success that they cannot understand the most obvious signs of the times—then we must indeed give up all hope of seeing a peaceful solution to the social question in England. The only possible outcome of this state of affairs is a great revolution and it is absolutely certain that such a rising will take place." Such "blindness" on the part of the industrial class was made all that much easier by the fact that the exploited labor was hidden, either literally or figuratively, below the ground—"in regions excluded from our sight," as Bulwer Lytton put it. By the time Wells wrote *The Time Machine*, the outlook had come to seem even more hopeless, and blindness to the future thus became a consciously chosen reaction to an inevitable evolution rather than merely a failure to see. Speaking at the end of the novel about the vanished Time Traveller, the narrator remarks: "He, I know—for the question had been discussed among us long before the Time Machine was made—thought but cheerlessly of the Advancement of Mankind, and saw in the growing pile of civilization only a foolish heaping that must inevitably fall back upon and destroy its makers in the end. If that is so, it remains for us to live as though it were not so." And in so choosing, the narrator and his kind seal their own fates. For it is precisely their refusal to look under the surface of their own existence—to go "down to the very bottom of things," as James says in *The Princess Casamassima*—that, in Wells's view, will result in the ultimate division between the Eloi and the Morlocks, between the thoughtless, carefree people of the surface and the beast-like but powerful creatures who live underground.

Forty years after *The Time Machine*, well into the twentieth century, George Orwell (who was in many ways a kind of anachronistic, time-traveling Victorian himself) described his visits to the mining country in *The Road to Wigan Pier*. As my earlier quotations from this work have shown, his viewpoint is basically sympathetic to these subterranean workers; yet there is also a strong suggestion that they are alien beings, different from "you or me" (to use the Orwellian rhetoric). Speaking of the miners' cramped physical position in the mines, Orwell says: "Certainly, it is not the same for them as it would be for you or me. They have done it since childhood, they have the right muscles hardened, and they can move to and fro underground with a startling and rather horrible agility. A miner puts his head down and *runs*, with a long swinging stride, through places where I can only stagger." Now compare Orwell's description to the Time Traveller's first encounter with a Morlock: "I know it was a dull white, and had strange large greyish-red eyes; also that there was flaxen hair on its head and down its back. But, as I say, it went too fast for me to see distinctly. I cannot even say whether it ran on all fours, or only with its fore-arms held very low. . . . It made me shudder. It was so like a human spider!" Wells's monster is more explicitly depersonalized: he refers to it only with the impersonal pronoun, gives it rabbit-like hair and eyes, and directly compares it to a spider. But the evident humanity of the creature—"It was so like a human spider"—is finally what makes the distortion so terrifying; whereas

Orwell's description, despite its overt admiration, consistently stresses the difference between the miners, on the one hand, and himself and his readers, on the other. The phrases "since childhood" and "right muscles hardened," though they do not profess to categorize biologically, nonetheless ring with a certain Lamarckian tone, a hint of instant evolution—something like Wells's earlier line about the effects of "being in contact with machinery." The fact that the miners can "*run*" whereas Orwell "can only stagger" makes them seem threatening rather than skillful (the stagger itself almost suggesting that the tall human has been drugged or beaten to put him at their mercy). And the frequent repetition of the collective "them" or "they"—especially in contrast to the singular sense of "you or me"—finally depersonalizes its subjects even more than Wells's flat "it" does. Orwell's whole passage stylistically builds on the idea presented in the first sentence: "it is not the same for them as it would be for you or me."

It is not quite fair of me to equate Orwell's strenuously self-revealing use of the phrase "rather horrible" with the Time Traveller's "shudder": one is a brave attempt to admit difference, the other a rather cheaply melodramatic shock effect. But the truth conveyed in them is similar. At the root of all these descriptions—those of the social novelists as well as those of Orwell, Engels, London, and Wells—is a strongly entrenched fear of the lower depths, and hence a tendency to bring together all the fearsome aspects of those depths: animals in pits, spiders in dark basements, cannibalistic alien races, ill-paid and finally uncontrollable laborers. What makes the Orwell book so quirky—beautifully written, superficially straightforward, and finally deeply disturbing—is the way in which this inbred (and occasionally acknowledged) anxiety wars with Orwell's attempts to take a man-to-man, non-technical, egalitarian look at the lives of miners. In the very act of attempting to bridge the "widening gap" Wells spoke of, Orwell demonstrates how vast the abyss still was by the 1930s.

Darkness and Invisibility

"Only I'm still in the tunnel."
—Ralph Ellison, *Invisible Man*

I FIND IT RELATIVELY EASY TO TALK ABOUT "ALIENATION" and "fear" and "avoidance" when discussing the nineteenth-century British and their class politics, but it is quite another thing for me to trace the same patterns closer to home. It is difficult, to say the least, for a white American of the late twentieth century to speak authoritatively about black American writing. This difficulty is not due to a lack of common culture, as it would be, for instance, if the same American tried to discuss Nigerian or Indonesian contemporary fiction. On the contrary, it is the simultaneous interweaving and separation of our two cultures—the fact that I can know exactly what Ralph Ellison or Richard Wright means, and yet be cut off from that meaning—that makes the task hard. Despite the developments which have taken place since Wright and Ellison wrote their major works—the nominal integration of the American army, the 1954 school desegregation decision, the fair housing effort, and the 1960s civil rights movement—very little has actually altered in the relations between black and white in this country. The disturbing issues of black oppression and resentment, white condescension and fear, that informed the novels of these black writers are still very much alive. Most of the time blacks continue to remain "invisible" to whites. Only occasionally are the two worlds brought into forced contact, and it is only at such moments that the meaning of black writing about the underground imposes itself viscerally on a white reader.

One of these moments came to me a few summers ago, when I found myself in the middle of what might have been a piece of Ellison's *Invisible Man* or Wright's *The Man Who Lived Underground.* I was staying alone in a friend's apartment in Greenwich Village. It was a hot summer month, and the streets in the neighborhood, along with the pier at the nearby river, were filled with people at all hours of the day and night. What surprised me about this scene was that it was both so urban and so white. These loungers and performers and strollers on the streets of the Village were certainly not the wealthy of the city—some seemed barely above survival level—and in San Francisco or Oakland they would have included a mixture of races. But New York is still a surprisingly segregated city (though perhaps my surprise is ingenuous), and only when I ventured down into the sweltering depths of the Sheridan Square or West Fourth Street subway station did I see any significant number of black people. The air-conditioned buses running on the surface streets were largely filled with white riders, but the inhabitants of the subway cars—who had to travel longer distances to get all the way home to Harlem, and therefore took the faster route—were mainly black. Down here was where one saw the city's huge population in full force: the subways were as crowded as ever, for they were filled with people who had not been able to leave the summer inferno for the country, as wealthier New Yorkers had done.

As is the habit with New York plumbing, mine went wrong early in my stay. The crisis came when I flushed the toilet and it overflowed. What seemed like gallons of fecal matter came pouring up out of the sewers and into that small, well-kept, neatly carpeted bathroom. It was a horrifying sight, this eruption from the literal bowels of the earth. I have never been good at small household maintenance tasks, and this one seemed far beyond me: even had I been able to locate my friend's "plumber's helper," I would not have had either the skill or the nerve to use it. The last thing I wanted to do, in any case, was to suction *anything* more out of the toilet bowl.

I therefore resorted to the perennial New York solution: the super. My friend had left a detailed note explaining how to get in touch with this mysterious being. The first step, I learned, was to take a special key (like Alice getting out of her underground room of tears) and let myself into the basement, which was accessible from only a single one of the four buildings that composed the apartment complex. In other words, it was significantly harder to get *below* ground (where one also did laundry and disposed of garbage) than it was merely to get down to ground level, as one could do in any of the four elevators. As I descended, I thought about the irony of the fact that the "super" is nearly always "sub" in Manhattan—always housed underground, or at least on the lowest floor, beneath all the other residents of the building.

I emerged into the laundry room, which resembled the place

where the second or third murder occurs in grade B horror movies. There was a lot of impersonal noise—washers rumbling, pipes hissing, some kind of machinery clanking in the background—but no sign of another living soul. It was also extremely hot, especially compared to my air-conditioned apartment five floors up. The room was lined with eye-level pipes and I followed them out of the laundry room, as I had been instructed to do. They led me down a long, narrow, cement-lined corridor with no visible destination. The pipes and the corridor made a right turn, and another right; so, of course, did I. I had lost all sense of direction and felt sure I must be getting back to where I started. Then suddenly I intruded on what were obviously the outskirts of the super's domain. ("You will know when you get there," my friend's note had ended.) Children's plastic toys lay strewn about, and a half-dismantled bicycle rested upside down on a piece of old carpet, with an open box of tools sitting on a nearby stool. I was shocked by the absence of a front door, of any boundary separating private from public territory: one moment I had been in a dimly lit tunnel, the next I was in this man's livingroom.

Through an adjoining door came the sound of daytime television. I knocked, and a black woman opened the door. Beyond her I could see a young woman and a couple of children. This, then, was the more private area, the "family room"—though even this was subject, on the slightest occasion, to importunate intrusions like mine. In so few words that I cannot accurately reproduce them, the woman let me know that the super was not at home, but that she would send him to my apartment when he returned. I felt as if I were throwing a message in a bottle out to sea: in this world without telephones, without appointments, without front doors, how would he know when and where to come?

He did, though, that same afternoon, and fixed the toilet so it worked. Such intrusions, such arrangements were a routine part of his life. I, however, was so traumatized by my journey into the lower regions (there was a moment, searching for the correct elevator, when I feared I might never get out) that I took all my laundry to a neighborhood laundromat and never threw out the garbage until the day I left.

The super of my story is a victim immolated in the underground, a trapped servant of the "upper" classes. Yet my horrified description, though it may be one of the visions to which Ellison and Wright speak, is not the same as the underground that appears in black fiction. Black American literature, as opposed to the British social novel, represents the world as seen from below, and hence the traditional values are turned at least partially upside down. In the works of Wright and Ellison, for instance, the underground is a means of escape as well as a trap, a place for rebirth as well as a tomb. The regions below the surface may seem frightening or repelling in these novels, but they are finally no more so than the world above, and they offer what may be the only chance for rescue. That the hoped-for salvation never comes is due to these authors' basic pessimism—some might say, to the accuracy of their social vision—as much as to the inherent "evils" of the underground.

Novels like *Invisible Man* and *The Man Who Lived Underground* have a dual ancestry. On the one hand, they go back to the nineteenth-century American tradition of black writing: to Frederick Douglass's autobiography and other slave narratives, with their tales of escape through the "Underground Railroad," movement "upward" to the free northern cities, black "uprisings" against injustice, and so on. But equally powerful, especially in the work of Richard Wright, is the influence of Dostoyevsky, whose *Notes From Underground* provides one model for twentieth-century stories of the lower depths.

There are a number of reasons why a mid-nineteenth-century Russian writer might have such a powerful appeal to the imagination of black Americans. For one thing, Russia was the equivalent of the "Third World" in the nineteenth century, the underdeveloped country inventing itself in competition against, but with necessary attention to, the more "civilized" culture of Western Europe. Russian authors, like black Americans, were used to being outsiders; James Baldwin could *not* have said about the Russians what he said of the Swiss in his 1953 essay "Strangers in the Village": "For this village, even were it incomparably more remote and incredibly more primitive, is the West, the West onto which I have been so strangely grafted. These people cannot be, from the point of view of power, strangers anywhere in the world; they have made the modern world, in effect, even if they do not know it. The most illiterate among them is related, in a way I am not, to Dante, Shakespeare, Michelangelo, Aeschylus, Da Vinci, Rembrandt, and Racine; the cathedral at Chartres says something to them which it cannot say to me, as indeed would New York's Empire State Building, should anyone here ever see it." Because the Russians were themselves newcomers to this European tradition, forced and only partial converts to the Continental culture imposed by Tsar Peter the Great, they provided for black American writers a sphere of references that did not depend on the traditional British novel. The heavy burden of the English literary tradition that sat on the shoulders of most American writers could thus be sidestepped if one turned instead to the Russians.

In addition, the nineteenth-century Russians were, like the black migrants from the south, an essentially rural people who had nonetheless felt obliged to settle in cities. The excitements and the horrors of Dostoyevksy's St. Petersburg, as sifted through the perceptions of a provincial like Raskolnikov, must have struck a chord for black American writers who felt both piercing nostalgia and bored hatred for their southern rural childhoods. And, finally, Russian literature was especially likely to attract the black writers who came of age in the 1930s and who almost universally joined the Communist Party. For novelists who were already being influenced by Marx, Lenin, and the events of 1917, it was only a short step to the Russian writers who preceded and seemed to forecast these events. Dostoyevsky, in particular, is one of those writers whose observations of social injustice under Tsarism have kept him permanently in print in the Soviet Union. For black writers seeking a way to reconcile intense aesthetic commitment with equally intense social concerns, Dostoyevsky must have seemed an ideal model.

In fact, Wright's and Ellison's response to both *Crime and Punishment* and *Notes From Underground* is, if anything, even stronger than their response to Frederick Douglass. Of course, this is partly due to availability: Douglass's three autobiographies were out of print for most of the century between their initial publication and their recent reissue. Nonetheless Douglass was a well-known figure among black writers earlier in this century (especially those who belonged to the Communist Party), and it is more than likely that they had direct access either to his autobiographies or to other "slave narratives" from the nineteenth century.

Certain images and events in Douglass's 1855 *My Bondage and My Freedom* (which, among the three memoirs, contains the most detailed description of his slave life) seem to be picked up directly in Ralph Ellison's *Invisible Man*. Thus, for instance, Douglass's experience as a speaker on behalf of abolitionism parallels almost exactly the lecture-work that the Invisible Man does for "the Brotherhood"; each man finds himself growing beyond the restricted role that has been assigned to him. "It was impossible for me to repeat the same old story month after month," Douglass explains, "and to keep up my interest in it. It was new to the people, it is true, but it was an old story to me; and to go through with it night after night, was a task altogether too mechanical for my nature. 'Tell your story, Frederick,' would whisper my then revered friend William Lloyd Garrison, as I stepped upon the platform. I could not always obey, for I was now reading and thinking. . . . It did not entirely satisfy me to *narrate* wrongs; I felt like *denouncing* them. . . . 'People won't believe you ever was a slave, Frederick, if you keep on this way,' said Friend Foster. 'Be yourself,' said Collins, 'and tell your story.' It was said to me, 'Better to have a *little* of the plantation manner of speech than not; 'tis not best that you seem too learned.' " What the abolitionists want, as the word "mechanical" suggests, is a black automaton who can give the appropriate speech. He should not have a mind of his own, lest he fail to move his audience in the correct way, for that audience must be able to look down on him and therefore pity him. He must give sense data and stories, not abstract analysis.

Ironically, the Brotherhood has exactly the same kind of complaint about the Invisible Man, but voiced in the opposite terms. The organization wants him to speak theoretically, while his instinct is to move his black audiences emotionally. But the criticism finally comes down to the same point: the Brotherhood wants the Invisible Man to submit himself entirely to the cause, speaking only within its rules, whereas he wants to say what he feels, when he feels it. After his first official speech, a pulpit-thumping tirade which produces wild applause from the crowd, one of the Brothers criticizes the speech by saying: " 'It was the antithesis of the scientific approach. Ours is a reasonable point of view. We are champions of a scientific approach to society, and such a speech as we've identified ourselves with tonight destroys everything that has been said before. The audience isn't thinking, it's yelling its head off."

Here the criticism is couched in terms of technique, but later it actually becomes an issue of differing opinions. On the occasion that causes his final break with the Brotherhood—his eulogy for the out-of-favor Tod Clifton, recently shot down by the police—the Invisible Man is reprimanded for giving a spontaneous speech that violates Brotherhood principles: " 'We furnish all ideas. . . . You say nothing unless it is passed by the committee. Otherwise I suggest you keep saying the last thing you were told.' " And then this Brother adds in a "fatherly" manner: " 'Let *us* handle the theory and the business of strategy. . . . We are experienced. We're graduates and while you are a smart beginner you skipped several grades.' " So it would seem that the Party finally wants from its black representatives much the same thing that the abolitionists wanted: a robot, an uneducated child, a speaker rather than a thinker. The argument has developed enormous sophistication between Douglass's time and Ellison's, and the Brothers are accusing the Invisible Man of stereotypical thinking rather than vice versa (" 'Now he's lecturing us on the conditioned reflexes of the Negro people' "), but the disagreement still comes down to the same point: the white organization's refusal to let the black instrument have any influence over strategy, any say in the ideas. And in both cases the black man's retort is the same: the writing of a book, the telling of his own tale as he wants it told.

If Douglass is less angry than Ellison at these manifestations of well-intentioned white condescension, he is no less aware of the power of physical resistance as a means of self-assertion. If anything, Ellison's Invisible Man is more conservative in his opinions about action, more fearful of the depths of rage that he perceives in himself and in other black people. At the scene of a near-riot against a white police officer, Ellison's character calms the crowd, explaining his motives as follows: "I saw them start up the steps and felt suddenly as though my head would split. I knew that they were about to attack the man and I was both afraid and angry, repelled and fascinated. I both wanted it and feared the consequences, was outraged and angered at what I saw and yet surged with fear; not for the man or the consequences of the attack, but of what the sight of violence might release in me. And beneath it all there boiled up all the shock-absorbing phrases that I had learned all my life. I seemed to totter on the edge of a great dark hole."

Where the Invisible Man sees rage and violence as a fall into this "great dark hole," Douglass views the same feelings in terms of lifting and raising. In *My Bondage and My Freedom* he says of a fight with a slave-owner: "Covey was a tyrant, and a cowardly one, withal. After resisting him, I felt as I had never felt before. It was a resurrection from the dark and pestiferous tomb of slavery, to the heaven of comparative freedom." Of course, Douglass is talking about defensive resistance whereas Ellison is describing active violence; still, in the one case a black man feels proud of his instinctive response, and in the other he fears it. Again, this is partly due to the degree to which black/white relations had become more complicated by Ellison's time. By 1947 it was no longer a simple case of black slaves beneath, seeking to rise, and white owners above, trying to keep them down. The heights and depths had gotten mixed, and an individual black man could feel them both battling within him. It was not so easy for a twentieth-century black writer to distinguish between the "dark and pestiferous tomb" and its opposite "heaven," for good and bad did not reside neatly in their appropriate high and low places.

It was Dostoyevksy, not Douglass, who gave black writers a vocabulary for this new reversal of experience. In Douglass's writing, the depths are almost always negative and the heights positive: he alludes to the "depth of poverty and physical wretchedness" that characterizes slave life, the "profounder depths of desolation, which it is the lot of slaves often to reach," and "the very depths of ignorance" in which a slave is brought up; conversely, when he talks about improving the lot of black people in America, he promises to "labor in the future, as I have labored in the past, to promote the moral, social, religious, and intellectual elevation of the free colored people." This is a vocabulary adopted from Christianity, with its sense of a low hell and a high heaven, and it is the language of an optimist who presumes that the heights can ultimately be accessible to all. But Ellison and Wright, contemplating the condition of "the free colored people" in the mid-twentieth century, could no longer be so sure that progress would involve upward movement. If the "depths" were where black people still remained after decades of supposed freedom, perhaps it made sense for black writers to turn their attention toward this lower world. And in seeking a guide to this aspect of existence—the buried, the invisible—they turned to Dostoyevsky as their Virgil.

For Dostoyevsky's Underground Man is a character who wallows in his degradation and harps on his obscurity. His attitude toward his own pain is too complex to be packaged neatly as "masochism": he both embraces the pain and resists it, has great pride and seeks utter abasement, becomes alternately mocking and self-mocking. The Underground Man has elevated suffering to a transcendent state, and at the same time he removes not one whit of its painful character. In attempting to "get to the bottom" of his "enjoyment" of his own pain, the Underground Man remarks: "I, for instance, have a great deal of *amour-propre*. I am as suspicious and prone to take offence as a humpback or a dwarf. But upon my word I sometimes have had moments when if I had happened to be slapped in the face I should, perhaps, have been positively glad of it. I say, in earnest, that I should probably have been able to discover even in that a peculiar sort of enjoyment—the enjoyment, of course, of despair; but in despair there are the most intense enjoyments, especially when one is very acutely conscious of the hopelessness of one's position." And a bit later he points out that "suffering is the sole origin of consciousness. Though I did lay it down at the beginning that consciousness is the greatest misfortune for man, yet I know man prizes it and would not give it up for any satisfaction. Consciousness, for instance, is infinitely superior to twice two makes four." The duality of Dostoyevsky's tone is perfectly illustrated by that last remark, which wryly undercuts all that came before while making its own special case for the argument (since humor, too, is consciousness).

The connection between suffering and consciousness is not Dostoyevsky's idea alone; in fact, Douglass was harping on a similar notion when he wrote that "to *understand*, some one has said that a man must *stand under*." But Douglass presents this initial oppression as the necessary preliminary to change, whereas for Dostoyevsky's character the condition of suffering is "sole" and unending. For the Underground Man, "the enjoyment was just from the too intense consciousness of one's own degradation; it was from feeling oneself that one had reached the last barrier, that it was horrible, but that it could not be otherwise; that there was no escape for you; that you could never become a different man." If *Crime and Punishment* is a novel about transformation, *Notes From Underground* is about the refusal to transform—a refusal that contains within it, however, extreme fluctuations between one side of a personality and its opposite, so that the character and tone in which the narrator tells his tale are anything but static.

Like the Underground Man, the central character in *Invisible Man* is a nameless figure narrating his own tale; and the main character of Richard Wright's *The Man Who Lived Underground* is also virtually without a name (though at one point he is identified as "freddaniels"). All three of these characters "live" underground in one way or another—Dostoyevsky's man in a mental and physical basement ("in its nasty, stinking, underground home our insulted, crushed and ridiculed mouse promptly becomes absorbed in cold, malignant and, above all, everlasting spite"), and the other two in subterranean hideouts (an abandoned basement in the case of Ellison's man, a sewer in the case of Wright's). Moreover, all three characters are obsessed with their own invisibility. For the Underground Man, this obsession forms the basis of the central encounter in his narrative: the one-sided battle with the officer who "moved me from where I was standing to another spot, and passed by as though he had not noticed me." For Wright's character, invisibility provides an opportunity to see without being seen: to peek through cracks at a black congregation, a mortician dressing a body, a movie-theater audience, a locked safe and its secret combination. Whereas invisibility represents powerlessness for Dostoyevsky's character, it represents a kind of power—albeit unrecognized and unrewarded power—for Wright's. And for Ellison's Invisible Man it simply becomes his whole identity: since his aboveground personality consists entirely of the false fronts given him by others, when he becomes invisible he also becomes nothing. For the two black writers, there is also a crucial connection between invisibility and blackness: they build on the idea of dark skin that fades into night, and of a whole black population that is ignored by whites.

In all three novels there is a clear political connotation to the idea of the underground. In *Notes From Underground* (as Marshall Berman has astutely pointed out in *All That Is Solid Melts Into Air*), this sense has less to do with actual political activity than it does with class. Dostoyevsky's narrator is viewed—or perhaps only views himself—as a mere mouse compared to those who are wealthier and more powerful. Spite and resentment, rather than open rebellion, constitute his "underground" response. *Invisible Man*, on the other hand, deals overtly with a political underground movement, in the form of the Communist Party (thinly disguised as "the Brotherhood"). And in *The Man Who Lived Underground*, the underground suggests the "underworld" of crime—though in fact this character's crimes are more like existential acts, less motivated by greed or need or desire than are any of the standard criminal activities they resemble. By the time he steals money and jewelry from a safe, Wright's underground man is so far removed from reality as to derive only aesthetic pleasure from his acquisitions: he papers his sewer wall with hundred-dollar bills and hangs gold watches up on nails. Yet like the futile resentment of Dostoyevsky's character or the abortive political activity of Ellison's, the gestures of Wright's underground man are also a kind of rebellion against the surface world—that conventional world where money is for buying things, where police officers are more powerful than the poor, and where blacks must take orders from whites.

Another kind of underground derived from *Notes From Underground* also informs both *Invisible Man* and *The Man Who Lived Underground*, and that is the world of dreams. This repressed material, welling up from the psychological depths, floats in and out of the Dostoyevsky novel, where it is difficult to tell the dream material from the character's reality. We only know that he does dream, for he makes remarks like "That night I had the most hideous dreams," "even while I was unconscious a point seemed continually to remain in my memory unforgotten, and round it my dreams moved drearily," or "Even in my underground dreams I did not imagine love except as a struggle." Such remarks, however, only serve as springboards to further discussions of the Underground Man's obsessional concerns: his victimization by others, his self-abasement, his spite. The Underground Man is so entirely a figure of consciousness that even his dreams are only an aspect of that consciousness. Either he has no independent unconscious, or else it has already taken over him entirely; in any case, there is no clear separation between his dream life and his waking life. (Note how different he is, in this respect, from Raskolnikov, whose dreams are both realistic and premonitory. In *Crime and Punishment*, the dream life represents a separate world that is nonetheless a lucid interpretation of waking life.)

For the Wright and Ellison men, however, dreaming is a form of access to a deeper world—one which may ultimately absorb the character who dreams, but which initially appears as a kind of vague, symbolic signal from an inaccessible part of the mind. Thus Wright's character dreams of being swept out to sea, where he tries to save a nude woman and her nude baby from drowning, and finally nearly drowns himself ("he began to doubt that he could stand upon the water and then he was sinking and as he struggled the water rushed him downward spinning dizzily and he opened his mouth to call for help and water surged into his lungs and he choked. . . ."). The dream is both heavily symbolic and psychologically realistic: it incorporates real material from the man's recent waking past—the dead baby he found floating in the sewer, his near-drowning when he first dropped into the water—but it also draws together more eternal ideas of death and rebirth. So the dreamer himself becomes identified with the drowning baby, the nude woman is thus both his mother and the object of his desire, and he himself is both a Christ/Savior ("he began to doubt that he could walk upon the water") and a mortal man who is about to die. If the dream foreshadows the future of this underground man—his mad desire to save humanity, his ultimate death in the sewers—it also marks the beginning of his transformation, the moment at which he begins to change from a mere fleeing suspect to a man governed by his unconscious.

In *Invisible Man*, the central dream-story is told to the black narrator and a white listener by a southern black man who has impregnated his own daughter. Telling the dream as a way of excusing his incestuous act, this man says: " 'I'm in a big white bedroom, like I seen one time when I was a little ole boy and went to the big house with my Ma. . . . Then I looks over in a corner and sees one of them tall grandfather clocks and I hears it strikin' and the glass doors is openin' and a white lady is steppin' out of it. . . . Then she starts to screamin' and I thinks I gone deef, 'cause though I can see her mouth working, I don't *hear* nothin'. Yit I can still hear the clock. . . .' " The lady grabs him, and in his fright he throws her on the bed, where the woman " 'just seemed to sink outta sight, that there bed was so soft. It's sinkin' down so far I think it's going to smother both of us. . . . I git aloose from the woman now and I'm runnin' for the clock. At first I couldn't get the door open, it had some kinda crinkly stuff like steel wool on the facing. But I gits it open and I gits inside and it's hot and dark in there. I goes up a dark tunnel, up near where the machinery is making all that noise and heat. . . . It's burnin' hot as iffen the house was caught on fire, and I starts to runnin', tryin' to git out. . . . Only I'm still in the *tunnel.*' " And when he wakes up, he finds himself raping his daughter.

Even more than the Wright dream, this dream shows the heavy influence of Freudian knowledge: the house that is also a tunnel that is also a woman, the intimations of birth and death that surround the clock, the guilty fear of punishment manifested in the hellish heat, the falling and sinking and running and flying (especially in the parts I've left out of my quotation) that create the sense of sexual movement. But, in part because of the incest story it is meant to explain, this dream seems far more graphic and intense than those described by Freud. The virginal door that won't open, covered with "some kinda crinkly stuff like steel wool," is almost *too* crudely symbolic: the old man is so ingenuous in his tale-telling that he seems to have no super-ego, no dream-censor. And the feeling this story creates in us is midway between fascination and horror, approaching (but not equalling) the horror felt by the novel's narrator, who feels humiliated that a white man is also listening: "How can he tell this to white men, I thought, when he knows they'll say that all Negroes do such things? I looked at the floor, a red mist of anguish before my eyes." The Invisible Man, at this point still a college boy, cringes at the implied connection between himself and this man from whom he feels so alien, who is like himself only in skin color (though that likeness is the only characteristic he expects the white world to notice).

But, as in *The Man Who Lived Underground*, the dream is more than just a realistic representation of unconscious material. It is also a forecast of the life that the Invisible Man himself will lead: the encounters with white women as sexual objects, the sense of being smothered (or gagged) by the Brotherhood, and finally the flight down a tunnel. And what's more, this dream sequence from *Invisible Man* moves and horrifies us because it describes not just the psychic life of one ignorant old man, not just the idiosyncratic psychology of the novel's main character, but a far deeper feeling about sex. The dream brings together two images of forbidden sex—between black man and white woman, and between father and daughter—and makes the sex all the more fascinating because of its illicitness. For a southern black man of the 1940s—at least as Ellison represents him—sex with a white woman might seem alluring partly *because* it was both forbidden and dangerous. Yet as the dream suggests, that kind of fear lies at the root of men's feelings about women in general: the fear of being lost in a "dark tunnel," of losing one's bearings, of smothering (of falling down a "manhole," so to speak). The illicit sex between black and white, between father and daughter, thus intensifies the usual sexual feelings, which involve overcoming one's fear of an enveloping otherness, and risking one's hard-won sense of adult separation from the mother's body. And in *Invisible Man*, the tunnel becomes a still more important image, encompassing as it does not only the release of sexuality but the escape from pursuit. If going down into the tunnel represents a frightening journey into the unknown, it also represents freedom, and apprehension is therefore mixed with hope. That these feelings are inevitably combined with a sense of guilt is crucial to both sex and escape—for, as one character in the novel says, " 'there's always an element of crime in freedom.' "

Invisible Man ends with exactly the same image that begins *The Man Who Lived Underground*: the picture of a black man, fleeing from his pursuers, who plunges down a manhole to temporary safety. Ellison's entire novel, which is framed by the experience of the underground, is a process of getting back to the point at which it starts, the point at which the invisible speaker says: "I live rent-free in a building rented strictly to whites, in a section of the basement that was shut off and forgotten during the nineteenth century, which I discovered when I was trying to escape in the night from Ras the Destroyer. But that's getting too far ahead of the story, almost to the end, although the end is in the beginning and lies far ahead." The circularity of the novel is crucial to its meaning, for part of what the Invisible Man discovers is that he is finally tied as helplessly to the cycles of existence as that ignorant old man who raped his own daughter and babbled about his dream. *Invisible Man*, the novel itself, is the central character's dream-story, his tale that he would once have been embarrassed to tell to white people. And he might almost be able to say, as Dostoyevsky's

Underground Man does at the end of *his* tale: "I have felt ashamed all the time I've been writing this story; so it's hardly literature so much as a corrective punishment. Why, to tell long stories, showing how I have spoiled my life through morally rotting in my corner, through lack of fitting environment, through divorce from real life, and rankling spite in my underground world, would certainly not be interesting; a novel needs a hero, and all the traits for an anti-hero are *expressly* gathered together here, and what matters most, it all produces an unpleasant impression, for we are all divorced from life, we are all cripples, every one of us, more or less."

I have said that Wright's novel begins where Ellison's ends, with a pursued man leaping down a manhole. Ellison shows us how his character got to that point; Wright tells us what happened afterward. In a way, this is also true of the two novels' styles. Ellison's Invisible Man, partly because he is the narrator, remains rationally in contact with us throughout the novel, whereas Wright's third-person character is alien from the start and only becomes more so. It is as if the two novels had split the narrative style of *Notes From Underground* between them: *Invisible Man* retains Dostoyevsky's duplicity of presentation—an apparently rational consciousness presenting outrageous events—while *The Man Who Lived Underground* brings the Underground Man's paranoia and craziness to an extreme. Ellison's novel takes the main character from innocence to experience, and the key question we ask ourselves as we read is how the optimistic, open young man of the early chapters could have become the cynical voice of the novel's first pages; what we observe, in the end, is the conscious sloughing-off of an acquired identity. In Wright's novel, on the other hand, we follow a character from semi-consciousness to madness: this Man Who Lived Underground is transfigured without being educated, and the product of his experience is death.

This difference becomes immediately apparent in the descriptions of the two descents. Like Lewis Carroll's Alice (another character who had to lose her identity to find out who she was), the Invisible Man plunges down unintentionally: "I was in strange territory now and someone, for some reason, had removed the manhole cover and I felt myself plunge down, down; a long drop that ended upon a load of coal that sent up a cloud of dust, and I lay in the black dark upon the black coal no longer running, hiding or concerned, hearing the shifting of the coal, as from somewhere above their voices came floating down." His first experience after the drop is one of peaceful release. He is in harmony with his new setting, and the repetition of the word "black" in "black dark" and "black coal" has a familiar, soothing quality. Here Ellison reverses the traditional bad/good connotations of black/white imagery, giving the positive values to blackness. In doing so, he conquers a sense of linguistic self-alienation that goes back at least as far as Shakespeare's *Othello*:

> *My name, that was as fresh*
> *As Dian's visage, is now begrimed and black*
> *As mine own face.*

Whereas Othello adopts white language, and with it the negative white attitude toward blackness, the Invisible Man puts pressure on the same language to make it yield an opposite sense.

In contrast to Ellison's protagonist, Wright's character intentionally climbs down his manhole to escape from the police. Yet this act of will results in far less immediate comfort than that gained by the Invisible Man—suggesting that the exertion of will itself, the failure to give oneself up to fate, may be likely to lead to unhappiness and danger. Wright's man is both more intentional and less self-conscious than Ellison's. First he peers into the open manhole, where he sees nothing but hears the sound of water "in the black depths." Then, as a siren sounds, terrifying him with its sudden nearness, he "swung his legs over the opening and lowered himself into the watery darkness. He hung for an eternal moment to the rim by his finger tips, then he felt rough metal prongs and at once knew that sewer workmen used these ridges to lower themselves into manholes. Fist over fist, he let his body sink until he could feel no more prongs. He swayed in dank space; the siren seemed to howl at the very rim of the manhole. He dropped and was washed violently into an ocean of warm, leaping water. His head was battered against a wall and he wondered if this were death." Unlike the Invisible Man, who rests against the "black dark" and the "black coal," merging his blackness with theirs, the Wright figure is frightened and repelled by the "black depths" and the "watery darkness." A black man himself, he has adopted the traditional white fear of darkness and thus begins in a state of self-alienation. But at this stage of the novel we don't yet know he's black. All we know is that he's a man chased by the police, and the manhole represents his only chance of escape.

The extent to which these images of escape through the underground are meant to invoke the original "Underground Railroad" is not entirely clear, but surely no educated, left-wing black writer of this period could have been unaware of that famous escape route for the slaves of the previous century. Any specific borrowing of the vocabulary of escape is far less likely; nonetheless, there are interesting parallels between Frederick Douglass's 1855 reference to the Underground Railroad and Wright's 1944 description. Douglass, in writing about this figuratively subterranean route, stresses the importance of secrecy—the *hidden* aspect of the word "underground." "I have never approved," he says, "of the very public manner, in which some of our western friends have conducted what *they* call the '*Underground Railroad*,' but which I think, by their open declarations, has been made, most emphatically, the '*Upper*-ground Railroad.' Its stations are far better known to the slaveholders than the slaves. . . . Nothing is more evident, than that such disclosures are a positive evil to the slaves remaining, and seeking to escape. . . . Such is my detestation of slavery, that I would keep the merciless slaveholder profoundly ignorant of the means of flight adopted by the slave. He should be left to imagine himself surrounded by myriads of invisible tormenters, ever ready to snatch, from his infernal grasp, his trembling prey. In pursuing his victim, let him be left to feel his way in the dark; let shades of darkness, commensurate with his crime, shut every ray of light from his pathway; and let him be made to feel, that, at every step he takes, with the hellish purpose of reducing a brother man to slavery, he is running the frightful risk of having his hot brains dashed out by an invisible hand."

Douglass begins by praising obscurity, by suggesting that only through secrecy and invisibility can the Underground Railroad succeed, and he keeps up this theme by repeatedly describing the forces of freedom as "invisible." But this passage is racked by the duplicity of his language, which insists on a negative connotation to secrecy and darkness, a positive one to openness and light. Thus even in the very act of condemning disclosure as a "positive evil," Douglass seizes on an oxymoronic description, the adjective warring against the noun it describes even as it seeks to intensify it. The same kind of contradiction riddles the rest of the paragraph, as when he uses the phrase "profoundly ignorant"—profundity being the opposite of ignorance as well as an indicator of depth or intensity. Later in the passage the values become utterly reversed, so that the desired obscurity of the means of escape gets confused with the "shades of darkness" through which the slaveholder must "feel his way in the dark": here it is the master, and not the fleeing slave, who is forced down a tunnel. Even in the "hellishness" he attributes to the slaveholders, Douglass confuses his metaphors. In the middle of a passage where he is supposedly trying to stress the benefit of an "Underground" as opposed to "Upperground" escape route, the reference to hell inevitably invokes the evil connotations of the lower regions. And even the attributes of the devil are spread around in a contradictory fashion: the slaveholder has a "hellish purpose" and an "infernal grasp," but it is those freeing the slaves who are described as his "tormenters." In valuing "every ray of light" over "shades of darkness" as he does in this passage, Douglass is forced into the same self-alienated position that afflicts Wright's character.

And, as in Douglass's vocabulary, a sense of the underground as hell or Hades pervades *The Man Who Lived Underground*. References to death and the dead run through the story, from the man's early encounter with the shriveled body of a dead baby, to his discovery of the "undertaker's establishment" and "the nude waxen figure of a man stretched out on a white table," to his own death at the novel's end ("He sighed and closed his eyes, a whirling object rushing alone into the darkness, veering, tossing, lost in the heart of the earth"). At one point he also walks into a basement with a "furnace glowing red"—a hellish image, and moreover one which recalls the doomed fate of that other Wright character, Bigger Thomas, who chopped up his unintended white victim and fed her to the roaring flames of her parents' furnace.

This belief in the deathly side of the underground, to which Wright finally seems to subscribe, is rejected by Ellison, who raises the spectre of death only to contradict it. In his general attempt to reverse or annihilate the usual poles of the argument, the Invisible Man merges life and death, remarking at the novel's beginning that "it is incorrect to assume that, because I'm invisible and live in a hole, I am dead," and at the end: "It's a kind of death without hanging, I thought, a death alive." For Ellison's character, burial can represent timelessness and eternity without making him feel frightened or condemned: "looking up, through black space, . . . I thought, this is the way it's always been, only now I know it—and rested back, calm now, placing the briefcase beneath my head." Where Wright's underground man "closes his eyes" to die, Ellison's closes his in a calm, restorative sleep.

Yet both novels hinge on rejection of the world above, and on a violent destruction of the surface world's "currency." In *The Man Who Lived Underground* it is literal currency—the money with which the thief papers his underground room. In Ellison's novel, what gets destroyed is the written evidence of identity, the papers the Invisible Man carries in his briefcase, from his high school diploma to the important letters he has received. Unlike the absurd gesture of Wright's character, the Invisible Man's act of burning his papers is purposeful and rational: he wants to illuminate the dark hole and thereby find his way out. But the burning papers also offer him another kind of illumination, for by their last light he discovers that Brother Jack, who gave him his Brotherhood name, also sent him a poisonous anonymous letter: "The handwriting was the same. I knelt there, stunned, watching the flames consume them. That he, or anyone at that late date, could have named me and set me running with one and the same stroke of the pen was too much." Whereas Wright's man, in his blatant misuse of currency, has lost the ability to comprehend words ("*This note is legal tender for all debts, public and private*. . . . He broke into a musing laugh, feeling that he was reading of the doings of people who lived on some far-off planet"), Ellison's becomes more aware than ever of the significance of writing, for it helps him to a knowledge he never had before. And while Wright's character, who earlier typed out a lowercase "freddaniels" on a stolen typewriter, now finds that he can't even remember his name when he wishes to type it again, Ellison's Invisible Man has consciously and angrily wiped out the name associated with his past. Poor Fred Daniels, deranged with his vision of a transcendent existence, comes across mainly as a victim, and we are tempted to agree with the brutal cops who casually write him off:

> *"What do you suppose he's suffering from?" Johnson asked.*
> *"Delusions of grandeur, maybe," Murphy said.*
> *"Maybe it's because he lives in a white man's world," Lawson said.*

The Invisible Man, on the other hand, has emerged from his degrading experiences with something like dignity. His is not an optimistic story—in the end he simply learns to embrace hopelessness rather than battle it—but one could never see him as a mere victim of the "white man's world." His invisibility, once forced on him, is now chosen, and his mad rejection of the aboveground world, if indeed it is madness, has the persuasive sound of sanity.

This difference in the tone with which Wright's and Ellison's characters reject the upper world carries over into their physical descriptions of their respective underground worlds. Ellison is far more concerned with the actual city that lies beneath the ground: the coal-filled basements, the subway stations and tunnels, the water mains. His Invisible Man stresses the simultaneous accessibility and inaccessibility of this other region, the solidity as well as the invisibility of its inhabitants: "I am not a spook like those who haunted Edgar Allan Poe," he says at the novel's beginning; "nor am I one of your Hollywood-movie ectoplasms. I am a man of substance, of flesh and bone, fiber and liquids—and I might even be said to possess a mind. I am invisible, understand, simply because people refuse to see me." For Wright's character, on the other hand, the gap between his world and the aboveground world grows wider and wider, so that eventually he can hardly even believe in the existence of that "far-off planet" where money has real value.

This image of the underground as a kind of science-fiction location, somewhere in outer space, begins to emerge within the first few pages of *The Man Who Lived Underground.* Just after he has climbed down into the manhole and walked several paces into the sewer, the character is "struck to wonderment by the silence; it seemed that he had traveled a million miles away from the world." The two levels of existence, however close they may be geographically, are two utterly different worlds—an obvious parallel with the situation of a black man living near to, but also very far from, the white world that surrounds him. (Demonstrating the general applicability of the metaphor, John Sayles's 1984 movie *The Brother From Another Planet*—about a black character from outer space who lands in Harlem—builds on the same idea.) After he has been down in the sewer for some time, Wright's character sits "brooding. Some part of him was trying to remember the world he had left, and another part of him did not want to remember it. . . . Emotionally he hovered between the world aboveground and the world underground." After he steals the money, the jewels, and the typewriter, the character finds himself even more committed to the world below. The objects he has stolen are virtually meaningless to him: "They were the serious toys of the men who lived in the dead world of sunshine and rain he had left, the world that had condemned him, branded him guilty." Here the phrase "the dead world of sunshine and rain" pointedly reverses our usual sense of the underworld as Hades, the aboveground world as the land of the living. Wright's man has by now become an underground man; he is no longer "hovering" between the two worlds.

It is typical of Wright that this transformation should be entirely psychological, and that it should take the form of a loss of reason. For this particular black author, the escape underground is primarily a mental rather than a physical act, and the underground itself represents the dark depths of the psyche, the buried regions in which man discovers himself to be an isolated rather than a social creature. Wright leans heavily on what might be called the "existential" side of Dostoyevsky: he is interested in pushing his character to the limits. The social message regarding race is not incidental to this tale—indeed, it is central—but it has been transformed into a kind of allegory by Wright's insistence on the "other-worldliness" of the underground.

In contrast, Ellison's Invisible Man retains a firm hold on the vocabulary and the rationality of the upper regions even when he is most separate from them. His rejection of that other world is conscious and active, not forced on him by the experience of separation. "They were all up there somewhere," he says, "making a mess of the world. Well, let them. I was through and, in spite of the dream, I was whole. And now I realized that I couldn't return to Mary's, or to any part of my old life. . . . I could only move ahead or stay here, underground. . . . Here at least I could try to think things out in peace, or, if not in peace, in quiet. I would take up residence underground." Unlike Wright's language, this is the language of rational behavior: "now I realized," "think things out," "take up residence." It does not matter that the act itself, the decision to live underground, seems *more* irrational than the mere decision to hide there temporarily (which is what Wright's character does); Ellison's character remains persuasively sane because he continues to speak in our aboveground vocabulary.

(Actually, the decision to take up residence underground may be rational and even sensible under certain circumstances, depending on what the alternatives are. As if to demonstrate that Ellison's is far from a purely literary device, a December 1986 edition of the *San Francisco Chronicle* carried a story about a group of people ousted from their underground dwelling on the eve of Christmas. "A small community of homeless men living in a sewer cave under a San Francisco street traded their soggy home for a dry hotel yesterday, but they made the switch reluctantly," the article begins. It goes on to describe the founding of the cave community "1½ years ago by a homeless man who had been sleeping in a field. . . . The dirt floor of the tiny cave was covered with a green carpet scavenged from a nearby dumpster; the walls are of mud. Foam mattresses and sleeping bags lie in a neat row."

The real reason for the "reluctance" to leave comes out later in the article: " 'What happens after eight or nine days when they kick us out of the hotel?' asked Jose Gonzalves, 40. 'We'll have to come back to the cave again.' If there is no cave to return to, the group will dig another one, Gonzalves said. . . .")

Unlike the Wright character, for whom such ease of movement back and forth would be impossible, Ellison's Invisible Man does not feel the existence of two worlds: what is up there is "the world," and the underground is a place to hide within it. The silence of the lower regions does not create an awed feeling of being "a million miles away," but simply an opportunity to think in "peace" and "quiet." That one can "take up residence" underground suggests that this region is subject to the same rules of social behavior as the one above.

This sense of the accessibility of the underground does not mean that Ellison has freed it from its frightening or alien connotations. On the contrary, he wants to make it both strange and ordinary. His underground does not consist only of foul sewers and abandoned basements which people rarely enter; it is a place into which hundreds and thousands of New Yorkers plunge every day. Some of Ellison's most extreme and terrifying language is reserved for the most ordinary experience of the underground, as when he describes the Invisible Man's first trip on a subway: "Moving into the subway I was pushed along by the milling salt-and-pepper mob. . . . Then the door banged behind me and I was crushed against a huge woman in black who shook her head and smiled while I stared with horror at a large mole that arose out of the oily whiteness of her skin like a black mountain out of a rainwet plain. And all the while I could feel the rubbery softness of her flesh against the length of my body. . . . The car roared and swayed, pressing me hard against her, but when I took a furtive glance around no one was paying me the slightest attention. . . . The train seemed to plunge downhill now, only to lunge to a stop that shot me out upon the platform feeling like something regurgitated from the belly of a frantic whale. Wrestling with my bags, I swept along with the crowd, up the stairs into the hot street. I didn't care where I was, I would walk the rest of the way."

Anyone who has ever ridden a New York subway at rush hour will acknowledge the realism of this scene. (Nor is the inhuman crush of humans a recent development in regard to the subway. A reporter for the *New York Tribune*, covering the opening of the first Manhattan subway line in 1900, wrote: "Indescribable scenes of crowding and confusion, never before paralleled in this city, marked the throwing open of the subway to the general public last night. . . . Men fought, kicked and pummeled one another in their mad desire to reach the subway ticket offices or to ride on the trains. Women were dragged out, either screaming in hysterics or in a swooning condition; grey-haired men pleaded for mercy; boys were knocked down and only escaped by a miracle being trampled underfoot." Apparently the underground has always brought out the devilish worst in New Yorkers.) The subterranean experience described by Ellison is not a solitary, isolating one, as in the Wright novel; it is filled with the noise and feel of a jostling, hurrying crowd. Ellison's underground is everybody's, and at the same time it represents an utterly alienating experience which invokes the private dream world of the "dark tunnel" (complete with intimations of sexual contact between a black man and a white woman). The Invisible Man's "horror" is a response to both the real experience of being trapped in the hot, crowded, noisy subway, and the allegorical experiences it suggests: Jonah's entrapment in the "frantic whale," the lurid dream of the incestuous old black man, the sense of "plunging" down into the land of death, and so on. Even when he becomes accustomed to traveling by subway, Ellison's narrator still retains these metaphorical associations (here converting the underground to underwater, as Jules Verne did when he wrote *Twenty Thousand Leagues Under the Sea*): "I wandered down the subway stairs seeing nothing, my mind plunging. . . . I stood there with the trains plunging in and out, throwing blue sparks. . . . A body of people came down the platform, some of them Negroes. Yes, I thought, what about those of us who shoot up from the South into the busy city like wild jacks-in-the-box broken loose from our strings—so suddenly that our gait becomes like that of deep-sea divers suffering from the bends?"

In *Invisible Man*, the subway comes to stand for all the "undergrounds" in the lives of the city's black people: the South from which they came (which, on a north/south axis, is "under" in the same way that Australia is "Down Under"); the long and uncomfortable subterranean commute from midtown or downtown jobs to homes in Harlem; the forced and disregarded proximity of black and white bodies; the sense of fatality in their lives, of being channeled through a previously existing tunnel. And by choosing such a common, public, everyday image of the underground to represent these "buried" things, Ellison manages to convey a simultaneous sense of crowd and isolation, access and inaccessibility, presence and invisibility—the very combination, that is, which characterizes the lives of black people in a white-run world.

In the last subway scene of the novel, the underground region also comes to represent "destiny," the closing of the circle, the end in the beginning. For in this scene the Invisible Man meets Mr. Norton, his one-time sponsor, the white man who was present at the telling of the "dark tunnel" dream. And of course Mr. Norton, seeking to learn from a stranger which subway train to take, fails to recognize the narrator, who is just another black man to him. At first the Invisible Man doesn't recognize this lost, elderly white man either, though he does notice him coming along the platform; this man is initially just an occasion for allegory. "Perhaps to lose a sense of *where* you are implies the danger of losing a sense of *who* you are," the Invisible Man comments. "That must be it, I thought—to lose your direction is to lose your face. So here he comes to ask his direction from the lost, the invisible. Very well, I've learned to live without direction. Let him ask." But when the man is only a few feet away "I recognized him; it was Mr. Norton." The two of them converse at cross-purposes, the Invisible Man asking " 'Don't you know me?' " and Mr. Norton countering with " 'Should I?' " " 'I'm your destiny,' " the narrator tells him, but Mr. Norton only wants to know the way to Centre Street. As the old white man gets on the train, the narrator begins to laugh hysterically, and continues to laugh "all the way back to my hole. But after I had laughed I was thrown back on my thoughts—how had it all happened? And I asked myself if it were only a joke and I couldn't answer. Since then I've sometimes been overcome with a passion to return into that 'heart of darkness' across the Mason-Dixon line, but then I remind myself that the true darkness lies within my own mind, and the idea loses itself in the gloom. Still the passion persists." Whether the darkness is internal or external, in his own mind or in the world at large, is in fact central to *Invisible Man*. The novel seems to suggest that it is both.

This refusal to separate psychological from physical reality is finally what makes Ellison's novel so powerful. By bringing together the underground and the aboveground, the interior life and the exterior life, the black world of victimization and the white world of conventional oppression, Ralph Ellison makes it impossible for us to ignore the fate of the Invisible Man. For, as he says to Mr. Norton, he is our destiny. Finally, the Invisible Man's escape into the underground is not an escape at all, but an acceptance of the inevitable. He does not retreat into madness, as Wright's character does, but holds firmly to his pessimistic realizations: "I'm an invisible man and it placed me in a hole—or showed me the hole I was in, if you will—and I reluctantly accepted the fact. What else could I have done? Once you get used to it, reality is as irresistible as a club, and I was clubbed into the cellar before I caught the hint." Perhaps the only difference between this character and those he addresses is that he knows he's in a hole, and we don't. But that it is our hole too becomes clear in another of his remarks: "Life is to be lived, not controlled; and humanity is won by continuing to play in the face of certain defeat. Our fate is to become one, and yet many—This is not prophecy, but description. Thus one of the greatest jokes in the world is the spectacle of the whites busy escaping blackness and becoming blacker every day, and the blacks striving toward whiteness, becoming quite dull and gray. None of us seems to know who he is or where he's going."

This universal fate perceived through the medium of individual misery echoes Dostoyevsky's "for we are all divorced from life, we are all cripples, every one of us, more or less." What makes us uncomfortable about both Dostoyevsky's Underground Man and Ellison's Invisible Man is that they are simultaneously alien from and part of one's own being. Separated from the middle-class reader by vast barriers of class or race or psychological attitude, they nonetheless represent a crucial aspect of everyone's personality: the dark, invisible, buried self. It is down at this level that the individual ego begins to lose its hold, giving way—in its affiliation with the rest of humanity—to both the conscience and the unconscious.

Depths of Self: The Body and the Unconscious

The story of Psyche may have been particularly attractive to Freud because she had to enter the underworld and retrieve something before she could attain her apotheosis. Freud, similarly, had to dare to enter the underworld—in his case, the underworld of the soul—to gain his illumination.

—Bruno Bettelheim, *Freud and Man's Soul*

BETTELHEIM WAS NOT THE FIRST TO POINT OUT THE SUBterranean quality of the psychoanalytic endeavor. Freud himself, when he first published *The Interpretation of Dreams* in 1900, used as an epigraph to the book a line from Virgil's *Aeneid*: "Flectere si nequeo Superos, Acheronta movebo"—"If I cannot move Heaven, I will stir up the underworld." As if to strengthen the connection between his own scientific discoveries and the workings of the underworld, Freud repeatedly alluded, in both his letters and his published writing, to Goethe's *Faust*—a parallel tale of a doctor who, in his search for answers about the nature of the human soul, makes a pact with the devil. And Freud drew upon other undergrounds to describe his work as well: we learn from Bettelheim, for instance, that "Freud frequently compared psychoanalysis with archaeology: the work of psychoanalysis consists in unearthing the deeply buried remnants of the past and combining them with other fragments that are more accessible." The father of psychoanalysis even structured his picture of the mind as a series of layers, with the *sub*conscious lying beneath the conscious mind, and the id, or unconscious, located even further down.

The tendency, in many discussions of Freud's legacy, is to disembody psychoanalysis, to make it a study of pure mind. But Freud himself was a medical doctor, and his conclusions about the unconscious were closely linked to his sense of bodily functions. One might even say that for Freud the id *is* the body, or an extension of it. The life forces that give impulse to the id—sexual desire and the aging process, the whole relationship between Eros and Thanatos—manifest themselves in the body and stem from the body. The id, containing vast reaches that cannot be plumbed by the conscious mind, essentially becomes part of the body: both are literally unconscious, incapable of thought or reasoning, but powerful enough to alter and invade and finally control the conscious life. It is this sense of "unconscious"—the underworld of the soul *and* the body—that I draw on throughout this chapter. Though I will be leaving Freud behind now, and only calling on him as a shadowy background figure, his shadow nonetheless remains a long and powerful one, for he was the first to journey so consciously into the underworld of the self.

The concept of the body itself as an "underground" is in fact a rather commonplace idea. Thus David Macaulay, in his children's book called *Underground*, uses a language that recalls the body to describe what takes place under a city's streets. Macaulay's sole purpose here is to present a direct, factual, clear picture of the physical underground; he is not aiming to create any sort of metaphor. Yet the language he employs to discuss water and sewage and electrical systems inevitably invokes internal bodily functions. Note, for instance, how his description of water pipes sounds like an account of the body's circulatory system: "To insure complete distribution throughout the city a constant pressure is maintained in the pipes by continuous pumping. . . . The largest water pipes . . . carry water from centralized pumping stations into predetermined districts of the city. Smaller pipes, called submains, are connected to the mains and carry water down each street. . . . Metal gates, called valves, are located inside the pipes. . . ." The structure of the digestive tract is similarly suggested by the sentence: "If a system is constructed for bringing water into a city, another system must be built to remove the dirty water and waste, which is referred to as sewage." And Macaulay's description of a city's electrical system borrows heavily from the physiological language of sex: "The electrical cable . . . is then fed through a protective flexible tube into the manhole. . . . A special lubricant is smeared on the cable as it enters the tube." Provocative as this may sound, it is not a case of authorially intended metaphor: I am quite sure that Macaulay is trying to be purely factual here. Nor is it likely that the metaphor has a larger kind of "intentionality" (as it would, for instance, if water and sewage systems had been explicitly designed to imitate the body's internal "pipes"). But whether our underground structures were named after bodily parts or not, the fact remains that they share the same vocabulary, so that in talking about the underpinnings of a city Macaulay seems to be talking about the human body.

Macaulay's matter-of-fact descriptions build on a metaphor that is so accepted as to be almost invisible. But a fiction writer seeking to re-ignite the metaphor can intentionally stress the connection between the body and the underground. This is what Herman Melville does in the second half of his 1855 story "The Paradise of Bachelors and the Tartarus of Maids," where he purports to be describing the location of a paper-mill that employs only women. After following a road at the bottom of a gorge, Melville says, "you stand as within a Dantean gateway. From the steepness of the walls here, their strangely ebon hue, and the sudden contraction of the gorge, this particular point is called the Black Notch. The ravine now expandingly descends into a great, purple, hopper-shaped hollow, far sunk among many Plutonian, shaggy-wooded mountains. By the country people this hollow is called Devil's Dungeon. Sounds of torrents fall on all sides upon the ear. These rapid waters unite at last in one turbid brick-colored stream, boiling through a flume among enormous boulders. They call this strange-colored torrent Blood River." Lest the reader unaccountably miss the fact that this passage also describes the female genitalia—lest he ignore the "sudden contraction" of the "Black Notch," the "shaggy-wooded mountains," the "Blood River"—Melville highlights the metaphor at the end of the story by stressing that the women who work in this factory are all virgins, "all maids." Only the intrusive narrator, a "seedsman" in search of a wholesale paper supply, has pushed his way into the female domain; otherwise it remains inviolate.

Melville's odd story is in part about the degree to which women are imprisoned by their biology. The very fact of their being women condemns these maids to the fearful "labor" described in this tale, a labor which takes "exactly nine minutes" to produce its finished product. And like the old man's subterranean dream in *Invisible Man*, this story is also about men's fear of women's bodies, their terror of being lost and enclosed in that deep gorge. The profound desire manifested in the Oedipus complex is the other side of a profound fear—that a man *will* have to reunite with his mother, go back down into the womb from which he came, re-enter that "first cavern, dark and moist" where "lover and mother melt into one figure" (as Thom Gunn puts it in "Bringing to Light"). Nor does the fear Melville expresses apply only to men: his maids, who work themselves to death in the factory, are "their own executioners; themselves whetting the very swords that slay them." The story told in "The Tartarus of Maids" embodies and confirms the Elizabethan pun on the word "die": sex *becomes* death, and that journey down into the body of the lover/mother is also a journey down to the grave, to Hades.

As with Thom Gunn's poem about memory and cells, works written about the unconscious often invoke the metaphor of the subterranean. This is certainly true of the books I will be looking at in the rest of this chapter: Oliver Sacks's *Awakenings* and Lewis Carroll's *Alice* adventures. On the surface, no two pieces of writing could seem more dissimilar. In Sacks's book, first published in 1973, a neurologist describes his treatment of an extreme form of Parkinson's disease, while the *Alice* books, composed in the 1860s, were ostensibly intended as an entertainment for little girls. Aside from everything else, one is a work of non-fiction, the other a fantasy; one presumes a self-conscious, highly literate adult audience, and the other apparently makes jokes for the as-yet-undeveloped mind. But such distinctions are precisely the sort that these books work to overcome. Both *Awakenings* and *Alice* are in part about the bridging of conventional barriers, the underlying cohesion of human experience. And both works share, among other things, a deep sense of the connection between body and mind (or soul), between the physical self and the inaccessible mental self, as joint elements making up the human "unconscious."

This aspect of *Alice in Wonderland* has been pointedly yet tactfully elucidated by the critic William Empson, who said in *Some Versions of Pastoral*: "To make the dream-story from which *Wonderland* was elaborated seem Freudian one has only to tell it. A fall through a deep hole into the secrets of Mother Earth produces a new enclosed soul wondering who it is, what will be its position in the world, and how it can get out. It is in a long low hall, part of the palace of the Queen of Hearts (a neat touch), from which it can only get out to the fresh air and fountains through a hole frighteningly too small. Strange changes, too, caused by the way it is nourished there, happen to it in this place, but always when it is big it cannot get out and when it is small it is not allowed to; for one thing, being a girl, it has no key." It is interesting, and typical of Empson, that even in this apparently "reductive" rendering of Alice's adventures as birth-trauma, he opens out Lewis Carroll's tale by suggesting its connection to other kinds of undergrounds. If conception is a "fall through a deep hole into the secrets of Mother Earth," then Aeneas visiting his father in Hades, Jules Verne's geological explorers, Graham Greene's Harry Lime, and Ralph Ellison's

Invisible Man are also creatures undergoing a process of rebirth: their hell, or earth's core, or sewer, or basement, is also a version of the womb, from which they will emerge changed in some crucial way. Empson makes the classical analogy explicit when he says of the tears in *Alice*: "I said that the sea of tears she swims in was the amniotic fluid, which is much too simple. You may take it as Lethe in which the souls were bathed before re-birth (and it is their own tears; they forget, as we forget our childhood, through the repression of pain) or as the 'solution' of an intellectual contradiction through Intuition and a return to the Unconscious." It is important to Empson's description that the metaphor work on both levels, that the tears be actual bodily fluid as well as soul-cleansing waters of forgetfulness. The *solution* is both liquid and idea; the Unconscious, in this sense, is both body and mind.

In Oliver Sacks's book *Awakenings*, that "solution" is a drug called L-DOPA which causes extreme changes, both mental and physical, in the patients to whom it is administered. Like a Faustian cure, L-DOPA brings both heavenly release and hellish punishment, offering hope and at the same time despair. Used as the cure for a devastating form of Parkinson's disease brought on by *encephalitis lethargica*, the drug has the appearance of a mythical potion applied to an enchantment: after years of entrapment in twisted, paralyzed bodies, the "souls" of Oliver Sacks's patients are temporarily freed to something approaching normality. But in almost every case the disease closes in again, often more harshly than before, so that the response to L-DOPA becomes an intensification of the illness it was designed to cure. And this is not purely a bodily illness. Both the symptoms of this form of Parkinsonism and the effects of the L-DOPA "cure" seem to be indications of the patients' psychological state as well as afflictions of their bodies.

The comparison between *Alice in Wonderland* and *Awakenings* is not entirely my own: Dr. Sacks himself suggests it in his discussions of both the condition of Parkinsonism and its reaction to L-DOPA. Describing one patient's response to the drug, he quotes her own analysis: " 'I've been up, down, sideways, inside-out, and everything else. I've been pushed, pulled, squeezed and twisted. I've gone faster and slower, as well as *so* fast I actually stayed in one place. And I keep opening-up and closing-down, like a human concertina. . . .' Miss D. paused for breath. Her words irresistibly depicted a Parkinsonian 'Alice' in a post-encephalitic Wonderland." And in a footnote about this patient, Sacks adds: "Miss D. (like half-a-dozen other highly articulate post-encephalitic patients under my care) has often depicted for me the strange and deeply paradoxical world in which she lives. These patients describe a fantastical-mathematical world remarkably similar to that which faced 'Alice.' Miss D. lays stress on the fundamental distortions of Parkinsonian *space*, on her peculiar difficulties with angles, circles, sets, and limits." (The italics, as elsewhere in my quotations, are Sacks's.)

The emphasis on "Parkinsonian *space*"—and, in particular, on the oppositions of height and depth—pervades *Awakenings*. In a footnote to the first edition, Sacks remarks: "Instinctively and intuitively all patients use certain metaphors again and again with regard to the transformations wrought by L-DOPA; one sometimes feels that such metaphors are an inherent part of our experience and heritage, like Borges' 'eternal metaphors' or Kant's *synthetic a priori*, or (though I dislike the mysticism which accrues to the notions) Platonic or Jungian 'archetypes.' Thus, there are the universal images of rising and falling, which come naturally and automatically to every patient: one *ascends* to health and happiness and grace, and one *descends* to depths of sickness and misery." Here Sacks is using the metaphor of depth in a different way from that found in Melville's "Tartarus of Maids" or Empson's version of *Alice*. Rather than representing the body itself—the body as sexual, reproductive entity, as it appears in Melville and Empson—the "lower depths" here refer only to the *sick* body, to illness. One does not go down into oneself, into the unconscious parts of oneself, but into one's illness; one "falls" sick.

Nor is the metaphor, as Sacks uses it here, strictly a subterranean one: "descent," after all, can refer to any downward motion (not necessarily into the underground), while "depth" may allude to a horizontal rather than vertical dimension (as in "depth perception"). The combination of words in "*descends* to depths of sickness and misery" does suggest penetration below the surface—but this could be the surface of a body of water or (literally) of a personality, without referring to an underworld as such. In metaphysical and medical discussions as well as in daily speech, notions of depth and descent have invaded our language to such an extent that they are not necessarily connected to a subterranean image. Throughout *Awakenings*, Dr. Sacks draws on this fund of common usage, as when he says of a patient that "his physical state was going downhill," or "I was shocked to find her very 'down'—hypophonic, somewhat depressed, rigid and akinetic," or "she sank naturally into a deep and almost comatose sleep"—sleep itself, perhaps in part through analogy with death, being something into which one often *sinks* or *falls*, or which one does *deeply*. (Such built-in metaphor may represent an age-old acknowledgment of the connection between sleep and the unconscious, that "deeper" level of being. Nor can one totally discount the effect of rhyme: perhaps English is a language particularly suited to the notion of a *deep sleep*.) In each of these remarks, the metaphor is so buried (as it were) in everyday language as to be virtually invisible; nor do any of these phrases have an explicit connection with the underground.

But elsewhere Sacks specifically employs the language of depth to describe a subterranean landscape, an underground region inhabited by both the illness and its supposed cure. Thus he says of one Parkinsonian woman: "She seemed to dwell in some unimaginably strange, inaccessible ultimity, in some bottomlessly deep hole or abyss of being; she seemed crushed into an infinitely dense, inescapable state, or held motionless in the motionless 'eye' of a vortex." And he describes this woman's reaction to L-DOPA as follows: "Completely motionless and submerged for over twenty years, she had surfaced and shot into the air like a cork released from great depth; she had exploded with a vengeance from the shackles which held her. I thought of prisoners released from gaol; I thought of children released from school; I thought of spring-awakenings after winter-sleeps; I thought of The Sleeping Beauty; and I also thought, with some foreboding, of catatonics, suddenly frenzied."

Here the after-effect description alludes to depths of water, out of which the cork-like personality "surfaced and shot into the air." Yet the initial landscape—that "bottomlessly deep hole or abyss," where the body is "crushed" into something "infinitely dense"—suggests rather a deep chasm in the earth itself. This metaphor of the underground is in turn mixed with that of a tornado ("the motionless 'eye' of a vortex"), while the second metaphor runs wildly over the terrain of prisoners, children, seasons of the year, fairy-tale princesses, and clinical insanity. Like the patients afflicted with Parkinsonism, Sacks seems to have lost his directions a bit here, and to be ricocheting aimlessly off various images.

Yet the dominant image in Sacks's mind, I think, is that of the "bottomlessly deep hole," and the others are chosen primarily because of their relationship to this image, sharing with it the characteristics of depth (the cork immersed in water), circularity (the vortex), entrapment (the prison), and immobility (the frozen winter, the enchanted sleeper). Part of my reason for assigning centrality to that image is Sacks's own evident obsession with the underground metaphor. It infects his writing almost unconsciously, and seems most likely to take control at the moments of greatest pressure. Thus the first edition of *Awakenings*, published just after Sacks had completed his initial three years of experimentation with L-DOPA, when he was most stunned by the drug's extreme and contradictory effects, is the one which contains the most references to the underground or the underworld; it is this edition from which I have taken the quotations in this chapter. As Sacks revised and refined his book, moving away from the initial experience, he eliminated some of the subterranean references and toned down others—as if he felt he had given away too much, or perhaps become overwrought, in the earlier formulations.

That Sacks is indeed giving away his own deepest sense of the world when he invokes subterranean images becomes clear in his autobiographical book *A Leg To Stand On*. An account of Sacks's near-death in a hiking accident and his slow, painful recovery, the story reaches its most melodramatic peaks at precisely the moments when Sacks alludes to "the abyss." For instance, he equates his own impending death with Death in general by saying: "There was something impersonal, or universal, in my feeling. I would not have cried 'Save *me*, Oliver Sacks!' but 'Save this hurt living creature! Save *Life*!,' the mute plea I know so well from my patients—the plea of *all* life facing the abyss, if it be strongly, vividly, rightly alive."

In *A Leg To Stand On*, Sacks also uses the metaphor of depth to describe the realm of dreams ("in the night, when I descended to the depths (or the depths erupted and surfaced in me) I had a dream of peculiar horror") and moments of sudden, terrifying awareness ("It seemed to me now, as I mused, more and more darkly, by myself, that the whole business was much deeper, much stranger, than I could have conceived. I felt abysses opening beneath me. . . ."). Sacks makes his most explicit reference to the underground—as *hell* and as *hole*—when he attempts to characterize his "scotoma," a stroke-like symptom. "The word 'hell' supposedly is cognate with 'hole,' " he says, "and the hole of a *scotoma* is indeed a sort of hell: an existential, or metaphysical, state, indeed, but one with the clearest organic basis and determinant. The organic foundation of 'reality' is removed, and to this extent one falls into a hole—or a hell-hole, if one permits oneself consciousness of this." In describing his sense of this Limbo, this nothingness, Sacks quotes a passage from Marlowe's *Dr. Faustus* and then goes on, rather melodramatically, to suggest that his own situation has a Faustian dimension: " 'If you stare into the abyss,' wrote Nietzsche, 'it will stare back at you.' The abyss is a chasm, an infinite rift, in reality. If you but notice it, it may open beneath you. You may either turn away from it, or face it, fair and square. I am very tenacious, for better or worse. If my attention is engaged, I cannot disengage it. This may be a great strength, or weakness. It makes me an investigator. It makes me an obsessional. It made me, in this case, an *explorer* of the abyss. . . ." (Moments like this, while they may superficially resemble Henry James's references to "the abyss," cause one to long desperately for James's leavening sense of humor).

A Leg To Stand On is a much less powerful work than *Awakenings*, in large part because it substitutes the author's own obsessive self-dramatization for the comparatively unmelodramatic, movingly sympathetic portraits he had earlier drawn of his Parkinsonian patients. But the book is interesting for the way it pointedly reveals, in moments such as those cited above, the same obsession with the underworld that shapes the language of *Awakenings*. For Sacks, "the abyss" clearly represents all the most frightening truths of existence: death, madness, nightmare, the hidden self. What he finds fascinating and moving about his patients in *Awakenings* is that they not only face this abyss (as he does in his *Leg* adventure), but that they actually seem to go down into it. At one point he even describes this descent in terms of a Jules-Vernian journey through an underground landscape, remarking of one patient's reaction to the drug that it brought about "*releases* or *exposures* or *disclosures* or '*confessions*' of very deep and ancient parts of herself, monstrous creatures from her unconscious and from unimaginable physiological depths below the unconscious, pre-historic and perhaps pre-human landscapes whose features were at once utterly strange to her, yet mysteriously familiar, in the manner of certain dreams."

The heroic, mythical quality of this quest, and at the same time its fearfulness, appear again in Sacks's reference to the Inferno, the image that seems to be at the base of much of his subterranean imagery: "The process of sickening, going-down, deteriorating, etc. has always been visualized as a circular process, with a peculiarly terrible force and shape of its own. Morbid process and propensity were classically identified with sin and peccability—hence Galen's vicious circle: the fundamental image of Dante's inferno." If the underworld is death, it is also hell, and in *Awakenings* the physical illness of Sacks's patients mixes oddly and inextricably with a sense of spiritual or moral condemnation. What lies "down there" is feared not only because it is life-threatening (a medical term), but because it is in some way evil (a moral term). So when Sacks uses words like "down" or "depressed" or "beneath," they are not merely directional or even clinical terms, but words that derive part of their meaning from that basic image of the Inferno: a hole that is also a hell, an underworld that is an exaggeration of life's punishments. Many doctors respond to continual exposure to pain or suffering by closing themselves off from metaphysical contemplation and spiritual concerns, but Sacks seems to have done the opposite: his close acquaintance with the body appears to have intensified his belief in a soul.

Toward the end of *Awakenings*, Sacks says of the drug's eventual effects: "Our patients, then, ascend higher and higher into the heights of exorbitance, becoming more active, excited, impatient, increasingly restless, choreic, akathisic, more driven by tics and urges and itches, continually more hectic, fervid and ardent, flaming into manias, passions and greeds, into climactic voracities, surges, and frenzies . . . until the crash comes at last. The form and tempo of 'crashing' are immensely variable in Parkinsonian patients; and in many of the stabler, more fortunate patients, there is more the feeling of gentle subsidence and detumescence, than of a sudden violent crash. But, whatever the form and tempo it takes, there is descent from the dangerous heights of pathology—a descent which is at once protective, yet also destructive. Patients do not descend to the ground, as a punctured balloon would sink to the ground. They sink or crash *below* the ground, into the subterranean depths of exhaustion and depression, or the equivalents of these in Parkinsonian patients."

In this description, both the "heights" of mania and the "depths" of depression are conveyed in negative terms. Yet the "exorbitance" and excitation are viewed as "dangerous" mainly because they inevitably precede the "crash": it is the "subterranean depths of exhaustion and depression" which are basically evil, and which contaminate with foreboding the states that came before them. The only positive aspect Sacks can find in this descent is that it is "protective"—but even this adjective is paradoxically linked with its opposite, "destructive," to indicate the fact that the only escape for these patients is in the direction of a death-like decline. Through the oddly inappropriate word "detumescence" (carried through in the image of "a punctured balloon"), the fall is also linked with post-coital exhaustion and melancholy—an analogy that turns out to be surprisingly appropriate, given the erotic cast of some of the patients' manias.

As if to imitate the course of the patients' illness, Sacks's sentences themselves take on a rise-and-fall quality, with the first phrase or sentence in each pair initiating an upward movement and the second half marking a fall of some kind. In the passage I've just quoted, the first sentence begins with a mounting list of adjectives (including "higher and higher") and ends, after the ellipsis, with a short, sudden crash. The next sentence begins on a level note ("The form and tempo of 'crashing' are immensely variable . . ."), moves slightly upward with the terms "stable" and "more fortunate," but again ends with "a sudden violent crash." The sentence after that moves upward toward the "heights of pathology," and then downward after the dash to the final word "destructive." And the last two sentences together form a depressed version of the rise-and-fall pair, the first alluding to the gentle descent of a balloon sinking to the ground while the second plunges "*below* the ground, into the subterranean depths."

The image of "the ground" is used as a complex metaphor in this context: it invokes not only the idiomatic sense of "ground zero," or a basic condition, but also, by contrast, the sensation of anti-gravitational flight that many of the L-DOPA patients experienced on the drug ("Look at me! Look at me! I can fly like a bird!" cried one female patient when she first found herself able to speak and move). The earth, in this sense, represents imprisonment as well as stability—not surprisingly, given the literal imprisonment of many of these patients in their heavy, paralyzed bodies. Sacks effectively manipulates the image of flight when he presents us with the personal histories of his patients, as when he says of one sixty-year-old woman's youth in the 1920s: "Airplanes, above all, appealed to her eager, volant, and irrepressible spirit; she flew to Pittsburgh and Denver, New Orleans and Chicago, and twice to the California of Hearst and Hollywood (no mean feat in the planes of those days)." This is the same young woman who, Sacks tells us, at twenty-one "was suddenly struck down by a virulent form of *encephalitis lethargica*—one of its last victims before the epidemic vanished." In the structure of this paragraph, her experience of being "struck down" by the disease is equated, in terms of unexpectedness and violence, with an airplane crash. Thus flight represents both freedom and danger, both escape (which is, after all, one meaning of the word "flight") and ultimate ruin. If flying *up* is in obvious ways the opposite of falling *down*, they are also connected: both flying and falling bodies are detached from the earth, surrounded purely by air, hence not "grounded" in their normal settings. One usually thinks of falling (especially with airplane crashes) as from a height *to* the earth; but with his image of the "crash *below* the ground," Sacks manages to link the act of falling with the act of descending underground: such falls, he implies, involve flying into the abyss.

The metaphor of the ground as surface and the subterranean as below the surface also raises another analogy: that between the individual self and the planet as a whole. To fly is thus to escape from oneself, while to plunge into the subterranean is to go deep into one's own mind, or soul, or being, or body. The earth is both the human head (which, like the earth, is spherical and generative) and the human body (Mother Earth, the underground as womb). Hence descent into the earth is an exploration of both mind (or soul) and body, of the mental interior and the physical interior. Sacks extends this geologic metaphor from the individual Parkinsonian patient to his whole experience with the disease when he says: "This sense of worlds upon worlds, of a landscape continually extending, reaching beyond my sight or imagination, is one which has always been with me, since I first encountered my post-encephalitic patients in 1966, and first gave them L-DOPA in 1969. It is a very mixed landscape, partly familiar, partly uncanny, with sunlit uplands, bottomless chasms, volcanoes, geysers, meadows, marshes; something like Yellowstone—archaic, prehuman, almost prehistoric, with a sense of vast forces simmering all around one. Freud once spoke of neurosis as akin to a prehistoric, Jurassic landscape, and this image is still truer of post-encephalitic disease, which seems to conduct one into the dark heart of being." While the heart of being may be a frightening place, it is also, finally, where all the most compelling things take place. *This* darkness, Sacks implies, is in reality the source of enlightenment, the region where one learns the truth about oneself.

The idea of an enlightening journey through a strange and sometimes frightening landscape lies at the center of Lewis Carroll's *Alice* books as well. In both *Alice in Wonderland* (originally composed as *Alice's Adventures Under Ground*) and *Through the Looking Glass*, the heroine journeys to a place that is simultaneously an opposite and a reflection of her normal world. In the first book, this dream-place is an underground realm inhabited by playing-cards; in the second, it is a mirror world populated by chess pieces. Though the two books are by no means identical in either tone or content, they do imply an equation between the underworld and the mirror world—both being places governed by game rules that are arbitrarily broken, where adults are represented by parodies of royalty, where animals and flowers speak, and where progress and regress are difficult to differentiate.

Though it makes sense to distinguish at times between *Wonderland*

and *Looking Glass*—for instance, as phases in Alice's development—Oliver Sacks alludes to the two books as if they were a continuous work, analogous as a whole to the experiences of his Parkinsonian patients. Following his lead, I will here be treating *Through the Looking Glass* as an extension of an underground tale, where the mirror represents the crevice, the lacuna by which one slips into the land of the shades. That these two sets of spatial oppositions—above and below the ground's surface, before and behind the mirror's surface—should come to seem nearly identical is perhaps a natural effect of the *Alice* books, which raise and strengthen dichotomies as preparation to overcoming them.

One of the important paradoxes expressed in the *Alice* books is the inextricable connection between life and death—between growing up and dying, between sexual development and eventual decline, between the first step in the cycle (birth) and the last step (death). Empson points out that both *Alice in Wonderland* and *Through the Looking Glass* "keep to the topic of death—the first two jokes about death in *Wonderland* come on pages 3 and 4—and for the child this may be a natural connection; I remember believing that I should have to die in order to grow up, and thinking the prospect very disagreeable." But if the process of growing up seems circular or at times even backward in the *Alice* books, it is still a kind of progress: from the helpless fall and inexplicable randomness of *Wonderland*, to the more purposeful (if confusing) progress across a chess board in *Looking Glass*, culminating with Alice (the pawn, the child) being crowned a queen (an adult woman) at the end of the second adventure.

Alice's journey, from child to adult, is actually the reverse of that performed by Sacks's Parkinsonians, who begin on the edge of the grave and work backward in time, under the influence of L-DOPA, to the period of their physical prime. Outwardly, then, the two stories of "rebirth" would seem to be opposites, at least in terms of the direction of their journeys. But one of the odd things about both the *Alice* books and Parkinsonism is that directional orientation becomes confused, so that the difference between moving forward and moving backward finally comes to seem slight, or arbitrary. Alice notably demonstrates this in *Through the Looking Glass* when she first arrives in the Garden of Live Flowers and tries to go meet the Red Queen:

> *"I think I'll go and meet her," said Alice, for, though the flowers were interesting enough, she felt that it would be far grander to have a talk with a real Queen.*

> *"You can't possibly do that," said the Rose. "I should advise you to walk the other way."*
>
> *This sounded nonsense to Alice, so she said nothing, but set off at once toward the Red Queen. To her surprise she lost sight of her in a moment, and found herself walking in at the front-door again.*
>
> *A little provoked, she drew back, and, after looking everywhere for the Queen (whom she spied out at last, a long way off), she thought she would try the plan, this time, of walking in the opposite direction.*
>
> *It succeeded beautifully.*

This mirror-like condition, in which movements must be calculated rather than just made, is precisely the kind of thing that afflicts Sacks's patients, whose motor coordination is so inhibited (or, in some cases, propelled) that they must literally steer themselves through life by a series of complicated maneuvers. Of one such patient, Sacks remarks (without referring at all to *Alice*): "This patient—Miss Z.—had long since found that she could scarcely start, or stop, or change her direction of motion; that once she had been set in motion, she had no control. It was therefore necessary for her to plan all her motions in advance, with great precision. Thus, moving from her arm-chair to her divan-bed (a few feet to one side) could never be done *directly*—Miss Z. would immediately be 'frozen' in transit, and perhaps stay frozen for half-an-hour or more. She therefore had to embark on one of two courses of action: in either case, she would rise to her feet, arrange her angle of direction exactly, and shout, 'Now!', whereupon she would break into an incontinent run, which could be neither stopped nor changed in direction. If the double-doors between her living-room and the kitchen were open, she would rush through them, across the kitchen, round the back of the stove, across the other side of the kitchen, through the double-doors—in a great figure of eight—until she hit her destination, her bed. If, however, the double-doors were closed and secured, she would calculate her angle like a billiard-player, and then launch herself with great force against the doors, rebounding at the right angle to hit her bed." The Sacks description seems much more bizarre and fantastic than the Carrollian fantasy, largely because it is true.

One of the basic symptoms of Parkinsonism, as analyzed by Sacks, is precisely this sense of not having any control over one's movements. It can take the form of extreme paralysis (accompanied by rigidity of various body parts) or of extreme compulsion to move. As Frances

D., one of Sacks's most articulate patients, told him: "I have various banal symptoms which you can see for yourself. But my *essential* symptom is that I cannot start and I cannot stop. Either I am held still, or I am forced to accelerate. I no longer seem to have any in-between states." This paradoxical mixture of opposites may remind us of the quality of motion in nightmares and dreams, where one is frequently either frozen or flying, imprisoned or propelled. And the same sense of compulsion by an external force, alternating with periods of imprisonment, characterizes the *Alice* books.

On the whole, *Wonderland* has more paralysis (Alice confined in the long, low room; Alice trapped in the little house with her leg up a chimney; the Caterpillar fixed on his mushroom; the Mad Hatter and the March Hare perpetually at tea) while *Looking Glass* has more hurrying (the Red Queen rushing Alice along, crying "Faster, faster!"; the White Queen hurtling out of the forest into Alice's arms; the King's Men running so quickly that they trip over themselves and each other; and all of those sudden leaps into the next chess square). In part, this difference in mobility can be traced to the nature of the game each book is based on. Card games take place primarily in the dimension of time (with the accumulation of a hand) rather than in space, and the immobilized, "blind" player must essentially depend on hidden, invisible, face-down cards for his progress; whereas in chess the visual layout is extremely important and one's strategy depends largely on the "moves" of one's opponent. Chess is thus a "mirror" game between two opposing minds, while card-playing is an "underground" game in the sense that its players rely on the dark, hidden forces of fate and chance; so perspective and movement are important in chess and relatively unimportant in cards. The contrast in degree of motion in the two *Alice* books can also be linked to phases of childhood development: *Wonderland*, a book about birth and infancy, naturally contains less mobility than *Looking Glass*, a growing-up fantasy written for an older Alice Liddell. But the difference is not consistent, and each book also contains examples of the opposite tendency (the hurrying White Rabbit, the sedentary Humpty Dumpty). Taken together, the two books seem to emphasize the opposition of speed and stillness rather than stressing either one. The overall tendency of the *Alice* books, as of *Awakenings*, is to view movement as a combination of starting and stopping. Thus a supposedly automatic or natural condition—the ability to move—is achieved through the willed joining of opposites.

For Sacks's patients, this contradictory relationship to space and movement is as much an effect of the curative drug as it is of their illness. And herein lies one of the central connections between *Alice* and *Awakenings*: the fact that both books are in some ways descriptions of "out-of-body" drug experiences. Like Sacks's drug, the *Wonderland* foods—the bottled liquid labeled "Drink Me," the cake that says "Eat Me," and the Caterpillar's mushroom—cause Alice to vacillate wildly between being "up" and being "down." And like L-DOPA's effects, the changes they bring about are unpredictable. "I know who I *was* when I got up this morning, but I think I must have changed several times since then," says Alice at one point, while Sacks remarks of a patient: "Her response . . . was exceedingly swift and dramatic, occurring within a few hours on one particular day. She experienced a sudden surge of energy and strength, and a complete abolition of her rigidity. . . . Her parents were summoned . . . her father embraced her with great gratitude and joy, and her mother exclaimed, 'A miracle from Heaven . . . a completely new person!' " In both cases, the potions bring mixed and exaggerated effects: the food and drink make Alice grow *too* large and *too* small, while L-DOPA creates in its subjects alternating conditions of mania and depression. What Sacks's Miss D. says of her disease—"I no longer have any in-between states"—is also true of its cure. And as with the Parkinsonians' response to L-DOPA, one might trace the extremes of Alice's adventures to the unusual personality of the girl herself, at once so grown-up and so charmingly childish.

Drugs and drug experiments themselves form a whole genre of the "underground" experience. The subterranean element appears not only in the source of the drugs (they are traditionally marketed by "underworld" characters, as in *The Third Man*), but also in their effects: they carry one down into the soul, into the "dark heart of being" (and sometimes into death). The revelations that come to Sacks's patients on L-DOPA are not merely about their disease, but about other and "deeper" layers of the self as well. Some of these underlying feelings take the most obvious Freudian form, as in the case of a patient called Hester Y. "What she did *not* express in her diary," Sacks says, "and which was perhaps still repressed, were sexual feelings and libidinous substitutes—the *voracities* which so many other patients showed during climactic excitations induced by L-DOPA. That she was consumed by such feelings, *under the surface*, was shown by her lascivious-nightmarish dreams at this time, and the quality of her hallucinations later this day." At times his descriptions of the Parkinsonians' revelations betray almost a note of envy in Sacks's voice, as if he too desired access to this underground realm of existence. But the conclusion that Sacks, as a medical man, eventually draws from this material is philosophically and psychologically less adventurous, though perhaps more humane, than the bare observations themselves. Shying away from the revelations brought about by L-DOPA, he says that the effects of the drug "must be seen as a summoning of possible natures, a calling-forth of entire latent repertoires of being. We see an actualization or extrusion of natures which were dormant, which were 'sleeping' *in posse*, and which, perhaps, might have been best left *in posse*."

Yet even his conscientious desire to heal, to avert pain, does not prevent Sacks from seeing the allure of such "extrusions." However dangerous and frightening drug experiments may seem, they do represent a basic and compelling desire to explore our own dark psychological interiors. That the awakenings in *Awakenings* are brought about by a drug makes them especially disconcerting: we want to see them as "reactions" to an external substance, but the nature of each response is so personal and so revealing as to call into question the distinction between external and internal chemistries. Even the term L-DOPA, which is merely a medical abbreviation of the drug's technical name, seems to represent the essence of "drugness"—El Dopa, The Dope, The Drug.

The adventure of the drug experience, its potential to reveal hidden aspects of the self, is of course intimately linked to the terror of the experience. As both Sacks and Lewis Carroll realize, the drug's capacity to enlarge life cannot be disentangled from its ability to wield death. Thus one of Sacks's patients repeatedly refuses to try L-DOPA for fear it will make her "blow up" (as indeed it eventually does), while Alice pauses a moment before drinking her first potion: "It was all very well to say 'Drink Me,' but the wise little Alice was not going to do *that* in a hurry. 'No, I'll look first,' she said, 'and see whether it's marked "*poison*" or not': for she had read several nice little stories about children who had got burnt, and eaten up by wild beasts, and other unpleasant things, all because they *would* not remember the simple rules their friends had taught them." Carroll's authorially self-conscious sneer at those "nice little stories" suggests his own awareness of the limitations of rules—and certainly the *Alice* books themselves do not demonstrate anything about which forms of real-life behavior will result in rewards or punishments. In fact, amidst the arbitrariness that prevails in *Wonderland* and *Looking Glass*, the only generalization that seems to hold up is that you should take the adventures that are offered to you. This means being willing to grow up—or, in the case of Sacks's patients, to come back to life—even if that growing is attended by pain and ultimately by death. It is *always* accompanied by death, as a sharp little story in *Through the Looking Glass* points out:

> *"Crawling at your feet," said the Gnat (Alice drew her feet back in some alarm), "you may observe a Bread-and-butter-fly. Its wings are thick slices of bread-and-butter, its body is a crust, and its head is a lump of sugar."*
>
> *"And what does* it *live on?"*
>
> *"Weak tea with cream in it."*
>
> *A new difficulty came into Alice's head. "Supposing it couldn't find any?" she suggested.*
>
> *"Then it would die, of course."*
>
> *"But that must happen very often," Alice remarked thoughtfully.*
>
> *"It always happens," said the Gnat.*

The Bread-and-butter-fly is presented as a special case: from Alice's viewpoint, the creature's unfortunate destiny is entirely attributable to the odd eating habits of this alien species. But it is a species which lives on the most ordinary food of her experience, something she probably encounters at least once a day. When Alice observes that this creature probably does not have easy access to such a common food, she is also perceiving its distinct *otherness*, its extreme difference from herself. Bread-and-butter-flies always die (the logic might be supposed to run), little girls with ample access to weak tea never do. But as with all Carroll's jokes, the sharpness has a double edge, and this comment on the specific mortality of a weird bug is also a comment on human mortality.

Like the Bread-and-butter-fly, Sacks's patients are in some ways an alien species to us. The daily life that is easily accessible to us (including walking, talking, and the rest of our equivalents to weak tea with cream in it) is utterly remote from them, and the drug that gives them life sounds like a poison to us. Yet their death-in-life affects us, as the Bread-and-butter-fly's fate affects the "thoughtful" Alice, as a chilling mortality tale, a reminder of the sameness beneath the difference. Whether we drink our poisons or fail to find them, death is always the ultimate result. It is only life which is variable, which can be lived in either a state of awakening or a state of sleep.

Even after they know the dangers of L-DOPA, it is almost impossible for Sacks's patients not to try it, for to refuse it would be to embrace their own living death. What for Alice is a potentially frightening but also adventurous process of growing older is for these patients a process of growing younger, of coming back to life, of returning from a state that is both early death and false infancy. And one cannot choose not to grow up for fear of dying—or rather, to resist growing is *also* to die, as another *Alice* story suggests:

> *"I never ask advice about growing," Alice said indignantly.*
> *"Too proud?" the other enquired.*
> *Alice felt even more indignant at this suggestion. "I mean," she said, "that one can't help growing older."*
> "One *can't, perhaps," said Humpty Dumpty; "but* two *can. With proper assistance, you might have left off at seven."*

Dr. Sacks's patients received just such murderous "assistance" in the form of the encephalitis which struck them down, and most of them *did* leave off at seven—or seventeen, or twenty-seven. And yet the most appealing of his patients, the ones who move us most intensely, are those who continued to develop and change and expand *within* the imprisonment of their wretched bodies. For these patients especially, but to some degree for all of them, life both continued and did not continue; they grew up and remained the same age (Sacks notes that his Parkinsonians are singularly youthful-looking); they suffered the extremes of intense illness, and yet they were in some ways removed from their own suffering.

The regression toward childhood that post-encephalitics experience is more than just a state of mind: it is a state of body as well, manifested in behavior and physical symptoms. Even their speech resembles the childlike babbling of the creatures who people Alice's imaginary world. One of the basic symptoms of Parkinsonism is "palilalia," the rapid, insistent repetition of a few words or phrases, often continued for long periods. Sacks's patients do this on many occasions, especially after being given L-DOPA. Alice encounters it in both *Wonderland* ("Here the Dormouse shook itself, and began singing in its sleep '*Twinkle, twinkle, twinkle, twinkle,*'—and went on so long that they had to pinch it to make it stop") and *Looking Glass* ("The White Queen only looked at her in a helpless frightened sort of way, and kept repeating something in a whisper to herself that sounded like 'Bread-and-butter, bread-and-butter' . . ."). Such behavior, when Sacks observes it in his patients, seems to exemplify the most terrible aspect of the start/stop syndrome: the patients feel that they have something urgent to say

("Doctor, doctor, doctor, doctor . . . help me, help, help, h'lp, h'lp"), but they are restricted to the first word or two of their urgent message and can only repeat it over and over again—almost as if the urgency itself has paralyzed them. Again, this has the quality of nightmare. But it is also quite close to what one finds in small children who are on the verge, or just over the verge, of language. They grasp a sound or a word that they know and repeat it over and over, as if to imitate the continuous, seemingly endless speech of adults. Thus one meaning of such repetition might be the wish for language at a pre-language state. This regressive, childlike nature of palilalia is pertinent to both *Alice* and *Awakenings*—one the story of growth away from childhood, the other a description of rebirth into a new youth.

Another kind of regression, this time phylogenetic rather than ontogenetic, also occurs in both books. For Sacks's patients as well as for Carroll's Alice, the possibility that people can turn back into animals—can work their way *down* the evolutionary ladder—is unusually real. In the *Alice* tales, a baby turns into a pig, a White Queen into a sheep, and a Red Queen into a kitten—all without occasioning much surprise or fear on the part of Alice herself. In fact, she is rather pleased than otherwise about the conversions: " 'If it had grown up,' she said to herself, 'it would have made a dreadfully ugly child: but it makes rather a handsome pig, I think.' " This sanguine refusal to view babies as automatically better than piglets—to rank the mammals hierarchically, with ourselves at the top—is of course true to the way children view the world. ("When I grow up I'm going to marry Ralph," announced the three-year-old daughter of a friend of mine, speaking of my cat.) Yet it would be ingenuous to suggest that such a state of innocence is easy or even desirable to recover: our adult sense of ourselves as humans comes with a hard-won knowledge of how frighteningly close we are to *not* being human. Thus the scenes in which Sacks shows his patients regressing to an animal-like state are among the most disturbing in *Awakenings*. Whether the regression is physical (the "flipper-like" hands of one woman) or behavioral (one patient lapped milk from a saucer; another pawed the ground with his right leg in a movement "suggestive of a high-spirited, impatient horse"), the fact that these men and women have come to resemble animals makes them "disgusting"—disgust being an emotion felt by those who consider themselves high up on the evolutionary ladder. (It is interesting to note that although Alice is a social snob, she does not seem to be an evolutionary snob: she would rather talk to a queen than a flower, but she would probably just as well talk to a flower as a commoner.)

Often the Parkinsonians' animal-like behavior is connected with eating, as if to mock in an extreme form the notion of civilized "manners." One of Sacks's patients herself commented on the terrible incongruity between her otherwise lady-like appearance and her inexplicable "inclination to munch and gnaw, . . . chew and over-chew her food, with a growling noise, like a dog with a bone": " 'I am a quiet person,' she expostulated on one occasion. 'I could be a distinguished maiden-aunt. And now look at me! I bite and chew like a ravenous animal, and there's nothing I can do about it.' " (As elsewhere in *Awakenings*, what makes this condition most distressing is the patient's own pained awareness of it.) The issue of table manners is central in *Alice* as well—children being, from an adult point of view, creatures who have not sufficiently left the animal-like phase to be worthy of dining at an adult meal. (Empson suggests that "the fascination of Soup and the Mock Turtle who sings about it was that soup is mainly eaten at dinner, the excitingly grown-up meal eaten after the child has gone to bed.") If the distinction between good and bad manners seems arbitrary and inaccessible in *Alice*, it is perhaps because all behavior in the subterranean dream-world springs from compulsions like those that afflict the Parkinsonians, so that the Dormouse can no more help falling asleep in his teacup than Alice can help falling down a vertical hole. Under such conditions, it makes as much sense to chop off someone's head as to issue a verbal reprimand, since no act has an intentional "cause," in the adult sense of the term.

The comatose Dormouse points up crucial ways in which the *Alice* books are both similar to and importantly different from *Awakenings*. In the world of Sacks's Parkinsonians, as in Wonderland and the Looking Glass world, sleep is frequently an unwilled and deeply inhibiting state. Many of Sacks's patients, before being given L-DOPA, were in a state that, if it was not sleep itself, resembled sleep in its immobility and removal from life. After the course of L-DOPA, if they were taken off the drug, they generally fell into a coma or near-coma, often much more extreme than their pre-drug state. And the disease itself, of course, sprang from an initial infection of "sleeping sickness." The Dormouse's behavior is in fact a joke version of the depressingly "dormant" life of Sacks's patients:

> *"You might just as well say," added the Dormouse, which seemed to be talking in its sleep, "that 'I breathe when I sleep' is the same thing as 'I sleep when I breathe'!"*
>
> *"It is the same thing with you," said the Hatter.*

Alice encounters a similar version of sleep in *Through the Looking Glass*, when she wonders why she's never heard talking flowers before: " 'In most gardens,' the Tiger-Lily said, 'they make the beds too soft—so that the flowers are always asleep.' " Besides invoking one of the images from which Sacks takes his title—the story of the perpetually Sleeping Beauty—Carroll's reference to soft beds and endless sleep manages to connect a range of ideas: sleep itself, and then growth and "flowering" (flower beds), hence sexual development (marriage beds), and finally death (death beds). This cycle, and its interruption by the onset of "sleeping sickness," is precisely the one that obsesses Sacks's patients, and on which they move forward and backward in response to the drug. Sleep is also, of course, the major activity of infancy—that babyhood from which Alice is trying to emerge, and to which Sacks's Parkinsonians have seemingly been reduced by their disease.

Despite their overlapping concerns, though, Carroll's and Sacks's books do not finally share the same attitude toward sleep, for the obvious and therefore easily forgotten reason that the two works bear different relationships to reality. A sleepy Dormouse or a soft flower bed is not a permanently ill patient or a hospital bed. To invoke allegory and symbolism in the case of fictional constructs is a very different thing from doing so with real people suffering real distress. Sacks's very humanism—his desire to link his patients' lives with the world of myth and literature, and to give larger meaning to their individual experiences of illness—is in part what makes his book strangely cruel. The more obvious cruelty of Carroll's humor, on the other hand, is what gives his *Alice* books their metaphysical and psychological largeness. If one begins on the metaphorical level, removed from the reality of actual human existences, one can be direct about the deep truths of sexuality and death and that near-death which is sleep. *Alice in Wonderland*, because it is fictional, can be a literal exploration of the underworld in a way that *Awakenings* never can. Even the title of Sacks's book suggests the manner in which he is continually pushing his "characters" toward allegory: their deep sleep is necessarily metaphorical, necessarily symbolic, rather than being the mere sleep of the Dormouse.

The problem here has to do with the degree of "fit" between what characters *are* and what they *stand for*. For the Dormouse, life *is* sleep ("It *is* the same thing with you"), and character is identical with behavior; whereas with Frances D., the mythical quality of her long "sleep," from which L-DOPA awakens her, is something imposed on her condition by both her own imagination and that of her doctor. Sacks is not more "cruel" to his patients, in his imposition of literary significance on their condition, than his most intelligent patients are to themselves: the cruelty arises from their (and his) ability to be both inside and outside at once, to see Parkinsonism and its cure as simultaneously an affliction and an enchantment. Alice can afford to be cruelly direct to the creatures she meets in Wonderland, not only because she is a child, but because *they* are safely shielded from self-awareness by their lack of projective imagination. They *are* literary or symbolic figures, and need not (indeed, cannot) imagine themselves to be so. Neither Lewis Carroll, Alice, nor the Dormouse is concerned with what the mouse stands for, merely with what he is; and the remarks about his character therefore do not seem a violation of his integrity. Sacks, on the other hand, is attracted to Parkinsonism precisely because of its metaphorical overtones—which also explain our own interest, as readers, in the "story" he has to tell. *Awakenings* can thus work its full magic only on readers who have some literary imagination, but in doing so it will also implicate them in what I have been calling the cruel humanism of its vision.

The numerous small factors that link the *Alice* books to *Awakenings* are all strands in the net that catches the imaginative reader. One notices, for instance, the Cheshire Cat grin on the face of one of Sacks's patients (the face "was profoundly masked, but when it broke into a smile that smile remained for minutes or hours—like the smile of the Cheshire Cat"), as well as the Parkinsonian habit of speaking in whispers or hoarse tones, like the Gnat in *Looking Glass*, or Alice herself in *Wonderland*, where "her voice sounded hoarse or strange, and the words did not come the same as they used to." The violent rages of the Parkinsonians, especially after they've been given L-DOPA, remind us of the unbridled anger of the Queen of Hearts, while their constant salivation (sometimes amounting to several gallons a day) calls to mind Alice drowning in her own sea of tears. Sacks's patients also experience "oculogyric crises" in which their eyes are rigidly focused upward, much in the manner of the Frog Footman who "was looking up into the sky all the time he was speaking" because his "eyes are so *very* nearly at the top of his head."

But as this last example suggests, the analogies to *Alice* consistently tend to dehumanize the patients. Like the disease itself, Sacks's (and our) literary vision has the effect of objectifying the Parkinsonians, making them into inert recipients of our projected ideas. This apparent cruelty is a necessary part of what gives *Awakenings* its power, for the duplicity of vision forces us to share something of the patients' own condition. At the very moment of greatest empathy we find ourselves reducing (or enlarging) Sacks's people to the level of metaphor—which gives us the same sense that they have, of being both inside and outside their physical bodies.

"*Wonderland* is a dream, but the *Looking-Glass* is self-consciousness," says Empson of the *Alice* books. *Awakenings*, strangely and movingly, is both. It is as if, through these victims walled up in their physiological and psychological prisons, we are able to gain an acute but momentary glance at a world we know well and not at all: the world of dreams, or death, or birth, or hell. Sacks's patients make concrete and visible the truths which we only grasp as metaphors and abstractions; they live in the shadow world that lies just beneath our own reality and, like others who have journeyed into the heart of matters, they bring us back knowledge we can never completely share. Moreover, like other voyagers to the underground—like Orpheus and Dante, for instance—they bring back this experience in the form of literature. It is as if the nightmare world they inhabit is so unimaginable that they can only grasp and convey it by comparing it to a work of imagination. Thus Leonard L.—perhaps Sacks's most learned and sophisticated patient—borrows from T.S. Eliot to describe the conditions of his illness:

Descend lower, descend only
Into the world of perpetual solitude,
World not world, but that which is not world,
Internal darkness, deprivation
And destitution of all property,
Dessication of the world of sense,
Evacuation of the world of fancy,
Inoperancy of the world of spirit . . .

There is a deep irony here, of course, in the fact that it is precisely the "world of fancy," Eliot's supposedly absent "world of sense," which has given Leonard L. the words in which to describe his internal darkness.

Another patient echoes Eliot's words, and also demonstrates her own need to grasp at metaphor, when she converses with Dr. Sacks about the uniquely Parkinsonian state of being:

"What are you thinking about, Rosie?"
"Nothing, just nothing."
"But how can you possibly be thinking of nothing?"

> *"It's dead easy, once you know how."*
>
> "How *exactly do you think about nothing?"*
>
> *"One way is to think about the same thing again and again. Like 2=2=2=2; or, I am what I am what I am what I am. . . . It's the same thing with my posture. My posture leads into itself. . . . Whatever I do or whatever I think leads deeper and deeper into itself. . . . And then there are maps."*
>
> *"Maps? What do you mean?"*
>
> *"Everything I do is a map of itself, everything I do is a part of itself. Every part leads into itself. . . . I've got a thought in my mind, and then I see something in it, like a dot on the skyline. It comes nearer and nearer, and then I see what it is—it's just the same thought I was thinking before. And then I see another dot, and another, and so on. . . . Or I think of a map; then a map of that map; then a map of that map of that map, and each map perfect, though smaller and smaller. . . . Worlds within worlds within worlds. . . . Once I get going, I can't possibly stop. It's like being caught between mirrors, or echoes, or something. Or being caught on a merry-go-round which won't come to a stop."*

There is something brave and Alice-like in this adventure into the self, some element of Carrollian black humor in the assurance that it is "dead easy" to think of nothing. Here it is the patient herself, and not Sacks or Carroll, who sets up the equation between a mirror world ("caught between mirrors") and a downward journey ("whatever I think leads deeper and deeper into itself"). In reaching out for these metaphors, Rose R. also arrives at that image of the body (or mind) as a world, the self as "map," which informs Melville's "Tartarus of Maids." And as if to confirm that what she describes is indeed a Tartarus, a hell, she reverts to the spiral metaphor (the merry-go-round, combined with that deeper and deeper descent) that Sacks elsewhere associates with disease and damnation, the "circular process" which he links to "the fundamental image of Dante's inferno."

Indeed, if you try to imagine who Sacks's patients *really* remind you of, you may finally arrive at the images of the damned souls in Dante's hell. Even in terms of physical appearance—in terms of their "posture," as Rose puts it—the Parkinsonians resemble certain of the tortured, distorted bodies in the Inferno. In particular, some of Sacks's descriptions sound remarkably like what Dante saw in the Eighth Circle:

And when I looked down from their faces, I saw
that each of them was hideously distorted
between the top of the chest and the lines of the jaw;

for the face was reversed on the neck, and they came on
backwards, staring backwards at their loins,
for to look before them was forbidden. Someone,

sometimes, in the grip of a palsy may have been
distorted so, but never to my knowledge;
nor do I believe the like was ever seen.

These are the twisted bodies of the seers, the diviners—visionaries who, like the people in *Awakenings*, saw into a world that did not yet exist, except in the deepest levels of the imagination.

If Dante's damned souls remind us of the Parkinsonians, they also recall Alice, who in *Through the Looking Glass* "came on backwards" when she wished to go forward. And there are many other resemblances that connect both Carroll's and Sacks's work to Dante's: the talking flowers in *Looking Glass*, for instance, that echo the suicides-turned-trees in Dante's hell, which in turn foreshadow the vegetative, "rooted" patients in Sacks's hospital; the way Alice, the Parkinsonians, and the souls of the damned are all bathed in their own "tears" (or saliva, in the case of Sacks's people); the regression from human to animal that appears not only in Alice's baby-turned-pig or Sacks's ravenously growling eaters, but also in Dante's spirits who "howl like dogs in the freezing storm"; and the numerous amputations and distortions in the bodies of hell's various sinners, which make them look like Sacks's twisted patients or Carroll's Humpty Dumpty.

But Dante gives us a reason for all this physical suffering, in Virgil's assertions that the sinners have earned their various punishments in the life aboveground. We may feel that the Inferno's tortures are harsh or inappropriate, but we cannot deny the sense of causal connection between moral behavior and physical condition; whereas the deep irony—the tragedy—for Sacks's patients is that, although they did nothing to earn their punishment, it is very difficult to think of the disease as a purely physiological accident. The Parkinsonian martyrdom takes such a mythical form that it *seems* to embody some kind of moral condemnation, however much our rational minds tell us otherwise. And this sense of hidden sin, of earned punishment, unavoidably affects the thinking of the patients themselves as well as that of the author and readers of *Awakenings*. It is the final element in their torture—this feeling that their physical state, which so resembles the punishments of the damned souls in Dante's hell, is actually the result of some unknown but inescapable sin. The Dantean quality that pervades their illness makes Sacks's patients feel that they are enclosed in a moral hell, when they are actually trapped, like Lewis Carroll's creations, in an arbitrary world without discernible causes or effects. In the underworld of the unconscious there can be no rational punishments—for the only sins in that realm are the unwilled sins of the body, over which the individual finally has no control.

The Child's Underground

Did you ever hear of Mickey, how he heard a racket in the night and shouted "QUIET DOWN THERE!" and fell through the dark, out of his clothes, past the moon & his mama & papa sleeping tight, into the light of the Night Kitchen?

—Maurice Sendak, *In the Night Kitchen*

ALICE IN WONDERLAND IS OF COURSE NOT THE ONLY work of children's literature featuring an underground adventure, though it is perhaps the best known. To talk about "children's literature" inevitably brings up the question of what defines that genre, the answer to which is usually provided by those who study it professionally. What constitutes a justifiable subject of study has, of course, altered over the years, and children's books have only lately been considered important enough to warrant academic attention. One eminent Princeton professor, explaining why this brand of literature was worthy of close examination, recently pointed out that it was written *for* children, not *by* children.

In salvaging the academic worth of his subject, though, the professor obscured an important point. The best children's literature, as any child will testify, is written from a point of view that resembles a child's—as if a child were given vast literary ability but were still restricted to the desires, the fears, and the knowledge possessed by a childish imagination. Reading such a work, the child feels he is being spoken to by an equal, or at least by someone who shares his way of looking at the world. This is what George Orwell meant when he said about his boyhood reading of David Copperfield: "The mental atmosphere of the opening chapters was so immediately intelligible to me that I vaguely imagined they had been written *by a child*."

David Copperfield is not, strictly speaking, a work of children's literature, and when Orwell re-read it years later he saw "the Murdstones, for instance, dwindle from gigantic figures of doom into semi-comic monsters." Because Dickens is writing for readers of all generations, Orwell points out, "the same scene can be wild burlesque or sinister reality, according to the age at which one reads it." But with real children's literature this is not the case: the re-reading process is more likely to transform the reader than the story. At least, so I found when I re-read a number of children's books as preparation for this chapter. I did not see the books with new, adult eyes: on the contrary, they carried me back (as certain smells or tastes will do) to the childhood self who had read them the first time—as if I, like the authors, were a child who had miraculously but unobtrusively acquired linguistic ability without the other trappings of adulthood.

I do not mean to make this sound romantic or nostalgic: there is nothing especially wonderful about being a child, and nobody has embraced the privileges of adulthood more eagerly than I. But the books we read as children do seem to have a particularly profound effect. Because a child's memory is relatively open and unmarked, the books of childhood leave a more permanent and more detailed record than anything we absorb as adults. I discovered this when I tried recently to re-read Dodie Smith's *I Capture the Castle*, a book about two sisters that my sister and I had read and loved and re-read many times during our childhood—a book which was so important to us as children that my sister can still allude to it merely with a brief gesture of her hand. I had not read *I Capture the Castle* for over fifteen years, but when I picked it up again I found every sentence so familiar that the book afforded no pleasure as casual bedtime reading. I knew each word in much the same way a monk knows his daily prayers, and therefore the "literary" element (of suspense, or at least discovery, as opposed to ritual) had fled.

With the underground adventures I read for this chapter—including George MacDonald's *The Princess and the Goblin*, C.S. Lewis's *The Silver Chair* (and, less obviously, Lewis's *The Magician's Nephew*), and the cave sections of Mark Twain's *Adventures of Tom Sawyer*—neither the memory nor the sense of "re-living" was that intense. After all, I had read each of these books only once or at most twice as a child. But given that fact, my recollection of them was startlingly complete, and in particular was far more visceral than my adult memories of well-loved books like *The Wings of the Dove* or *Howards End*. Though I have read the James and Forster novels several times each, I do not, on re-reading, get a sudden visual image of the scene that is about to take place; my memories of them are mostly psychological, or moral, or sometimes linguistic. But when I began to re-read *The Silver Chair*, and came to the part where the two schoolchildren, chased by bullies, approached the wall that surrounded their school, I had a sudden mental image of a vast and beautiful open space lying on the other side of that wall. And I think this visceral memory came not only from C.S. Lewis—who did indeed provide a magical world just beyond the school wall—but also from my own childhood wish that I would one day open a familiar door and find a beautiful unexplored world on the other side. (As adults, our only experiences of such wishes come in dreams, where we suddenly discover whole new, previously unknown rooms or even floors in our houses—as Les Murray did in his old grandfather's house.) What made C.S. Lewis a brilliant story-teller for children was his ability to tap into these existing wishes and fears—to write about things that the child-reader had already explored in her imagination, so that even the first reading had the resonance of a re-reading.

A similar sense of felt recollection colored my recent re-reading of *The Princess and the Goblin*. As a child, I used to be entranced by the shallow pools of water that accumulated on the street after a rain. What I loved about these still pools was the way you could look down into them, on a clear day, and see the faraway blue sky reflected in their depths, so that you seemed to be looking down into an infinitely deep hole, but a hole filled with light and color rather than darkness. This was a giddy experience—entrancing but also a little terrifying—and it probably explains, to some degree, my present fascination with the underground. As with most childhood discoveries, I thought this was an original and unique invention, and was therefore amazed to find, as an adult, the following passage in *The Princess and the Goblin* (first published in 1872):

> *The princess looked, and saw a large oval tub of silver, shining brilliantly in the light of the wonderful lamp.*
>
> *"Go and look into it," said the old lady.*
>
> *Irene went, and came back very silent with her eyes shining.*
>
> *"What did you see?" asked her grandmother.*
>
> *"The sky and the moon and the stars," she answered. "It looked as if there were no bottom to it."*

Whether I originally borrowed this image from my childhood reading of MacDonald, or he borrowed it from me (and all the other children who have ever imagined it), is an unanswerable question; probably the power of the image lies in our mutual yet independent fascination with it. Another use of bottomless pools appears in Lewis's *The Magician's Nephew*, where such pools of water form the entrance to various magical worlds. It was partly that possibility—that the mirrored sky in my reflecting pools was in reality another world—that made those rain-puddles of my childhood so entrancing. Those puddles combined, for me, Alice's rabbit-hole and her looking-glass—a reflected world that was also an underworld.

I now want to say a few things about what the underground seems to mean (or do, or suggest) in the children's books I mentioned above. But even as I descend into literary or sociological or psychological analysis, I would like not to leave behind the sense of the miraculous "felt" memories I have described. The dry analysis and the vivid recollections are all of a piece, I hope; they are just different adult ways of getting at elusive childhood experiences. Like H.G. Wells, we really need a Time Machine to get at the full significance of the underground—but in this case a machine that will take us back to our own pasts rather than into the human race's future.

One of the striking things about underground adventures in children's books is how much they have in common. Whether the book is written by a nineteenth-century American or a twentieth-century Englishman, an atheist or a devout Christian, the way the author chooses to employ the underground follows a relatively rigid pattern. It is always a testing ground for the child-adventurer, a place where one must go to prove oneself. The visit is always temporary, but there is always the threat of eternal imprisonment, or at least death. And although the subterranean experience is a frightening one, it is almost never a solitary adventure: for the most part, the children of these stories venture underground in pairs—in boy-girl pairs. (Alice is the notable exception—and if the biographical evidence contains even a shred of truth, Lewis Carroll clearly had his own reasons for not wanting Alice Liddell to undergo quite that kind of underground adventure.)

It does not take a psychoanalyst to perceive the sexual overtones to the underground experience, and I have already discussed this aspect of the subterranean metaphor in relation to adult literature (particularly, for instance, *Invisible Man* and "The Tartarus of Maids"). In children's literature, the sexuality of the underground is obviously linked to the overall process of growing up, of becoming an adult: to pass through the underworld is in some way to undergo sexual development. This premise is never made explicit, but it is nonetheless made obvious. For instance, in *The Princess and the Goblin* the Princess Irene goes down into the earth to save Curdie, her youthful protector whom she will eventually reward with a much-discussed kiss. Her great-great-grandmother tells her that this trial is a necessary part of becoming a princess like the grandmother herself (an old, old woman who is still beautiful—not a bad metaphor for a child's image of an adult). Irene's path to her grandmother's room, where she will go delightfully to bed, leads (by way of a magic thread) through the goblins' subterranean dominions. Curdie and the princess each work to protect the other (implicitly, to demonstrate their love for each other) by going down under the ground.

The sexual overtone is equally strong in Mark Twain's *Tom Sawyer* (which first appeared in 1876, only four years after MacDonald's book). Here Tom sees the picnic trip to the caves as a prime opportunity to court Becky Thatcher; and they define themselves as youthful lovers by going off without the others, smoking their names with candles on the wall, surviving on their "wedding-cake" (as they call the remainders of their lunch), and kissing each other for reassurance when they are lost. The cave trip is Tom's first (and nearly last) chance to spend substantial time alone with Becky.

In the two C.S. Lewis stories (published in the 1950s), the pattern is slightly different. This post-Freudian author can't afford to be quite so sanguine about puppy-love among children, and indeed he seems eager to avoid all "mushy" overtones in the comradely relationship he depicts between boys and girls. But the sexual suggestion persists nonetheless—not only in the boy-girl pairing of the adventurous team, but more particularly in the explicit sexuality of the underground monarch. In both cases, this powerful figure of evil is a beautiful woman who seeks to control men through sexual attraction. In *The Silver Chair* this sexual creature—who sometimes takes the form of a bright green snake—is literally called "the Queen of the Underland"; and in *The Magician's Nephew*, though the witch Jadis does not come from a literal underworld, the two children do find her by falling downward through a pool ("Down and down they rushed, first through darkness and then through a mass of vague and whirling shapes") into a cheerless land where "the sky was extraordinarily dark." In both cases, Lewis projects sexuality away from the children and onto a witch-figure, but the result is still that the children acquire a knowledge of sexual power through their subterranean adventure, even if that power is exhibited by and on someone other than themselves. If anything, the projection onto adults—onto the Queen of the Underland and her captive, Prince

Rilian, or the witch Jadis and Digory's foolish Uncle Andrew—makes the issue of sexuality *more* prominent in these books, in that those adults' behavior is far more lustful than the innocent kissing of the princess and Curdie or Tom and Becky.

The sex difference is not the only common attribute of the adventure-seeking pair; the two children are usually of different classes as well. Here the children's stories pick up the class connotations of the underground as used in nineteenth-century social novels and H.G. Wells's *Time Machine*—but they do so in an unusual way. Instead of confirming class difference, as Wells's fantasy does, the children's books use the underground to eliminate or confuse the issue of class. Thus the children begin by coming from separate classes and end by being joined or equalized through their underground adventure. Sometimes the distinction between them involves class as we know it: a princess and a miner's son in MacDonald, the town rapscallion and the judge's daughter in Twain. But sometimes it is class as children define it: a bully's victim joins forces with a former toady in *The Silver Chair*, a domestically secure child journeys underground with a domestically insecure child (a near-orphan living with his uncle and aunt) in *The Magician's Nephew*. In addition to joining these initially disparate pairs, the underground adventures tend to turn the whole notion of class on its head. In *The Princess and the Goblin*, for instance, Curdie the miner is a far more "princely" figure—physically as well as morally—than the ugly goblin prince who aspires to Princess Irene's hand. The very fact that there can *be* goblin royalty casts doubt on the meaning of royalty, and the princess is repeatedly told that being a "true" princess depends on actions rather than birth. In *The Magician's Nephew*, the final voyage down through the magic pools results in the creation of a new world (Narnia) where a Cockney cabby and his wife become the first king and queen. (This is the same cabby, by the way, who immediately interprets the fall into a magic realm in light of his urban experiences of the subterranean: " 'Now if we've fallen down some diggings—as it might be for a new station on the Underground—someone will come and get us out presently, see! And if we're dead—which I don't deny it might be—well, you got to remember that worse things 'appen at sea and a chap's got to die sometime.' " His manner of reassuring the children is both selflessly "noble" and aitchlessly working-class—a good example of the kind of paradox the underground stories abound in.)

The class issue, in these stories as in the Victorian social novels, becomes explicitly linked to ideas of oppression and rebellion. But whereas

Victorian novels were written for adults who had something to lose in a revolution, children's stories are aimed at a class of people who often feel themselves "oppressed" by rules and laws, and who are therefore likely to side with the underdog. For children, in other words, rebellion is an opportunity rather than a threat, a vision of freedom rather than chaos. In their play on the various connotations of the word "under," as well as their portrayal of power relationships, children's stories use the fact that children are smaller and weaker than adults to confuse the normal class allegiances. The question thus becomes whether a middle-class child is more middle-class or more child—and the variations on the attitude toward rebelliousness within each book come partly from this persistently unresolved question. Only the most insipid children's books counsel utterly lawful behavior; such books are written more for the parents than the children, and their appeal is correspondingly low. The good children's books—as all four of these are—come out at least partly on the side of rebellion.

Sometimes this attitude is explicit, as when the enchanted underground workers in *The Silver Chair* suddenly react to the wicked queen's death. A gnome called Golg explains to the children: " 'Then there came a great crash and bang. As soon as they heard it, everyone says to himself, I haven't had a song or a dance or let off a squib for a long time; why's that? And everyone thinks to himself, why, I must have been enchanted. And then everyone says to himself, I'm blessed if I know why I'm carrying this load, and I'm not going to carry it any further: that's that. And down we all throw our sacks and bundles and tools.' " The rhetoric of this speech—the fact that the workers are manual laborers, that they progress from subversive thoughts to self-addressed words to action, and that they finally "throw down" their burdens—clearly links it to a Marxist tradition of throwing off one's chains, or a slave tradition of rebellion. Yet far from being the frightening figure he might be in a Gissing novel, Golg is quite an appealing character. He was "enchanted" when he worked too hard, and he is himself only now that he recognizes the need to have "a song or a dance or let off a squib." This is the revolutionary as child: all work and no play makes Jack a dull *boy*.

Whereas Lewis's sentiments for the oppressed class come through clearly—perhaps because, as a Christian, he can align such sentiments with Christ's teachings rather than Marx's, and thereby make them acceptable—MacDonald's are much more confused. In *The Princess and the Goblin*, the goblins are both the villains and the victims. They are ugly and self-centered and alternately frightening or ridiculous, and it is from them that the princess must be protected. On the other hand, they have obvious affinities with the two most sympathetic characters in the book, Curdie and the princess herself. Like the princess, they are small of stature and have physically delicate extremities (the goblins have soft feet; the princess hurts her finger). Like Curdie the miner, they work underground and are shunned by Lootie, the princess's nurse. That is, the miner and the goblins both earn the silly, snobbish nurse's disdain: the former because he belongs to a "lower" class, the latter because they live in the "lower" regions. It is part of Irene's growth as a princess to learn to reject the class snobberies of her nurse. Yet though she comes to love Curdie, she remains filled with fear and dislike for the goblin-prince, who sees her as a potential wife (as Curdie himself also seems to do—or at least that is what Lootie's fear suggests). Evidently the parallelism between the miner and the goblin has a useful function in the story: to divert onto a dispensable monster some of the sexual disgust a young girl might otherwise feel for her human suitor.

MacDonald's goblins remain villainous and frightening to the end—these are not reformable opponents—but the book gives them good reasons for hating aboveground people. In the first chapter we learn that "in these subterranean caverns lived a strange race of beings, called by some gnomes, by some kobolds, by some goblins. There was a legend current in the country that at one time they lived above ground, and were very like other people. But for some reason or other, concerning which there were different legendary theories, the king had laid what they thought too severe taxes on them, or had required observances they did not like, or had begun to treat them with more severity, in some way or other, and impose stricter laws; and the consequence was that they had all disappeared from the face of the country." For an American child, the references to "too severe taxes" and "required observances they did not like" bring to mind the Boston Tea Party and the Pilgrims, and therefore link the goblin race to the highly sympathetic rebels of the American revolution. This interpretation will not come through as strongly to other English-speaking readers, but even for British children living in the *laissez-faire* atmosphere of nineteenth-century liberalism, reference to "stricter laws" (note the verb "impose") and other government interference is bound to sound like tyranny, or at least government harassment. And the child's basic tendency to identify with rebels—especially those who hide when they are angry (in closets, under bedclothes, or under the ground)—will make the passage an especially strong argument in favor of the goblins. MacDonald's book is interesting because it exploits two opposing childhood fantasies: the desire to be, or marry, or at least emulate a princess, and the identification with the underdog. Curdie's role in the novel is clearly to stake a claim on all the "good" underdog characteristics while leaving the less desirable traits to the goblins; but once joined in the imagination, the good miner and the bad goblin can never be entirely separated, especially since they are both such obvious representatives of the underground. (The title of MacDonald's subsequent book, *The Princess and Curdie*, further stresses the parallel by placing the miner's name in the position previously occupied by "the Goblin.")

As in Wells's *Time Machine*, the description of how the goblins came to be an underground race is bound to involve the relatively new idea of evolution. And indeed we soon learn about them that "they had greatly altered in the course of generations; and no wonder, seeing they lived away from the sun, in cold and wet and dark places. They were now, not ordinarily ugly, but either absolutely hideous, or ludicrously grotesque both in face and form." Later in the book, MacDonald humorously invokes a Lamarckian notion of evolution when he has Curdie ponder the goblins' rumored lack of fingers and toes: "One of the miners, indeed, who had had more schooling than the rest, was wont to argue that such must have been the primordial condition of humanity, and that education and handicraft had developed both toes and fingers—with which proposition Curdie had once heard his father sarcastically agree, alleging in support of it the probability that babies' gloves were a traditional remnant of the old state of things; while the stockings of all ages, no regard being paid in them to the toes, pointed in the same direction."

MacDonald's book was first published a mere thirteen years after *The Origin of Species*, when evolution—of both the Darwinian and Lamarckian varieties—was still a hot issue. None of the other children's books I discuss here (except, of course, *Alice*) focuses on the topic to the same extent. But lingering concern with the subject appears in the C.S. Lewis books—and indeed in many other children's stories—in the form of talking animals. The sense that people are part of a continuum that includes all other animals is much stronger in children than in adults (witness the little girl who wanted to marry my cat). Because they have so recently emerged from languagelessness themselves, it is not difficult for children to perceive that speaking creatures could emerge from the dumb animal world.

The Narnia world of the C.S. Lewis books has a chain-of-being hierarchy that groups talking animals and humans above non-talking (and therefore, by implication, non-intelligent) animals. The link between the idea of talking animals and the idea of children as animals is made explicit in a passage from *The Silver Chair*, where the two children and their "native" guide, trapped in a castle full of giant cannibals, discover that they have unwittingly been eating a talking deer: "This discovery didn't have exactly the same effect on all of them. Jill, who was new to that world, was sorry for the poor stag and thought it rotten of the giants to have killed him. Scrubb, who had been in that world before and had at least one Talking beast as his dear friend, felt horrified; as you might feel about a murder. But Puddleglum, who was Narnian born, was sick and faint, and felt as you would feel if you found you had eaten a baby." Like Curdie's father's theory of "babies' gloves," this reference strengthens the parallel between ontogeny and phylogeny: as babies grow into adults (it suggests), animals have developed into humans, and therefore ought under certain circumstances to be considered, like babies, part of the same species. This is an appealing theory for children, who tend to identify with the cossetted-but-powerless-pet status of animals, and who therefore welcome any attitude which raises this status to a level closer to equality with adults.

Another motif that seems to run through all underground children's books is the subterranean sea or lake. This occurs in *Alice*, of course, in the form of the Pool of Tears from which she is "born" (through that too-small door) into the world of "adult" playing cards and eccentric animals. Elsewhere it is not so clearly an amniotic pool combined with life-generating ocean, but I think its vestigial appearance in every children's story I've mentioned here has something to do with this original function. In *The Adventures of Tom Sawyer* it is "a subterranean lake . . . which stretched its dim length away until its shape was lost in the shadows"; in *The Silver Chair* it is a sunless sea, a seemingly endless expanse of "smooth, dark water, fading into absolute blackness," on which the children sail to the underground palace. This is a familiar image in adult underground works as well: think of the sea on which Jules Verne's underground travelers sail, or the River Styx across which Phlegyas ferries Dante and Virgil, or Dante's sea of tears. But whereas the image is associated with death in those works, it tends to be associated with birth and rebirth in the children's books. For instance, the two children in *The Magician's Nephew* (as I've already pointed out) repeatedly enter new worlds by jumping into various magic pools. In children's books, the hidden sea buried deep in Mother Earth *can* be a frightening place, but it is just as likely to be a useful passageway to a new existence: children, that is, do not seem to fear regression to the womb as much as adults do, nor to equate such retreat exclusively with death.

Which is not to say that death is absent from the child's underground. On the contrary, it is the ever-present threat inherent in the subterranean adventure. This is particularly obvious in *Tom Sawyer*, where Tom and Becky—like the townspeople who are searching for them—fear that they will die in the cave. When Becky wakens from a brief sleep, she says:

> *"Oh, how* could *I sleep! I wish I had never waked!* No, *no, I don't, Tom! Don't look so! I won't say it again."*
>
> *"I'm glad you've slept, Becky; you'll feel rested, now, and we'll find the way out."*
>
> *"We can try, Tom; but I've seen such a beautiful country in my dream. I reckon we are going there."*

Her dream of death-as-heaven vaguely echoes a passage from MacDonald's book, where Princess Irene is sleeping in the attic bedroom of her great-great-grandmother:

> *"Oh, dear! this is so nice!" said the princess. "I didn't know anything in the world could be so comfortable. I should like to lie here forever."*
>
> *"You may if you will," said the old lady. "But I must put you to one trial—not a* very *hard one, I hope."*

Aside from the ominous phrase "lie here forever," a number of things associate Irene's beloved great-great-grandmother with death or heaven. One, of course, is her advanced age; another is her ghostly quality of appearing only to certain people. There are also her magical attributes, her supernatural powers over the world. And finally there is the heavenlike height of her attic—the fact that it is far above the normal part of the house, and only selectively accessible.

Books like Twain's and MacDonald's, while they basically present life as desirable and death as fearsome, also borrow a sort of *Pilgrim's Progress* quality in scenes like those I quoted above. In such scenes, death is a passageway to heaven—a sure thing for children, who are too innocent to be guilty of sin. Twain mocks this kind of attitude in *Huckleberry Finn*, when Huck is staying with the death-and-heaven-obsessed Grangerfords; but he mocks it gently and a bit sentimentally, as he seems to do here with Becky. In both Irene's and Becky's cases (as in Dante's), the way to heaven lies through the underground, and while they seem to long for that beautiful heaven, they fear the experience that will bring them to it. Perhaps this dissociation—death as the fearful underworld, heaven as the beautiful sky—is characteristic of Christianity in general, which has very mixed attitudes toward mortality.

As might be expected, these conflicts and confusions reach the greatest pitch in C.S. Lewis's works, with their avowedly Christian underpinnings. In *The Silver Chair*, the paradoxical link between heaven and hell, between death and the afterlife, is pointedly drawn in the children's respective fears. Scrubb, the boy, fears heights, and his most terrifying experience occurs when he falls off an incredibly high cliff—a cliff which turns out to be the home of Aslan (the lion who stands in for God and Christ in these books). Jill, on the other hand, fears the underground, and the parallel between these two fears is made explicit in the book: "Now it happened that Jill had the same feeling about twisty passages and dark places underground, or even nearly underground, that Scrubb had about the edges of cliffs." As it turns out, the story confirms Jill's position by placing all the wickedness underground and all the virtue in the heights. But Lewis does not justify one set of fears over another: that is, he seems to condemn (and sympathize with) the two children equally, as if to assert that the underground trial and the heady cliff-edge are inextricably linked in the progress toward virtue, and that neither can be avoided if the final end is to be attained. This is a reasonable acknowledgment of the fact that both death and salvation represent a parting with mortality, a loss of the human self. Eternity is not the province of heaven alone; if one fears endings, one might equally well opt for the underworld. Both God and the Devil are immortal—as is suggested in a discussion about the relative ages of Aslan and the Queen of the Underland. " 'Our guide is Aslan,' " one of the good characters asserts,

> "*and he was there when the giant king caused the letters to be cut, and he knew already all things that would come of them, including* this."
>
> "*This guide of yours must be a long liver, friend,*" *said the Knight with another of his laughs.*

> *Jill began to find them a little irritating.*
> *"And it seems to me, Sir," answered Puddleglum, "that this Lady of yours must be a long liver too, if she remembers the verse as it was when they first cut it."*

The verse in question, the remains of which have served to guide the children and Puddleglum into the underworld, crucially exposes the various connections among death and immortality, God and the Devil, the world and the underworld. The signpost words that constitute "a message on the stones of the City Ruinous" (again, shades of Bunyan) are "UNDER ME," but apparently the original verse ran:

> *Though under Earth and throneless now I be,*
> *Yet, while I lived, all Earth was under me.*

According to the Knight (who is in thrall to the evil Queen, and therefore an unreliable witness), these lines were cut in the stone over the sepulchre of a powerful giant king. And indeed the verse can be read this way, in which case the first "under" (in "under Earth") refers to the physical burial of a dead body, while the second one ("under me") refers to the power relationship between a "high" king and his "low" subjects—augmented, in this case, by the physical suggestion of power and height inherent in the fact that the king was a giant. But the lines can also be read as a message from Lucifer (for whom the Queen of the Underland is obviously a stand-in). He was once an angel, and a powerful one at that—hence Earth was literally "under" him as he flew over it or lived in heaven, and metaphorically "under" his control because of his influence as God's right-hand man. Now he is "under Earth" not because he is dead and buried, but because he occupies the underworld of hell. There are certain problems with this reading—Lucifer is not exactly "throneless" in hell, and it would be difficult to say he "lived" any more before his fall than after—but *some* sense of the Devil is nonetheless buried in those lines. And the very words that the new interpretation puts pressure on ("throneless," "lived"—one invoking power, the other mortality) reach toward the concepts that make us uncomfortable with the heaven/hell dichotomy. If God is omnipotent, why does the Devil have so much power? And if heaven is so desirable, why do we fear loss of life so intensely?

It may seem strange that such deep and troubling issues should emerge from a reading of children's literature. But children are interested mainly in the significant—it's the irrelevant details (like multiplication tables or irregular word spellings) that they find boring and difficult to comprehend. Moreover, children's books offer a relatively hopeful way to deal with these issues. Like *Pilgrim's Progress* or Arthurian legends, and unlike most serious adult novels of the past century, children's books offer a vision of self-salvation: a trial set and passed, a frightening experience (of loss, of near-death, of chaos) endured and conquered. This is especially apparent, I think, in works about the underground, where the subterranean adventure itself constitutes the trial. In each of the books I've discussed here, the children save *themselves* from danger, even while adults may be simultaneously (and ineffectually) trying to save them.

In *Tom Sawyer*, for instance, the whole town turns out to search for the two lost children in the cave, yet it is Tom himself who finds the way out by exploring until he sees a "far-off speck that looked like daylight." As in the other children's stories (and some adult tales too —notably Jules Verne's and Virgil's), the exit from the underworld is not the same as the entrance; the subterranean adventurers have covered miles underground before coming up to the surface again. In Tom's case, he has not only saved himself and Becky, but has done so by discovering a new point of access between the cave-world and the daylight-world. This sense of progress and discovery is the underground tale's version of optimism. As in the progress from childhood to adulthood, one can't solve problems by going backward to the point of origin, but one *can* still hope to emerge from the darkness.

The issue of saving oneself (and others) is broadened in the MacDonald book to include a kind of mutual self-salvation. Curdie goes underground first to work for the benefit of his family, and second to help save the princess and his fellow miners from the goblins. When he gets captured there, he needs to be saved by the princess. She goes underground essentially because her great-great-grandmother leads her there, and ends up rescuing him unwittingly: what she sees as her own "trial" ends up being an effort directed toward another's benefit. Neither would have gotten trapped underground if it were not for the other; neither would have gotten out without the other. The invisible thread that guides Irene in and both of them out—the magic thread woven by her grandmother—literally becomes a lifeline. (Tom Sawyer uses a similar lifeline to get himself and Becky out of the cave—only in his case it is merely an everyday piece of string.) And like the fortune-telling lifeline on the palm of one's hand, the princess's thread knows where its owner is going even before she does. In this sense the thread is fate as well as guide—but a fate that requires intelligent pursuit if it is not to lead to a bad end.

Like the process of growing up, the thread is unidirectional: when Irene feels backward along it, it disappears, and she can only use it to move forward. The fact that the underground is Irene's "trial," the necessary preliminary to becoming an adult "princess" (like Alice's "Queen" at the end of *Through the Looking Glass*), is made obvious at the point when she follows the thread into the goblins' subterranean world: "she became more and more sure that the thread could not have gone there of itself, and that her grandmother must have sent it. But it tried her dreadfully when the path went down very steep. . . . Through one narrow passage after another, over lumps of rock and sand and clay, the thread guided her, until she came to a small hole through which she had to creep. Finding no change on the other side, 'Shall I ever get back?' she thought, over and over again, wondering at herself that she was not ten times more frightened, and often feeling as if she were only walking in the story of a dream." As that last phrase suggests, Irene's descent, like Alice's, is a process of going down into her own unconscious as well as into a frightening real-world hole. That the two realms overlap is an essential element of subterranean children's stories.

In MacDonald's book, the usefulness of the unconscious is pointedly apparent in the weapon used to ward off the goblins: that is, rhyme. As the narrator says, "the chief defense against them was verse, for they hated verse of every kind, and some kinds they could not endure at all. I suspect they could not make any themselves, and that was why they disliked it so much." To make verse is to tap into that subterranean world of the unconscious which also generates dreams (as Robert Duncan, among others, has pointed out). Perhaps the goblins, because they have gone entirely underground, have no further underworld to tap into: hence their fear of language which comes from that deeper level. MacDonald tells us that nonsense verse is less effective against them than meaningful verse, and that new rhymes work better than old. This suggests that the very act of manipulating language, rather than any reliance on pure sound or pure memory, is what frightens them: they can't stand to confront a poet in the process of generating poetry.

As the adult world gets more complicated, self-salvation or even mutual salvation becomes an inadequate rite of entry. The more difficult adulthood is to attain, the more people one must demonstrably save to get there. In *The Silver Chair*, the two children, by finding their way out of the underground, save not only themselves, each other, and their accomplice Puddleglum, but also a kidnapped prince of Narnia. Indeed, their whole adventure takes the form of a quest for the prince, with obscure signs to follow and frightening barriers to overcome. They knowingly enter the underworld because it is part of their assigned task. One can't write this off as merely C.S. Lewis's Arthurian preoccupations, since that would not account for the popularity of the Narnia books among children who never heard of medieval literature. What the Arthurian overtones do, I think, is to show the appeal of knight-errantry in a new light—to connect those medieval tales explicitly with the process of growing up (as T.H. White's *Once and Future King* does as well). Lewis seems to be suggesting that present-day England doesn't provide clear enough rites of passage for young men and women: it is only by going back to a medieval world, imbued with the powers of both Christianity and royalty, that they can find strong enough standards to test themselves by. Before entering Narnia, both Jill and Scrubb are suffering from a kind of existential angst (as well as a very concrete victimization) brought about by the lawlessness of their experimental school. The clear rules of Narnia and the absolute authority of Aslan are in stark contrast to the world of the school, where the people in charge "had the idea that boys and girls should be allowed to do what they liked." (This need for clear definitions of merit also seems to be at the root of Don Quixote's chivalric longings—and to be a similar response to the social confusion of Cervantes' own period.)

It is interesting that the two children never consider refusing to do what Aslan asks of them. Though frightened at times, they embrace their quest with a remarkable degree of enthusiasm, as if they have been waiting all their lives to follow orders. Unlike Princess Irene, they occasionally get their instructions wrong, and have to muddle forward under less-than-desirable circumstances. Making mistakes thus becomes an integral part of the quest for adulthood. This confused following of obscure directions lends a new sense to the idea of the underground: a dark place where one can't see what one is doing but must plunge ahead anyway. If this sounds like adolescence, it also sounds like certain periods of history. And indeed, Lewis's book—by making the children's quest deal with the whole fate of a nation, in the form of Narnia's royal heir—draws a clear parallel between personal and historical development. In addition, the author's frequent references to twentieth-century conditions suggest that he views his own century as a "dark age" of sorts. So if the Arthurian period corresponds to England's—one might even say, to Europe's—childhood, the twentieth century is the dark adolescence through which the culture must go, surviving only if it can hark back to the rules and fantasies of childhood, as Jill and Scrubb do when they enter Narnia. For both the children and Narnia (and, by implication, post-war Europe), adulthood is something that must be achieved with difficulty, wrested from the subterranean and brought up to light.

Nor will it always be easy to tell when one is trapped underground, for the subterranean realm may disguise itself as the whole world. The Queen of the Underland tries to persuade the travelers that hers is the only reality: " 'How?' said the Queen with a kind, soft, musical laugh. 'Is there a country up among the stones and mortar of the roof?' " Paradoxically, the best response to such tactics turns out to be a belief in the world of dreams, as Puddleglum shows when he answers: " 'Suppose we *have* only dreamed, or made up, all those things—trees and grass and moon and stars and Aslan himself. Suppose we have. Then all I can say is that, in that case, the made-up things seem a good deal more important than the real ones. Suppose this black pit of a kingdom of yours *is* the only real one. Well, it strikes me as a pretty poor one. And that's a funny thing, when you come to think of it. We're just babies making up a game, if you're right. But four babies playing a game can make a play-world which licks your real world hollow.' " On one level, of course, this is just Lewis's transparent defense of faith. But it is also an argument in favor of fantasy, and in particular children's fantasy ("babies making up a game"), and thus constitutes a defense of the very work in which it is embedded. Like MacDonald's notion of rhyme-as-weapon, Lewis's idea of fantasy-as-weapon advocates the power of the imaginative work of literature as a way of dealing with a distressing reality. And in both Curdie's and Puddleglum's cases, a great deal rests with the ability to speak up—to voice one's poems or one's fantasies in the face of the opposition. What makes the passage quoted above so moving is not just its content, but Puddleglum's assertive rhetoric in expressing that content: the act of speech itself establishes the other world.

When the four travelers from Narnia do eventually emerge from the underground, it is not into the kind of bright daylight that we think of as the "opposite" of the subterranean world. They come out at night, and are immediately taken into a cozy cave, where "the warmth of the cave, and the very sight of it, with the firelight dancing on the walls and dressers and cups and saucers and plates and on the smooth stone floor, just as it does in a farmhouse kitchen, revived them a little." In other words, the frightening underground is not rejected, but domesticated: what had been ominous (the absence of sunlight, the enclosure of stone ceilings) becomes harmless and even protective. This tendency is taken even further in the last paragraph of the novel, where the underground is made recreational. *The Silver Chair* ends: "The opening into the hillside was left open, and often in hot summer days the Narnians go in there with ships and lanterns and down to the water and sail to and fro, singing, on the cool, dark underground sea, telling each other stories of the cities that lie fathoms deep below. If ever you have the luck to go to Narnia yourself, do not forget to have a look at those caves." Far from being vanquished and ignored, the underground becomes an aspect of daily life, an interesting rather than frightening element. In part this ending represents a willful attempt to soothe, an assertion that good can triumph and convert bad. But it also, I think, has a similar quality to the social incorporation of the Eumenides at the end of the *Oresteia*: that is, it acknowledges that we cannot rid ourselves of our demons, so we may as well learn to live with them. The underground may have become domesticated, but it still has the power to awaken fantasies of "the cities that lie fathoms deep below."

In *Tom Sawyer*, the children also revisit the underground (at least, Tom and Huck do), but in this case it is for the purpose of retrieving buried treasure. Buried treasure is a frequent theme in children's underground stories. It is, for instance, the reason behind the employment of Curdie and the other miners in *The Princess and the Goblin*—in that case, the treasure consisting of natural ores buried in the mountain. "Buried" (in the sense of being underground) treasures of a material sort surround the enchanted Prince Rilian in the C.S. Lewis Underland—indeed, he is physically confined, during his rebellious periods, in the silver chair of the title, just as he is morally confined by the riches the Queen offers him. And the deeper one goes, the more attractive the treasure is. As Golg the gnome says about the far-deeper land from which he comes: " 'I have heard of those little scratches in the crust that you Top-dwellers call mines. But that's where you get dead gold, dead silver, dead gems. Down in Bism we have them alive and growing. There I'll pick you bunches of rubies that you can eat and squeeze you a cup full of diamond-juice.' " And the children, peering down into the abyss, see "blues, reds, greens, and whites all jumbled together: a very good stained-glass window with the tropical sun staring straight through it at mid-day might have something the same effect."

For the most part treasure represents a false attraction—a lure that traps the avaricious, or that ends up being worthless. To prefer the treasure to the underground experience itself—as Digory's greedy Uncle Andrew does in the new-found Narnia—indicates a lack of enlightenment and usually leads (as it does with Andrew) to some kind of imprisonment. At first, *Tom Sawyer* seems to reverse this pattern: the boys go down into the cave on a second trip, *after* the self-rescuing experience Tom has with Becky, and successfully retrieve Injun Joe's treasure box. This makes them rich, and that would seem to be the requisite happy ending. But even this treasure turns out to be something of a prison. As Huck says: " 'Lookyhere, Tom, being rich ain't what it's cracked up to be. It's just worry and worry, and sweat and sweat, and a-wishing you was dead all the time.' " To appease Tom, he promises to stick with his wealthy life at the widow Douglas's a while longer—but, as we learn in *The Adventures of Huckleberry Finn*, that solution is only temporary.

If buried treasure is not the reward of most underground adventures, it is still a primary lure. The association between riches and the underground goes back as far as Pluto, whose name (as I mentioned in the thriller chapter) literally means "wealth." But Pluto was also, of course, the god of death; and it is the encounter with death, rather than any material wealth, that most strongly affects the children in these underground stories. They grow toward adulthood by facing and temporarily defeating the prospect of dying; the underground enables them to confront the darkness and perhaps begin to understand it. By saving themselves from death, they gain faith in their own powers of survival, and at the same time they begin to comprehend the existence of forces beyond their control. As part of their education in survival, they learn to follow a lifeline thread, or a set of rules, and thus they start to acknowledge the constraints of adult life.

But like the Princess Irene's thread, their lives still have a mysterious course: the end is not yet in sight. This is perhaps what makes children's underground books so different from other underground stories—that sense of unfinished possibilities, of things still to come. As Mark Twain says at the end of *Tom Sawyer*: "So endeth this chronicle. It being strictly a history of a *boy*, it must stop here; the story could not go much further without becoming the history of a *man*. When one writes a novel about grown people, he knows exactly where to stop—that is, with a marriage; but when he writes of juveniles, he must stop where best he can." As Twain's syntax shows, the difference can be as subtle as the shift from the definite article ("*the* history of a man") to the indefinite ("*a* history of a boy").

This kind of openness in turn makes it possible for children's books about the underground to deal with dark, potentially horrifying material without finally being frightening or depressing. For instance, in Maurice Sendak's books for small children—including not only the dream-tale *In the Night Kitchen*, from which I have drawn this chapter's epigraph, but also *Outside Over There* (which is in some ways a retelling of *The Princess and the Goblin*) and *Where the Wild Things Are*—the deep, nightmarish terrors that characterize his works are vanquished by the stories' endings, in which the children all end up safe at home, having successfully combatted the terrors and solved the nightmare problems. These endings are not pat resolutions, because they do not claim to resolve permanently: they are of the moment, but that moment is all that matters to children. The grown-ups who read these works to their progeny are likely to be horrified by the images of lost, stolen, and runaway children, of babies turned to ice or married to goblins, of little boys baked in ovens or alone among monsters. But the kids themselves will merely be interested. Death and destruction are only temporary threats to children; it is the return to daily life which seems real and important. And that fact gives the books about children's subterranean adventures an optimistic tone that is utterly inaccessible to adult books about the underground—even (or especially) when those "serious" adult works are also works of fantasy.

Three Underground Fantasies

Why, to tell long stories, showing how I have spoiled my life through morally rotting in my corner, through lack of fitting environment, through divorce from real life, and rankling spite in my underground world, would certainly not be interesting. . . .

—Fyodor Dostoyevsky, *Notes From Underground*

THROUGHOUT THE REST OF THIS BOOK, WORKS OF LITerature have been brought forcibly into conjunction with other kinds of writing—geology texts, newspaper reports, sociological surveys, and so on—to elicit a sense of the underground. This approach, like the practices of mining and archaeology, has been fruitful but destructive: I have violated what I excavated, mined the literary works for what I needed and abandoned the rest. Yet even this purposeful pursuit was somewhat self-defeating. For the underground metaphor tends to flee or dissolve when examined too schematically. To retain its full force, it must function *as* a metaphor, existing organically within its own context; it will die, or at least wither, when plucked from that context. In this final chapter, therefore, I have allowed the metaphor to speak for itself—to *remain* itself—in three individual stories that treat the topic: E.M. Forster's "The Machine Stops," Graham Greene's "Under the Garden," and Franz Kafka's "The Burrow." Here the fictional works are looked at in themselves (to the extent that's possible), rather than merely as examples or proofs of a particular historical or cultural tendency; and here the underground metaphor becomes, not a container from which meaning can be scooped out, but a tunnel through which one must journey to arrive at meaning.

Another problem that I've sensed in the rest of the book, and that I want to rectify here, is what you might call the problem of seepage. It's very easy, when examining the idea of the underground, to let it drip and overflow into all the other senses of "depth"—to let, for instance, the subterranean metaphor overlap with the underwater metaphor (as I do in the Proust quotation cited in the chapter "Journeys Into the Underground"), or to see shades of the underground in every use of the word "down" or "below" (as I sometimes do in my analysis of Oliver Sacks's writing). In this final chapter, therefore, I feel a need to draw a tighter ring around the definition, and to focus on the essential metaphor in its narrowest forms—forms that nonetheless pull together all the overtones of the previous chapters, stressing the positive connotations of "underground" (as foundation, stability, source of knowledge, place of refuge) as well as the more obvious negative ones.

Nor is it arbitrary or coincidental that the final perceptions presented in this book should be extremely literary ones. For each preceding chapter has individually contributed to the overall notion of a connection between the underground and writing—from Jules Verne's Runic inscriptions and Poe's hieroglyphic chasms, through Hyacinth Robinson's poetic sensibility and the Invisible Man's burning documents, to the labels on Alice's magical foods and the inscriptions on the stones of C.S. Lewis's City Ruinous. Writing, or literature (or art, Henry James would say) *is* the domain of "the Devil himself—who is nothing but the sense of beauty, of mystery, of relations, of appearances, of abysses of the whole" (as Henry James *did* say). Orpheus is not only the ancestor of poets: he is the literary progenitor of all attempts to bridge the gap between life and death, and hence the parent of virtually all serious literature.

In this I will be seen to have something in common after all with James Hillman, who in *The Dream and the Underworld* views all underground images as Jungian symbols for death. I would not go that far, of course, but I do concur with Hillman's belief that dreams (and fictions or poems that resemble dreams) are the only access we really have to the deepest underworlds. And for this reason, all three works examined in this last chapter are explicitly works of fantasy—pieces of literature that self-consciously imitate the manner or content of dreams.

One might well ask how this differentiates them from many of the other works discussed in previous chapters. Indeed, you might wonder how it is possible to write an underground tale that is *not* in some way a fantasy, given the otherness of the setting. Very well, let me grant that point. It helps explain why this has turned out to be, not a book on the underground itself, but a book on imagining the underground. Finally, what has interested me about the underground is its role as an active metaphor—a bringing together of something solidly in the world (an archaeological excavation, a coal mine, a sewer, a subway, a hole in the ground) with some abstraction (life after death, working-class rebellion, fear, escape, psychological growth). When the metaphor loses one of its essential elements—when it becomes mere abstraction, as in the label applied to the late-twentieth-century "Weather Underground," or mere solid reality, as in the BART subway train I ride under San Francisco Bay—it ceases to interest me. In the former case it is a dead metaphor, in the latter it is no metaphor at all.

What these three "fantasies" do is to push the metaphor as far as it can go toward eternity without being dead. In the earlier chapters of this book, the subterranean image was generally tied in some way to a specific historical development, and the underground derived part of its power from the temporal strength of that issue. Verne's underground adventures meant more in the heyday of geology than they do in the space age; Victorian social novels and H.G. Wells's *Time Machine* mattered at the height of coal-mining and sewer construction in a way they cannot matter today; thrillers, as Graham Greene's Rowe pointed out, have greater significance for a post-war audience than for the comparatively naive readers who died before World War Two. Because the underground metaphor is a living one, it changes in response to historical reality, and the passage of time makes a difference. But in this final chapter, though I've confined myself to the twentieth century, I've abandoned chronology, leaping from pre-World-War-One Forster to post-World-War-Two Greene and then back to Kafka. This approach seems appropriate to the stories themselves, which deal with time in a different way from the rest of the literature about the underground, focusing on the deepest and most persistent versions of the subterranean experience and ignoring contemporary metaphors in favor of eternal ones.

What strikes you immediately about "The Machine Stops," which was written prior to 1914, is its extremely modern sensibility. The language of this "futurist" story—where human beings exist underground in an artificial environment, their lives controlled by an all-powerful Machine and its supporting social conventions—is that of the most recent science fiction, as is Forster's anti-technology moral. In its condemnation of centralized power and its celebration of instinctive man, the story goes beyond Orwell's 1948 novel *Nineteen Eighty-Four*. Yet Forster wrote "The Machine Stops" before "airships" were a form of transport, before radio and television brought mass culture into individual residences, before two world wars had signaled the likelihood of the human race's self-destruction. That Forster could envision all these events before they happened is not necessarily due to prescience. His fantasy delves downward, into an existing core of subconscious material, as much as it reaches forward into the unknown. The imagined world in "The Machine Stops," if it is accurate, is timelessly so, and the volume of fantasies in which the story first appeared was aptly named (after its title story) *The Eternal Moment.*

The opening of "The Machine Stops" itself suggests a suspended state of animation, a machine-enforced variety of timelessness as opposed to a more traditional notion of eternity. "Imagine, if you can," it begins, "a small room, hexagonal in shape, like the cell of a bee. It is lighted neither by window nor by lamp, yet it is filled with a soft radiance. There are no apertures for ventilation, yet the air is fresh. There are no musical instruments, and yet, at the moment that my meditation opens, this room is throbbing with melodious sounds. An armchair is in the centre, by its side a reading-desk—that is all the furniture. And in the arm-chair there sits a swaddled lump of flesh—a woman, about five feet high, with a face as white as a fungus. It is to her that the little room belongs."

The very language of this first description sets the tone for the entire story. The initial imperative, "Imagine . . .," and the later reference to a "meditation" define the material as a fantasy, and yet the solidity of the description, as well as the attribution of ownership ("It is to her that the little room belongs"), imply an existence in reality. ("And yet," the core of my sentence, is also the operative phrase of Forster's paragraph: the key to the description is apparent paradox.) The "Imagine, if you can" and the reference to "my meditation" also introduce two individuals, the reader and the writer, who appear to be so fully cognizant of each other's thoughts that one's imaginings are identical with the other's meditations. This degree of communication, reinforcement, and shared assumption seems at first totally alien to this isolated world in which "people never touched one another." But then it turns out that shared "ideas" are precisely what flourish in this underground world. The very notion of an imperative "imagine"—a command to have a vision, an insistence on willed fantasy—is eerily reflective of the atmosphere of the tale, in which people frantically insist on hearing new ideas from each other. So the author, despite his seeming warmth and individuality, is already participating, in this first paragraph, in the authoritarian mode that marks the world he describes. The link between author and authoritarian is forged in that word "imagine": the enterprise is doomed in quite an interesting way from the start, because the fantasist will be insisting on the values of independent thought and tangible reality even as he forces us to share his abstract moral "idea."

The limits of Forster's technique, as well as some of its specific aims, can best be seen by contrasting this opening passage with one from a somewhat similar but finally quite different work, Samuel Beckett's *The Lost Ones*. Beckett begins: "Abode where lost bodies roam each searching for its lost one. Vast enough for search to be in vain. Narrow enough for flight to be in vain. Inside a flattened cylinder fifty metres round and eighteen high for the sake of harmony. The light. Its dimness. Its yellowness. Its omnipresence as though every separate square centimetre were agleam of the some eighty thousand of total surface. Its restlessness at long intervals suddenly stilled like panting at the last. Then all go dead still. It is perhaps the end of their abode. A few seconds and all begins again. . . ."

"No ideas but in things": William Carlos Williams' dictum, which aptly sums up the moral point Forster is striving to make in "The Machine Stops," is as fully achieved in the Beckett piece as one imagines it could ever be. The fragmented sentence structure reflects the absence of the authoritative tale-teller—not that every word isn't exactly placed, but the verbal exactness seems to come from the same impersonal source as the exact measurements, to be dictated by natural laws rather than human art. Instead of Forster's "It is lighted neither by window nor by lamp, yet it is filled with a soft radiance," Beckett gives us: "The light. Its dimness. Its yellowness. Its omnipresence . . .," the absence of verbs conveying and reinforcing the absence of an evident light source.

Against this impersonal background, the creatures who inhabit Beckett's world are both less recognizable and more pitiable than Forster's "swaddled lump of flesh"—which is, after all, "a woman" of nearly average height, who "sits," like a normal person, in an armchair, with a face which is merely "white *as* a fungus"—has not *become* a plant, like Beckett's dry leaves in the following passage. Beckett's bodies are felt rather than seen: "Consequences of this climate for the skin. It shrivels. The bodies brush together with a rustle of dry leaves. The mucous membrane itself is affected. A kiss makes an indescribable sound. Those with stomach still to copulate strive in vain." Though they are not described as human, they are presented from within—through touch and sound, as if we were among them, rather than as a picture we see through a transparent wall. They are simultaneously reduced and elevated to their mere physical parts: reduced because the parts are disembodied (a kiss here, a stomach there—and a metaphorical stomach at that), but elevated because the gestures are after all still human, are of the body in a very central way. Though "celebration" is hardly a word one would associate with the deeply distressing vision in *The Lost Ones*, that work does celebrate the very bodily-ness of humanity in a way that Forster's parable urges. "The sin against the body—it was for that they wept in chief," says Forster at the end of "The Machine Stops"; "the centuries of wrong against the muscles and the nerves, and those five portals by which we can alone apprehend—glozing it over with talk of evolution, until the body was white pap, the home of ideas as colourless, last sloshy stirrings of a spirit that had grasped the stars." It is the inflation of language which defeats Forster here—the "five portals," the "spirit that had grasped the stars." Beckett's moment of epiphany (itself far too inflated a word for the delicate but powerful shift in his story) is far more compelling: "And sure enough there he stirs this last of all if a man and slowly draws himself up and sometime later opens his burnt eyes. . . . He himself after a pause impossible to time finds at last his place and pose whereupon dark descends and at the same instant the temperature comes to rest not far from freezing point. Hushed in the same breath the faint stridulence mentioned above whence suddenly such silence as to drown all the faint breathings put together. So much roughly speaking for the last state of the cylinder and of this little people of searchers one first of whom if a man in some unthinkable past for the first time bowed his head if this notion is maintained."

I have skipped some sentences in this quotation—but then, I have also left out the sixty pages of the story that precede this ending, and they are equally essential to the understanding of its tone. "The Machine Stops" and *The Lost Ones* are both about the intrusion of time on a situation of timelessness, the grinding-down-to-a-halt of a seemingly eternal machine. But whereas Forster only describes such an event, Beckett creates one: we feel that final suggestion of death and darkness, that closing silence, as a blessed release from the preceding sense of endlessness and repetition. This "last" creature ("last" echoing the title's "lost," but also mirroring the final "first") may be only uncertainly human—"if a man"—but he seems far closer to us than Forster's ironically presented "swaddled flesh." If Forster has told his story in a language at odds with its evident moral, Beckett has given us a pared-down language (*sans* verbs, *sans* subjects, *sans* everything

—to paraphrase Shakespeare, Beckett's nearest literary relative) that matches the pared-down existence he describes, and that enables us to sense even the subtlest changes as major transformations.

The flattened cylinder in which Beckett's story takes place is not an imagined part of a world, an obscure segment of reality; it is, within the story, the whole world. Very crucially, *The Lost Ones* is not an underground fantasy (though that cylinder *is* reminiscent of Dante's circular Inferno), whereas "The Machine Stops" is. The sense that there has been and could be a wholly different life outside of the artificial underground world is central to Forster's intention. Thus the alienated tone in which he conveys the story corresponds to a physical alienation of setting: part of the reason we cannot sympathize much with Forster's characters is that they inhabit a world which is defined as strictly other than ours.

The underground "cells" or rooms in "The Machine Stops" are actually more familiar to later generations than they would have been to Forster's contemporaries, for they resemble nothing so much as a bomb shelter. As a self-enclosed unit of existence, complete with its own heat, light, and air system, the bomb shelter represents the same ideological trend as Forster's cells: a movement toward individualism and isolation on a physical level, combined with an increasing subjugation to mass beliefs and an ever-rising likelihood of technological apocalypse. The question that pervaded the bomb-shelter discussions of the 1950s and early 1960s—that is, would a survivor's life be worth living?—is basically the one raised by Forster. Yet "The Machine Stops" was written three decades before the development of the atom bomb, and nearly that long before the British experience with air-raid shelters (the Second World War's predecessors to a later generation's bomb shelters—though these predecessors lacked the crucial and most ludicrous element, because they were never viewed as semi-permanent dwellings). This coincidence says as much about the fantastic nature of bomb shelters as it does about the accuracy of Forster's imagined world. Both represent irrational responses to a fear of annihilation, technological attempts to combat technological self-destruction; the fact that one was actually built in the 1950s whereas the other was merely imagined in the 1900s is less important than the obvious futility of both. To escape annihilation by moving permanently underground (the plan recommended by Dr. Strangelove in Stanley Kubrick's movie) is, as Forster points out, to leave off being human. Part of what defines us is that we live on the surface of the earth.

That the people in "The Machine Stops" are becoming something other than human is suggested in several places. Describing Vashti's evening ritual, Forster says: "Then she fed, talked to many friends, had a bath, talked again, and summoned her bed"—"fed," as opposed to "ate," being a verb usually applied to animals. There is also a strong suggestion that this buried human city is like a hive of bees (creatures with a stronger sense of social organization and a correspondingly lower level of individual intelligence than we habitually attribute to ourselves). Thus Vashti's room is shaped "like the cell of a bee," and when she leaves it for a trip to her son Kuno she gets a vision of the whole hive: "Beneath those corridors of shining tiles were rooms, tier below tier, reaching far into the earth, and in each room there sat a human being, eating, or sleeping, or producing ideas. And buried deep in the hive was her own room." And when the civilization is destroyed, Forster says (in the last paragraph) that "the whole city was broken like a honeycomb." Physically, this is the same structure as Dante's Inferno, as the inverted Tower of Babel in Thom Gunn's "Bringing to Light":

craters
like a honeycomb bared
. . . . . .
In one cellar, a certain manikin
terribly confined

Forster's is the Inferno created by technology, life in earth (not life *on* earth) as hell.

In fact, the journey taken by Kuno in "The Machine Stops" is the inverse of the one Dante takes in the *Inferno*. Dante loses his way ("I went astray/from the straight road") and enters into the lower regions, a living tourist in the land of the dead and damned. Kuno also finds a break in the path, an irregular route, but his leads upward to the open air: he is a tourist from the land of death and damnation visiting the upper world of light and life. For poets and archaeologists (as I suggested in an earlier chapter), the past lies downward and one must dig downward to get at it; but for Kuno the way to the past is upward. Only on the surface do the old place names like "Wessex" and "Cornwall" have any meaning; only there does a history exist that the machine has been unable to wipe out. Kuno feels that as he climbs upward he is coming into contact with the spirits of the past: " 'I loosened another tile, and put in my head, and shouted into the darkness: "I am coming, I shall do it yet," and my voice reverberated down endless passages. I seemed to hear the spirits of those dead workmen who had returned each evening to the starlight and to their wives, and all the generations who had lived in the open air calling back to me, "You will do it yet, you are coming." ' " Because he begins below and moves upward, Kuno sees the underground workmen, the builders of tunnels and sewers and subways, as representatives of the open-air race—the opposite of H.G. Wells's vision, in which these same workers were progenitors of the underground Morlocks.

In more ways than just this one, "The Machine Stops" is *The Time Machine* in reverse. The concept of evolution—the biological transformation of the human race into something other than its familiar self—is central to both, as is the influence of technology on the evolutionary process. Moreover, both works see the future as a decline from the present; in this sense they are both conservative documents, emphasizing the value of old ways over new, the past (or our present) over the future. But here the similarity ends and the opposition begins. For if Wells sees the hypothetical future as a period of barbarism, in which all intellectual achievement has been lost and mankind is reduced to an animal-like form, Forster foresees it as a state of pure intellectualism, totally out of touch with the body. And while technology has given the Morlocks their edge over the Eloi ("being in contact with machinery, which, however perfect, still needs some little thought outside habit, [they] had probably retained perforce rather more initiative"), it has reduced Vashti's and Kuno's race to a condition of utter dependence.

Class conflict, the central issue in *The Time Machine*, is absent from "The Machine Stops," at least on an explicit level. It has been replaced by the conflict between machine and human—which, like Wells's class battle, is a fight that can only end in the destruction of both parties. The only note of class awareness that comes through in Forster's story is the positive role accorded to the workmen of the past, and indeed to manual labor and physical activity in general. This classless society of the future sadly lacks the virtues which in Forster's own time were associated with the working class: a preference for the concrete over the abstract, a close relationship to the physical world, bodily strength and self-sufficiency, the rejection of abstract "ideas." In this sense "The Machine Stops" has an obvious political affinity with *Nineteen Eighty-Four*, where only the ideology-resistant "proles" hold out any hope for the human race. But there are no such proles in Forster's world, and therefore no hope for that civilization. The only possible salvation, in Forster's story, lies in a return to the superficial—literally, to the surface of the earth. Both Wells and Forster view the underground race negatively, but whereas it represents the downward evolution of the working class in Wells, it is instead the outcome of bourgeois intellectuality in Forster. Finally, Forster's story champions surfaces (skin, hair, bodies, the senses) over depths (abstractions, language, ideology), and this moral preference is reflected in the topography of the imagined landscape.

Between the composition of Forster's "The Machine Stops" and the 1963 publication of Graham Greene's "Under the Garden" came two world wars, the second of which intrudes heavily on Greene's story (as it does on much of his other work). In this sense "Under the Garden" can hardly be called a timeless fantasy, a detached contemplation of "eternal moments." Yet the very issues of time and fantasy—what changes or remains the same, what is dreamed or really happens—are at the core of Greene's story. Moreover, the concerns that give the story its power—the relationships of the unconscious to death, of death to childhood, of childhood to adult reality, and of adult reality to the unconscious—are as timeless as anything I have explored in this book.

The three-part fantasy is structured as a journey into and then out of the underground, which is simultaneously a journey into and out of an individual imagination. Part One, told in the third person (but from within the consciousness of the main character), describes William Wilditch's discovery that he has lung cancer, his decision to revisit his childhood summer home, and his re-reading of a boyhood tale, a "little fantasy" he published in his school newspaper that describes an underground adventure. But the adult Wilditch is dissatisfied with this inaccurate, evasive version of a dream or an experience he still remembers vividly, and therefore he sets down the "true" adventure exactly as he recalls it; this constitutes Part Two, the longest section of the story, told in the first person. The very brief Part Three, once again narrated objectively, describes Wilditch's actual visit to the site of the adventure, his discovery of physical evidence that may or may not confirm the truth of the tale, and his sense of the possibilities (of life, or of death) that have been reawakened by the memory and its reconsideration.

Thus there are at least three different levels of fantasy or dream or fiction here: the school story which appeared in *The Warburian* under the signature W.W., the account or story which the adult William Wilditch sets down in Part Two, and the story "Under the Garden" written by Graham Greene about a fictional character named Wilditch. But each of these fictions also possesses a level of reality that is subject to debate—that in fact constitutes the major debate of the story itself. The school story, which had enraged Wilditch's Fabian-minded mother because of its overtones of fantasy and religion, bothers the adult Wilditch because of its conventional adherence to a simpleminded "boy's adventure" format: "He read with growing irritation, wanting to exclaim again and again to this thirteen-year-old ancestor of his, 'But why did you leave that out? Why did you alter this?' . . . Of course it had all been a dream, but a dream too was an experience, the images of a dream had their own integrity, and he felt professional anger at this false report. . . ." Wilditch's objections are in some way the opposite of his mother's: where she disliked the story for its attraction to the vague mysteries of spiritual and psychological imagination, he feels these mysteries are precisely those slighted by W.W.'s conventional account. Yet both condemn the story for its failure to be accurate, for its lack of attention to reality.

Whether that reality is merely a dream becomes the central question in Part Two. Telling the story as he remembers it, Wilditch continually finds himself checking the remembered facts against the probabilities of reality—and then catches himself up for taking a dream so seriously as to believe it has "facts." "I dreamed that I crossed the lake, I dreamed . . . that is the only certain fact and I must cling to it, the fact that I dreamed. [That is Greene's ellipsis, not mine.] How my poor mother would grieve if she could know that, even for a moment, I had begun to think of these events as true," Wilditch says near the beginning of his tale. But later he marvels at the kind of information he remembers—"still to this day I wonder how it was that a child could have invented these details, or have they accumulated year by year, like coral, in the sea of the unconscious around the original dream?"—and near the end he stands fast on the side of the dream's reality, even if only *as* dream. Describing the precious gems he saw, or dreamed he saw, underground, Wilditch says: "And there again I find myself adjusting a dream to the kind of criticism I ought to reserve for some agent's report on the import or export value of coloured glass. If this was a dream, these were real stones. Absolute reality belongs to dreams, and not to life. The gold of dreams is not the diluted gold of even the best goldsmith, there are no diamonds in dreams made of paste—what seems is." By the end of Part Two, after a long night of writing, Wilditch is willing to accept a dream itself as the strongest version of reality. The borderline between the imagined and the real has become fuzzy; and it gets even fuzzier in Part Three, when Wilditch discovers, half-buried in the garden, an old yellow-painted tin chamberpot that could well be the "golden po" he remembers from his adventure. On the other hand, "there was no certainty; perhaps years ago, when the paint was fresh, he had discovered the pot, just as he had done this day, and founded a whole afternoon-legend around it."

As for the way in which Graham Greene's story itself wavers between the fictional and the real, I will have more to say on this after a bit. Let me just say now that to someone who has read all of Greene's novels, this one story seems pointedly and disturbingly to get at "the heart of the matter" in Greene's fiction. In contrast to the pronounced evasiveness of Greene's interviews and autobiographies, "Under the Garden" seems nakedly direct, courageously self-revealing ("though I suppose it is arguable whether one can really show courage in a dream," as Wilditch says). If Wilditch is not identical with Greene (and obviously he is not), still, it makes a great deal of sense to view the child to whom this adventure (or dream) occurred as the father of both Wilditch and Greene.

In fact, "Under the Garden" is, among other things, a dark, deep, and serious consideration of Wordsworth's epigraph to his Immortality Ode. This is not childhood as bland, innocent goodness, but childhood as ancient knowledge, as connection to the infinite (which means death as well as, or as, immortality). There is a definite sense in which the child-Wilditch (the seven-year-old who had the adventure, the thirteen-year-old who wrote it up for his school paper) is older and more knowledgeable than the man in his late fifties who is about to die. Not only does Wilditch-the-adult think of W.W. as "this thirteen-year-old ancestor of his"; he also feels that the child will in some way survive him, like the ageless old man he discovered underground. "Now the dreaming child was dying of the same disease as the man," Wilditch realizes. "He was so different from the child that it was odd to think the child would not outlive him and go on to quite a different destiny." It is this "dreaming child" who, Wilditch decides, has shaped his own destiny, has made it impossible for him to settle into the routines of everyday life. That seven-year-old's dream (or experience) of the underground cavern, his remembrance of the extremely old man and woman who live down there, of their beautiful daughter, their buried jewels, and above all the old man's strange conversation—these are the memories which have driven Wilditch: "If it had not been for his dream of the tunnel and the bearded man and the hidden treasure, couldn't he have made a less restless life for himself, as George in fact had done, with marriage, children, a home?" The world his child-self encountered underground provided a tantalizing vision of life as it might have been. He recalls his childhood impression of the couple's beautiful daughter, known to him only through her photographs as "Miss Ramsgate": "With that girl for my wife I could take anything, even school and growing up and life. And perhaps I could have taken them, if I had ever succeeded in finding her."

From the details I've given thus far, it may seem as if "Under the Garden" borrows all the traditional elements of the child's fantasy-tale: the buried treasure, the beautiful princess, the scary underground creatures. And indeed the story has much in common with such children's literature. The boy enters the underworld through a pool of water, as the two children do in *The Magician's Nephew*. Like Tom Sawyer's experience in the cave with Becky Thatcher, his adventure is associated with childhood sexuality, with a search for treasure, and with a frightening pursuer embodying a darker, "older" race (Injun Joe/the gypsy-like Maria). The jewels he sees underground, like the living jewels in *The Silver Chair*, are brighter and more intense than anything in the upper world. This boy-adventurer sees himself as a miner ("I remembered how miners carried canaries with them in cages to test the freshness of the air, and I wished I had thought of bringing our own canary with me"), like Curdie in MacDonald's *The Princess and the Goblin*, and in W.W.'s reconstruction he even provides the hero with "a pick and a spade" with which he digs into the tunnel. Like the subterranean creatures in the MacDonald book, the people Wilditch meets underground are distorted and ugly. Maria (the old woman) has a roofless mouth and can only quack for speech, while Javitt (the old man) has a single leg, like a tree trunk: " 'Do you think I lost this leg in an accident?' " he asks the boy. " 'I was born that way just like Maria with her squawk. Generations of us uglier and uglier. . . .' " In fact, the fear of this kind of physical deformity seems linked in some way to more general childhood fears about the underground. Where MacDonald's goblins are repulsive (though also vulnerable) in part because they have soft, squishy, toe-less feet, Wilditch-the-child is terrified at meeting an underground man whose feet, like those in an aboriginal cave-painting, are "badly executed." "A foot which looked like a foot was only human," Wilditch thinks, "but my imagination could play endlessly with the faults of the painter—a club-foot, a claw-foot, the worm-like toes of a bird."

(In this context, I should note that a little boy of my acquaintance was for some months afraid to accompany his parents on the BART subway, and when asked why, he told his father that he was disturbed by all the people he saw in wheelchairs down there. I suppose a psychoanalyst would attribute this anxiety to an early manifestation of castration fear, perhaps set off by the notion of a return to the womb, a regression back into the female earth; Greene rather supports this notion when he has Wilditch recall about Javitt, " 'I'll cut you off,' he cried at once and I pictured him lopping off one of my legs to resemble him." But then in *The Silver Chair* it is the girl-adventurer rather than the boy who is particularly frightened of the underground, and *she* has no extra limbs to lose.)

At any rate, Javitt's odd shape gives him a mythical, dryadic quality—"When he stood upright he looked like a rough carving from a tree-trunk where the sculptor had not bothered to separate the legs"—which in turn seems to bear some relation to the adult Wilditch's vision of the garden at dawn: "the trees of the garden became visible, so that, when he looked up after some hours from his writing, he could see the shape of the broken fountain and what he supposed were the laurels in the Dark Walk, looking like old men humped against the weather." This amalgamation of the human shape and the natural landscape occurs, strangely enough, in most of the underground tales I've read, where men (or goblins, or giants) get mistaken for trees or rocks, or vice versa. Think, for instance, of the souls embodied in trees that Dante finds in the upper reaches of the Inferno, as well as the giants turned to rock he encounters lower down. In part, I suppose, this kind of description conveys the middling state of people who reside underground, their status falling somewhere between the known human and the alien. But it also seems to suggest the way in which darkness and the underground make even humans question their own humanity—make them fear that they might turn to rock or tree at a moment's notice. The fear of life's amorphousness—the sense that neither oneself nor the external world can be counted on to "hold its visible shape," as Shakespeare's Antony worried—is especially central to the child's imagination, which can create bogeymen out of inanimate objects. Whether this perception of the terrifying underside of life is the result of an overactive imagination or a particularly acute perception is a key argument in "Under the Garden"—and unlike Steven Spielberg's *Poltergeist* (a movie based on the same question), Greene's story refuses to come down on either side.

Greene's subterranean world, more extremely than any of the children's-story undergrounds, is both terrifying and attractive, disgusting and fascinating. All of the suppressed elements of existence—defecation, lust, incest, ugliness, deformity, greed—are active in this underworld, embodied in the figure of Javitt (" 'You can call me Javitt,' he said, 'but only because it's not my real name. . . . If you had a dog called Jupiter, you wouldn't believe he was really Jupiter, would you?' "). Javitt is in fact a sort of Jupiter of the underworld, a gross, aging but ageless, invective-hurling egomaniac who nonetheless possesses all the secrets of life. And like Jupiter, he has given birth to a beautiful Venus—" 'Miss Ramsgate to you and the whole world upstairs.' " His is the ancient knowledge of the gods, intermingled (as theirs is) with a great deal of filth and ribaldry. He peppers his speech with references to "fucking" and "shitting," and he discourses at length about sex and death to the seven-year-old who has intruded on his domain. All the while, he sits on a throne which is really a lavatory seat, under which is a deep, dark hole in which he hides, he says, his best treasures. In the underground, wealth is the same as excrement: the one treasure Wilditch takes away with him, aside from knowledge, is his "golden po," his shining chamberpot.

In most underground stories, the child ventures into the underworld to pass some kind of test that will enable him or her to move toward adulthood; these undergrounds are something like well-behaved ids, potentially dangerous areas kept under control by adult rules. But in "Under the Garden," the concerns of adulthood and the concerns of childhood get confused, and true knowledge is portrayed as wild and anti-social. Far from turning him into a more mature or adult-like boy, Wilditch's experience insures that he will always stay a child, in the sense that he will continue searching for things that the "upstairs" adult world doesn't believe in, or chooses to ignore.

In this respect the boy-Wilditch *does* remain permanently underground, despite his remembered (or dreamed) escape at the end of two or three days. That he will be kept there forever is what he fears at first, and what Javitt threatens:

> *"But I don't really want to be kept," I said. "I really don't. It's time I went home."*

> *"Home's where a man lies down," he said, "and this is where you'll lie down from now on."*

But phrases which denote time, like "always" or "from now on," don't mean the same thing below ground as they do above. Time itself has a different value there—as Javitt points out when Wilditch first arrives: " 'Where's the light? There aren't such things as mornings and evenings here.' " Hence the old man's attitude toward the passage of time tends to be disdainful: " 'Time,' he exclaimed, 'you can——time,' using a word quite unfamiliar to me which I guessed—I don't know how—was one that I could not with safety use myself when I returned home." Sometimes his contempt seems merely the inevitable attitude of the old, as when Javitt says, " 'When I was born, time had a different pace to what it has now' "—an opinion echoed almost exactly by the "real-life" gardener Ernest at the story's end. At other points Javitt's remarks clearly refer to the different nature of above-ground and below-ground time. When Wilditch reads his fortune through his tea leaves, interpreting five leaves as indicating five days, "Javitt shook his head. 'You don't count time like that with us,' he said. 'That's five decades of years.' "

Five decades turns out to be exactly the period that elapses between Wilditch's boyhood adventure and his recounting of it—or between his first visit to the underground and his discovery of his approaching death. For what comes to Wilditch in fifty years is not Javitt's beautiful daughter (this being his interpretation of the tea leaves), but cancer. The timelessness of the underworld, which the boy thinks of as immortality or at least immense longevity, can also be seen as death; hence the frightening overtones of Javitt's "Home's where a man lies down . . . and this is where you'll lie from now on." Like the visit to the underworld, the prospect of death alters the meaning of time. Note how the word "always" gets twisted in this conversation between Wilditch and his doctor, which takes place at the story's beginning:

> *"It's really very lucky. If caught in time. . . ."*
> *"There's sometimes hope?"*
> *"Oh, there's always hope."*

Here the doctor's use of the supposedly reassuring "always" counteracts its own good intentions, removing the probabilities of hope from Wilditch's particular case. (And perhaps there is also an echo here of Alice's conversation about the Bread-and-butter-fly: "Then it would die, of course." "But that must happen very often. . . ." "It always happens.") The connection between the distortions of time-measuring language and the issue of longevity/mortality is made explicit when Wilditch elsewhere recalls one of his underground dialogues with the old man:

> *"It'll take a long time," Javitt warned me.*
> *"I'm young," I said.*
> *I don't know why it is that when I think of this conversation with Javitt the doctor's voice comes back to me saying hopelessly, "There's always hope." There's hope perhaps, but there isn't so much time left now as there was then to fulfill a destiny.*

By the end of the story, however, Wilditch seems much more sanguine about the possible approach of death. It has become equated for him with his underground adventure, as the story's final paragraph suggests: "Wilditch shook the loose earth out of the po, and it rang on a pebble just as it had rung against the tag of his shoelace fifty years ago. He had a sense that there was a decision he had to make all over again. Curiosity was growing inside him like the cancer." This comparison of his most lively emotion to the disease which is killing him is the closest Wilditch ever comes to taking possession of that disease. Early in the story, it is described as something happening at a great distance from him: "Dr. Cave [note the subterranean names Greene chooses—a *cave* to match Wil*ditch*] had lined up along one wall a series of X-ray photographs, the whorls of which reminded the patient of those pictures of the earth's surface taken from a great height that he had pored over at one period during the war." Pointing out the condition of Wilditch's lungs, the "doctor's finger moved over what might have been tumuli or traces of prehistoric agriculture." Wilditch's body, in other words, has become an earth or planet invaded by "underground" forces of illness that will ultimately destroy the host. This tendency to see disease as simultaneously external and internal, to confuse what is inside one's body and outside it, is typical of the progress of an extreme and lingering illness, as Sacks's Parkinsonian patients make clear. For Wilditch, the confusion comes full circle when he leaves the doctor's office and notices taxis pulling up "outside the tall liver-coloured buildings." The external world is like a body, and his body is like an external world. Given this confusion, the metaphor of illness as a journey toward death becomes particularly concrete: "He supposed that it was the effect of his disease that he was so tired—not sleepy but achingly tired as though at the end of a long journey." For the traveler Wilditch, who has lived "in Africa and another time in Chinese parts," no real-world journey can ever quite live up to that first underground adventure. It may well be the possibility of its recurrence, the prospect of a second journey into the underworld, that fills him with a curiosity which is "like the cancer."

The places Wilditch has traveled, and indeed the rootless life he has led, noticeably recall the life journey of his author. The references in "Under The Garden" are a geographical recapitulation of the settings Greene has used in his fiction: the Africa of *The Heart of the Matter* and *A Burnt-Out Case*, the East of *The Quiet American* and *Stamboul Train*, the Latin America of *The Honorary Consul* and *The Power and the Glory*. These are all places that Greene himself has visited, and the restlessness of both Greene and Wilditch seems to come together in the response to Javitt's remark about seeking his daughter: " 'You'll have to take a look in Africa,' he said, 'and Asia—and then there's America, North and South, and Australia—you might leave out the Arctic and the other Pole—she was always a warm girl.' And it occurs to me now when I think of the life I have led since, that I have been in most of those regions—except Australia where I have only twice touched down between planes."

There are other and perhaps even more telling connections between the fictional W.W. and the real G.G. The one experience (other than the underground journey) which has affected Wilditch—and which seems oddly out of place and therefore particularly noticeable in this novel—is the Second World War, the war which heavily shaped Greene's own imagination as a writer. I have already noted the way Wilditch associates his medical X-rays with wartime aerial photos; elsewhere he compares his attempts to elicit information from his brother George to "the apparently harmless opening gambit of a wartime interrogation." His response to Javitt's strange conversations is voiced in terms of military intelligence work: "I haven't made sense of them all yet: they are stored in my memory like a code uncracked which waits for a clue or an inspiration." And Wilditch's adult explanation of the evasiveness and inaccuracy of W.W.'s school story also borrows from wartime experience: "He remembered how agents parachuted into France during the bad years after 1940 had been made to memorize a cover-story which they could give, in case of torture, with enough truth in it to be checked. Perhaps forty years ago the pressure to tell had been almost as great on W.W., so that he had been forced to find relief in fantasy. Well, an agent dropped in occupied territory was always given a time-limit after capture. 'Keep the interrogators at bay with silence or lies for just so long, and then you may tell all.' The time-limit had surely been passed in his case a long time ago, his mother was beyond the possibility of hurt, and Wilditch for the first time deliberately indulged his passion to remember." This contrast between the "lies" told to interrogators and the passionately remembered truth might almost describe Graham Greene's attitude toward his own writing—only in his case it is the autobiographies (*A Sort of Life* and *Ways of Escape*) which are the "cover-story," while his fictions or fantasies are closer to the truth. When Wilditch responds to Javitt's concern about revealing the buried treasure—" 'I swear I'd say nothing' (and at least I have kept that promise, whatever others I have broken, through all the years until now)"—we can hear in that fleeting "whatever others I have broken" the voice of Graham Greene himself. "I've betrayed a great number of things and people in the course of my life," he has said to Marie-Françoise Allain in an interview, "which probably explains this uncomfortable feeling I have about myself, this sense of having been cruel, unjust." (We do not need the interview to tell us this, since the novels themselves are filled with betrayals.) And we even have Greene's own assertion (for whatever it's worth) about the connection between himself and Wilditch: he tells Allain that " 'Under the Garden' evoked fragments of my childhood (that's always a wrench) and the painful recollection of a recent operation."

To say that Wilditch is really Greene, however, is like saying that the events in "Under the Garden" are real rather than a dream: the truth of both statements finally lies in their emotional accuracy rather than any connection to observed event. If the story says something important about the underground to Graham Greene, it says even more about its importance to fiction in general. For fiction (as Greene himself has elsewhere suggested) lies somewhere in that fertile ground where dream and observed reality meet. In "Under the Garden" this notion is best expressed in Wilditch's paragraph about the connection between his own writing and the process of listening to (or dreaming of) Javitt's conversations: "I sat on the golden po and looked at the photograph [of Javitt's daughter] and listened to Javitt as I would have listened to my own father if I had possessed one. His sayings are fixed in memory like the photograph. Gross some of them seem now, but they did not appear gross to me then when even the graffiti on walls were innocent.

Except when he called me 'boy' or 'snapper' or something of the kind he seemed unaware of my age: it was not that he talked to me as an equal but as someone from miles away, looking down from his old lavatory-seat to my golden po, from so far away that he couldn't distinguish my age, or perhaps he was so old that anyone under a century or so seemed much alike to him. All that I write here was not said at that moment. There must have been many days or nights of conversation—you couldn't down there tell the difference—and now I dredge the sentences up, in no particular order, just as they come to mind, sitting at my mother's desk so many years later." It is the fecundity of the "mother's desk" merging with the "father's" talk that produces fiction, which is not a made-up series of events but a kind of dream or memory "dredged up" from elsewhere. Typically, Greene reverses the traditional sex roles here, making the mother represent order and rationality and the ability to write, while the father embodies the wild unconscious. Javitt is both a god and a dirty old man (Jove/id?), a king and a Beckett-beggar on a lavatory-seat; he is, in this respect, the source of literature.

If the visit to the underground has made Wilditch into an eternal child—always restless, never settling down to reality—it has made Graham Greene a writer. As in *Alice in Wonderland*, Greene's child-as-writer is associated with the dark side of the imagination—the side closest to death and filth and greed and fear—as well as the playful side. Yet that playfulness is crucial too; it is a key aspect of the poet as well as the child, for both of whom (in Randall Jarrell's words) "a word has the reality of a thing: a thing that can be held wrong side up, played with like a toy, thrown at someone like a toy." Linguistic play in "Under the Garden" appears in the form of Javitt's puns about fête and fate, his willful misinterpretation of the White Elephant stall, his remarks about the reality or unreality of names. Javitt's mistakes or misinterpretations are like those the unconscious makes in Freud's *Interpretation of Dreams*: they chip away at the authority of language even as they use its multi-sidedness for their own purposes. So perhaps in the underground the dark side and the playful side—of childhood, of language, of memory, of death—are not so far apart after all; "you couldn't down there tell the difference."

If "Under the Garden" is in part about Graham Greene's approach to fiction, then "The Burrow" is even more intensely a meditation on what writing meant to Kafka. To make this kind of statement is not, I hope, to narrow the power of either work. I certainly do not belong to the school of critics (if indeed any such school still exists) which insists that all writing is about the act of writing rather than—or as the only accessible substitute for—the "real" world. On the contrary, it seems to me that when an author begins to suggest comparisons between his act of composition and the tangible events of his plot, he is usually doing so *not* to create a self-serving distinction between writers and doers, or writers and non-writers, but to bring them into closer relation. The self-referentiality of a good writer is not an end in itself, but a means of forging a link between writing and other forms of behavior; and far from glorifying the act of writing as a preeminent or "privileged" activity, such references more often denigrate it to a parasitic (or useless, or voyeuristic) role. If the subjects of reading and writing become part of the conversation between author and reader (as indeed they are likely to do, since the only fact each can be sure of knowing about the other is that he is, respectively, writing or reading), this by no means makes such topics the endpoint or justification for the conversation itself.

Nevertheless, they occasionally make a good starting place, and this is particularly true in the case of a writer like Kafka. One of the things that makes Kafka's writing "difficult" is that it does not offer an easy suspension of disbelief, a smooth transition from one's own world to the fantastic world of fiction. One is unable to forget oneself while reading Kafka. Despite the imaginative power of the Kafkaesque universe, it never overwhelms the reader's reality, but rather strains in constant tension with that reality. Even in translation, Kafka's language has the opacity of poetry: it calls attention to its own phrasing, its own obsessions, its own act of writing, even as it struggles to write about something beyond itself.

Even more than other Kafka tales, "The Burrow" seems unremitting in its focus on the act of creation. Ostensibly a description by some unidentified creature of the underground hiding place he has constructed for himself, "The Burrow" over and over again suggests the image of Kafka himself in the act of writing fiction (the Kafka, I mean, whom we have come to know from his other acts of writing—including the published letters, which have the same obsessional, paradoxical tone as the stories). Consider, for instance, the creature's discussion of the "whole little maze of passages" at the burrow's exit: "it was there that I began my burrow, at a time when I had no hope of ever completing it according to my plans; I began, half in play, at that corner, and so my first joy in labour found riotous satisfaction there in a labyrinthine burrow which at the time seemed to me the crown of all burrows, but which I judge today, perhaps with more justice, to be too much of an idle *tour de force*, not really worth the rest of my burrow, and though perhaps theoretically brilliant . . . in reality a flimsy piece of jugglery that would hardly withstand serious attack. . . ." Here, certainly, is the mature author criticizing his "brilliant" but "flimsy" early work; and yet in another place he is able to read his juvenilia as if he had not himself written it: "I am both exasperated and touched when, as sometimes happens, I lose myself for a moment in my own maze, and the work of my hands seems to be still doing its best to prove its sufficiency to me, its maker, whose final judgment has long since been passed on it."

For the writer—especially for Kafka—it is finally his own judgment of his work which matters. And yet this cannot be entirely true, for to write presumes the hope of an audience. Kafka's ambivalence toward potential readers—the same ambivalence which caused him to designate Max Brod as the executor who was to burn his manuscripts after his death, knowing (as Walter Benjamin has suggested) that Brod would be the one man least capable of doing so—appears in the creature's attitudes toward visitors to his burrow. He wants and needs a "confidant" to guard the entrance and warn him of possible intruders, yet he is afraid to cede even this amount of power to someone else: "For would he not demand some counter-service from me; would he not at least want to see the burrow? That in itself, to let anyone freely into my burrow, would be exquisitely painful to me. I built it for myself, not for visitors, and I think I would refuse to admit him, not even though he alone made it possible for me to get into the burrow would I let him in." For Kafka, the reader is both a banned outsider and the person who "alone makes it possible" for the writing to come to life. However much he wants the writing to have a self-contained inviolability, he is constantly reminded that it must not be a totally closed world: like the burrow, it must have an open entrance even if that entrance weakens the burrow's security and therefore undermines the very purpose for which it was constructed.

In his vacillations over leaving and entering the burrow, Kafka's creature is like a creator with writer's block: he leaves it "for only a short spell," but once outside, "spoiled by seeing for such a long time everything that happened around the entrance, I find great difficulty in summoning the resolution to carry out the actual descent. . . . So I give up the attempt and do not make the descent." As in "Under the

Garden"—or, for that matter, the *Inferno*—the act of writing here becomes an equivalent to making a physical descent. The prospective journey is both alluring and frightening; the creature wants to return to his burrow, but feels he will risk everything—especially the burrow—in doing so.

Even when he is "at work," safely inside the burrow again, the creature's habits are those of an obsessional writer. While he worries endlessly over the major steps required in his enterprise, planning and replanning the construction of a vast new "experimental" trench, he finds the minor rewriting and revision comparatively soothing: "so I begin by shoveling the soil back into the holes from which it was taken, a kind of work I am familiar with, that I have done countless times almost without regarding it as work, and at which, particularly as regards the final pressing and smoothing-down—and this is no empty boast, but the simple truth—I am unbeatable." This writer-creature is clearly a master of the small details.

And like all such writers—like Proust in his cork-lined burrow—he is obsessed with the interference of noise. Finally, it is the destruction of the burrow's silence that causes him to become frantic. He wishes for complete insulation from intruders: "then I would not have to listen with loathing to the burrowing of the small fry, but with delight to something that I cannot hear now: the murmurous silence of the Castle Keep." In the reference to the Castle Keep, the holy-of-holies storeroom at the heart of his burrow, lies another allusion to Kafka's writing, which includes among its major constructions that famous maze *The Castle*. And in the remark about "the burrowing of the small fry" there is a suggestion that the noise which disturbs the creature/creator is not just physically irritating sound, but the clamor of lesser writers with whom he unwillingly finds himself competing. The very fact that there are other writers who impinge on his awareness, if only in his own imagination, makes it impossible for him to write. "Even if it should be such a peculiar beast that its burrow could tolerate a neighbor," he thinks of a hypothetical fellow-burrower, "my burrow could not tolerate a neighbor, at least not a clearly audible one."

If this narrator's voice sounds eerily familiar, it is not just because he resembles the Kafka of the letters and other writings, but also because his tone shares so much—including paranoia, pride, self-laceration, intense ambivalence, pathos, tragedy, and great wit—with the narrator of Dostoyevksy's *Notes From Underground*. Recall the way in which that creature, too, refers to the writing process itself: "I have felt ashamed all the time I've been writing this story; so it's hardly literature so much as corrective punishment." Both the Underground Man and Kafka's Burrower are experts at self-punishment: they throw themselves in the path of a fate which will inevitably crush them. In the case of the Dostoyevsky character, this fate is embodied in another individual, the officer who fails to acknowledge him; in the Kafka story, the source of laceration is the burrow itself. To create the burrow/fiction, Kafka's creature/creator must do damage to himself: "But for such tasks the only tool I possess is my forehead. So I had to run with my forehead thousands and thousands of times, for whole days and nights, against the ground, and I was glad when the blood came, for that was a proof that the walls were beginning to harden."

This gladness at the arrival of pain is characteristic of both Kafka's narrator and Dostoyevsky's. In neither case is it a matter of simple masochism (if masochism can ever be described as simple), for these creatures do not derive sensory pleasure from the pain itself. Rather, they are interested in self-degradation or self-mortification for a purpose beyond the enjoyment of the experience—for what one might call a spiritual purpose. Dostoyevsky's character expresses this in the axiom that "suffering is the sole origin of consciousness," consciousness being the thing that provides him with the abiding (albeit painful) sense of superiority to others. Kafka's character seems to view punishment as a literal "corrective," a necessary response to his own weaknesses. Thus he tries to re-enter his burrow "but I cannot, I rush past it and fling myself into a thorn bush, deliberately, as a punishment, a punishment for some sin I do not know of." The Underground Man's self-punishment is a response to a world (and a self) that he understands all too well, whereas the Burrower's behavior is dictated by something that he does not profess to understand. Of course, given the paradoxes that both Dostoyevsky and Kafka subscribe to, this assertion of ignorance might well make the Burrower the more self-aware of the two.

In any case, what results from this psychological difference between the two characters is a vast difference in the way they view the outside world. For the Underground Man, "spite" is an overwhelming emotion: his self-dislike turns outward against the other people in his world as well as his hypothetical readers ("I have only in my life carried to an extreme what you have not dared to carry halfway, and what's more, you have taken your cowardice for good sense, and have found comfort in deceiving yourselves," he snaps at his readers in the closing paragraph). For Kafka's character, on the contrary, spite does not exist—not only because there are no tangible figures in his world to turn it against (the Underground Man, after all, was able to manufacture *his* targets out of nothing), but also because he does not seem to have the capacity to hate. Anxiety, rather than spite, is his dominating emotion, and anxiety is basically a passive emotion: its objects are its causes rather than its victims. Kafka's Burrower muses remorselessly on the sources of his various problems, but he does not blame anyone for them, not even himself. He too has "enemies" who threaten his security; he too can mock himself, in a tone that sounds a great deal like the Underground Man's sarcastic wit ("If it should really break through to the burrow I shall give it some of my stores and it will go on its way again. It will go on its way again, a fine story!"). But there is finally no rancor in his attitude toward either himself or these enemies. The fact of his victimization is accepted as a problem to be worried over, not resented and resisted.

This does not mean that Kafka's character is any closer to solving his dilemma than Dostoyevsky's is. For both, the essence of their situation is its continuity, its lack of change. The time distortions that appear in other underground fantasies (from "Under the Garden" and *Alice in Wonderland* to *The Man Who Lived Underground* and *The Time Machine*) appear in "The Burrow" as well, but here they signal the meaninglessness of "objective" time rather than the possibility of dual time schemes. For Kafka's character, underground time and aboveground time are not separate realities: they are merged into the subjective perceptions of the Burrower himself. Thus time does not represent eternity on the one hand and mortality on the other, but rather the capacity of the individual to create his own endless hell. For the Burrower, time measures only his emotional relationship to the burrow: when he feels secure he imagines he can leave it "for a short spell," when he is outside he feels that "it was really impossible to go down into the burrow." It is he himself who controls (and yet cannot consciously control) the passage of time, as he implies when he says that "somehow or other I shall quite certainly find myself in my burrow again. But on the other hand how much time may pass before then, and how many things may happen in that time, up here no less than down there? And it lies with me solely to curtail that interval and to do what is necessary at once."

The accumulation of detail in "The Burrow," the vacillations from one possible course of action to its opposite, the plethora of anxieties, all lend the story a kind of pressure in the face of time, an insistence that something must break. Yet the story ends with the sentence: "But all remained unchanged." Following upon all the vacillation of the previous pages, this line has the finality of a death-knell. Just as the build-up of repetition and immobility in Beckett's *The Lost Ones* makes the final, minute transformation powerful by contrast, the uncertainty and insecurity presented throughout "The Burrow" heighten the stolidity of that last line. And just as a change toward death and closure represents hope for Beckett's creatures, the absence of such a change represents the absence of hope for Kafka's burrower. As long as his situation remains unchanged, he will continue to impose on himself the suffering induced by the thought of *potential* change.

The arrival at paradox is crucial to "The Burrow," as it is to all of Kafka's work. Unlike the paradoxes of mathematics, which suggest that an error of logic has been made somewhere along the line, the paradoxes in Kafka's writing signal that a core of truth has emerged. For the narrator of "The Burrow," paradoxes usually arise out of his too-great ability to envision the opposite alternative—his fear (so strong a fear that it becomes almost a desire) that things will change from their present position of stasis. Thus, having built his burrow to provide security for himself, he becomes so anxious to prevent his enemy's discovering the burrow entrance that he spends hours *outside* the burrow, guarding its (therefore useless, since it does not enclose him) secrecy. The thing built for an apparent purpose has become an object in itself. A similar pattern governs the creature's behavior with his "stores," his buried treasure of food. He alternates between distributing these stores at various points in the burrow and grouping them together in the Castle Keep—each alternative, once enacted, striking him as less secure than the other one. Occasionally the food itself, the thing which he hides from his enemies and which enables *him* to hide from his enemies, becomes an enemy itself, as when "my road is so blocked by all this flesh in these narrow passages, through which it is not always easy for me to make my way even when I am alone, that I could quite easily smother among my own stores; sometimes I can only rescue myself from their pressure by eating and drinking a clear space for myself."

Like several other fleeting references in the story (allusions to his need to transport food in his mouth, or to firm up walls with his forehead), this mention of raw "flesh" emphasizes the fact that the creature who lives in the burrow is some kind of non-human animal. Yet to call this a "fact" is too clumsy for Kafka's technique: to say that the Burrower is really an animal is no more factual (and no less so) than to say that Gregor Samsa really turns into a cockroach. What Kafka does is to take the figurative language of most underground tales, which in one way or another stress the animal-*like* qualities of below-ground dwellers, and turn it into something more concrete. To posit the burrow-dweller as an animal makes new sense of the basic attributes of underground life, as they have been outlined by the various writers I discuss in this book. It explains why the creature's hands are powerless (like those of Sacks's patients); why his "stores" have no exchange value in the upper world (like the buried treasures of Wright's "freddaniels" or Greene's Javitt); why he finds security in below-ground darkness (like Harry Lime or the Invisible Man); why he eats raw flesh and cannibalizes the "small fry" (like the Morlocks, or the Victorian vision of the working class); why he sounds so much like Dostoyevsky's "insulted, crushed and ridiculed mouse"; and why he seeks, rather than abhors, the isolation from humanity that is a concomitant fact of subterranean existence.

And yet it is not accurate to say that all this is true "merely" because he is an animal, for Kafka's Burrower is surely no mere animal. He speaks, for one thing; but that alone would not be enough to explain why he seems more human than the talking animals of *Alice in Wonderland* or the other children's stories. The Burrower is not only the primary sensibility of this story, he is its *only* sensibility, and as such he forces us into a direct and curiously equal relationship with him. It is not exactly that we too are animals, or that he is really a human, but that we can't fully discount either possibility. Moreover, as I pointed out earlier, this animal-narrator is closely identified with the figure of the writer, and in particular with the writer who composed this fiction. Just as with Dostoyevsky's character, our disdain for the anxieties and obsessions of this pathetic narrator gets mixed with our profound admiration for the sensibility that could compose such a narrative—a sensibility which, we are forced to realize, depends utterly on the possession of anxieties and obsessions.

In the attribution of typical underground "bestiality" to an actual beast lies an apt metaphor for Kafka's use of metaphor. I said near the beginning of this chapter that these three fantasies push the underground metaphor to an extreme, converting its figurative possibilities to concrete realities and at the same time loosening the tie between fiction and reality. In obvious respects Kafka's story does this even more than Forster's or Greene's: it is simultaneously more fantastic (because narrated by an animal) and more mundane (because it simply documents the uneventful, unchanging anxiety of a fearful creature's daily life). Detaching the underground experience from anything that resembles our idea of a lived reality, Kafka nonetheless gives us back a devastatingly familiar psychological picture. He destroys, and then remakes in a more resilient form, the very notion of metaphor.

In her essay "The Aesthetics of Silence," which attacks the idea of allegory by questioning the concept of "meaning" in art, Susan Sontag says: "The narratives of Kafka and Beckett seem puzzling because they appear to invite the reader to ascribe high-powered symbolic and allegorical meanings to them and, at the same time, repel such ascriptions. Yet when the narrative is examined, it discloses no more than what it literally means." On one level, of course, this remark rings true: nothing is more irritating than the kind of interpretation which suggests that Kafka is "really" writing about the forthcoming Holocaust, or the mystical authority of Jewish law, or the tyranny of his father, or whatever (though he *may* be writing about these things as well). Part of me wants to join Sontag in insisting that Kafka's stories are concrete, not symbolic; direct, not allegorical. But anyone who thinks hard about what Kafka's works "literally mean" must surely begin to doubt the concept of literal meaning. Sontag herself seems uncharacteristically nervous about her own assertion, positing the hypothetical wrong reading in a series of distancing phrases that attenuate the misinterpretation to virtual nonexistence ("*seem* puzzling," "appear," "invite," "ascribe"). Such phrases suggest confusion somewhere along the interpretive line—*maybe* Kafka is saying this or that, *maybe* the reader is introducing an incorrect meaning—but they do not pin down the source of confusion. The easy answer would be to say that the confusion lies in language itself, which by its very nature is ambiguous and multifarious and therefore . . . (etc., etc.). But that answer does an injustice to Kafka (and Beckett), whose fictions, however much they focus on language, are powerful because they also have something to say. That this "something" cannot be boiled down to a form beyond or beside the language itself is inherent in the nature of great fiction.

Most of us have been taught to think of metaphor as something with two separate parts: the tenor, or meaning, and the vehicle which carries that meaning. Such an image—of a passenger in a car, or a wad of money in a bank robber's suitcase—suggests the priority of the tenor over the vehicle, the subservience of the transmitter to the meaning it transmits. What Sontag's revision does, in focusing on the importance of "art's language as autonomous and self-sufficient," is to reverse the values. Metaphor becomes a Louis Vuitton bag stuffed with old newspapers, or a Mercedes-Benz occupied by a test dummy, in which case the tenor can easily be discarded. But what Kafka's writing does is far more radical: it calls into question the very metaphor for metaphor, the whole idea of two separable elements. Kafka's narratives do not "seem puzzling," they *are* puzzling, because we are used to separating out symbol from meaning, allegory from described event. The puzzle is in some ways the heart of the story for Kafka, because it is what forces us to think on both levels at once—as E.M. Forster would say, to "connect."

I have digressed into this seemingly theoretical discussion because I think its issues are crucial to what makes the underground such a rich metaphor. The subterranean is not an inviolable symbol hidden away from human touch, like Forster's Marabar Caves or Kafka's alternative Castle Keep ("One of these favorite plans of mine was to isolate the Castle Keep from its surroundings," the Burrower says at one point). It is a physical place in the world, visited or occupied at various depths and in various ways by innumerable people. On the other hand, the underground is more than just its physical being—not only because it remains somewhat inaccessible (despite Verne, we cannot physically go all the way to the earth's center), but also because some of its most important embodiments—in particular hell, or Hades—never did take a physical form. It is a "vehicle" which has become so enriched by its various passengers—who altered through time, and who thereby altered the vehicle—that even when it lies "empty" it is still extremely full. So the author who chooses to journey in it will inevitably be jostled and frightened and comforted and entertained by all the ghosts of past passengers—however much he believes (like Kafka's Burrower) that he is basically alone down there.

Bibliography

ALLAIN, MARIE-FRANÇOISE. *The Other Man: Conversations With Graham Greene*. New York: Simon & Schuster, 1983.

AMBLER, ERIC. *A Coffin for Dimitrios*. New York: Alfred A. Knopf, 1943.

BALDWIN, JAMES. "Strangers in the Village," in *Notes of a Native Son*. Boston: Beacon Press, 1955.

BARKER, T.C. and MICHAEL ROBBINS. *A History of London Transport, Volume One: The Nineteenth Century*. London: George Allen & Unwin, 1975.

BEAVER, PATRICK. *A History of Tunnels*. Seacaucus: The Citadel Press, 1973.

BECKETT, SAMUEL. *The Lost Ones*. New York: Grove Press, 1972.

BELLOW, SAUL. *Mr. Sammler's Planet*. New York: The Viking Press, 1970.

BERMAN, MARSHALL. *All That Is Solid Melts Into Air*. New York: Simon & Schuster, 1982.

BETTELHEIM, BRUNO.*Freud and Man's Soul*. New York: Alfred A. Knopf, 1982.

BOBRICK, BENSON. *Labyrinths of Iron*. New York: William Morrow, 1981, 1986.

BRIGGS, ASA. "The Language of Class," in *Past and Present 15* (November 1955).

BULFINCH, THOMAS. *Bulfinch's Mythology* (aka *The Age of Fable*). New York: Collier Books, 1962.

BULWER LYTTON, EDWARD. *The Coming Race*. Santa Barbara: Woodbridge Press Publishing Company, 1979.

CARLYLE, THOMAS. *Sartor Resartus*. London: Everyman's Library, 1908.

CARROLL, LEWIS (aka CHARLES DODGSON). *Alice in Wonderland* and *Through the Looking Glass*. In *The Annotated Alice* (Martin Gardner, ed.). New York: Clarkson N. Potter, 1960.

CERVANTES, MIGUEL DE. *Don Quixote* (Tobias Smollett, tr.). New York: Farrar, Straus & Giroux, 1986.

CHANDLER, RAYMOND. "The Simple Art of Murder," in *Pearls Are a Nuisance*. Harmondsworth: Penguin Books, 1964.

CHEEVER, JOHN. *The Wapshot Scandal*. New York: Harper & Row, 1964.

CLARK, GRAHAME. *Archaeology and Society*. London: Methuen, 1939.

CONRAD, JOSEPH. *The Secret Agent*. Garden City: Doubleday Anchor, 1953.

DANIEL, GLYN. *The Idea of Prehistory*. Baltimore: Penguin Books, 1962.

Dante Alighieri, *The Divine Comedy* (John D. Sinclair, tr.). New York: Oxford University Press, 1939.

Dante Alighieri, *The Inferno* (John Ciardi, tr.). New Brunswick: Rutgers University Press, 1954.

Dickens, Charles. *Our Mutual Friend.* Harmondsworth: Penguin Books, 1971.

Dickens, Charles. *Hard Times.* New York: Holt, Rinehart & Winston, 1958.

Dickens, Charles. *Great Expectations.* Harmondsworth: Penguin Books, 1965.

Dickens, Charles. *Bleak House.* Boston: Houghton Mifflin, 1956.

Diva, a film directed by Jean-Jacques Beinix, 1981.

Dostoyevsky, Fyodor. *Crime and Punishment* (tr. David Magarshack). New York: Penguin Books, 1966.

Dostoyevsky, Fyodor. *Notes From Underground.* In *Three Short Novels by Fyodor Dostoyevsky* (Constance Garnett, tr.). New York: Dell Publishing Company, 1960.

Douglass, Frederick. *My Bondage and My Freedom.* New York: Dover Publications, 1969.

Dr. Strangelove, a film directed by Stanley Kubrick, 1964.

Drabble, Margaret. *The Middle Ground.* New York: Alfred A. Knopf, 1980.

Dressed to Kill, a film directed by Brian De Palma, 1980.

Duncan, Robert. "From the H.D. Book," in *Ironwood 22* (Fall 1983).

Dyos, H.J. and Michael Wolff. *The Victorian City: Images and Realities.* Boston: Routledge & Kegan Paul, 1978.

Eliot, T.S. *Four Quartets.* London: Faber & Faber, 1944.

Eliot, T.S. *Selected Poems.* London: Faber & Faber, 1954.

Ellison, Ralph. *Invisible Man.* New York: Vintage Books, 1972.

Emerson, Ralph Waldo. *Selected Writings* (William H. Gilman, ed.). New York: New American Library, 1965.

Empson, William. *Some Versions of Pastoral.* London: Chatto & Windus, 1935.

Engels, Friedrich. *The Condition of the Working Class in England* (W.O. Henderson and W.H. Chaloner, tr.). Stanford: Stanford University Press, 1968.

Forster, E.M. *The Eternal Moment.* New York: Harcourt Brace Jovanovich, 1928.

Freud, Sigmund. *The Interpretation of Dreams* (A.A. Brill, tr.). New York: Random House, 1950.

Fussell, Paul. *The Great War and Modern Memory.* New York: Oxford University Press, 1975.

Gaskell, Elizabeth. *North and South.* Harmondsworth: Penguin Books, 1970.

GEDDES, PATRICK and J. ARTHUR THOMSON. *Evolution*. New York: Henry Holt & Company, 1912.

GISSING, GEORGE. *Demos: A Story of English Socialism*. Brighton: The Harvester Press, 1972.

GISSING, GEORGE. *The Nether World*. Brighton: The Harvester Press, 1974.

GOULD, STEPHEN JAY. *Ever Since Darwin*. New York: W.W. Norton & Company, 1977.

GREENE, GRAHAM. *Collected Stories*. New York: The Viking Press, 1973.

GREENE, GRAHAM. *The End of the Affair*. New York: The Viking Press, 1951.

GREENE, GRAHAM. *The Ministry of Fear*. New York: The Viking Press, 1943.

GREENE, GRAHAM. *The Power and the Glory*. New York: The Viking Press, 1940.

GREENE, GRAHAM. *The Quiet American*. New York: The Viking Press, 1956.

GREENE, GRAHAM. *A Sort of Life*. New York: Simon & Schuster, 1971.

GREENE, GRAHAM. *The Third Man*. New York: The Viking Press, 1950.

GREENE, GRAHAM. *Ways of Escape*. New York: Simon & Schuster, 1981.

GREENE, MOTT. *Geology in the Nineteenth Century*. Ithaca: Cornell University Press, 1982.

GUNN, THOM. "My Life Up To Now," in *The Occasions of Poetry*. London: Faber & Faber, 1982.

GUNN, THOM. *Selected Poems*. New York: Farrar, Straus & Giroux, 1979.

HAWKES, JACQUETTA (ed.). *The World of the Past, Volume 2*. New York: Touchstone (Alfred A. Knopf/Simon & Schuster), 1963.

HILLMAN, JAMES. *The Dream and the Underworld*. New York: Harper & Row, 1979.

Indiana Jones and the Temple of Doom, a film directed by Steven Spielberg, 1984.

JAMES, HENRY. *The Princess Casamassima*. New York: Thomas Y. Crowell Company (Apollo Edition), 1976.

JAMES, HENRY. *Letters, Volume IV, 1895–1916* (Leon Edel, ed.). Cambridge: Harvard University Press, 1984.

JARRELL, RANDALL. *Selected Letters* (Mary Jarrell, ed.). Boston: Houghton Mifflin, 1985.

JARRELL, RANDALL. "An Unread Book," in *The Third Book of Criticism*. New York: Farrar, Straus & Giroux, 1969.

KAFKA, FRANZ. *The Complete Stories* (Nahum M. Glatzer, ed.). New York: Schocken Books, 1972.

LAWRENCE, D.H. "Edgar Allan Poe," in *Studies in Classic American Literature*. New York: The Viking Press, 1964.

LE CARRÉ, JOHN. *The Naive and Sentimental Lover*. London: Pan Books, 1972.

LE CARRÉ, JOHN. *Smiley's People*. New York: Alfred A. Knopf, 1980.

LEWIS, CLIVE STAPLES. *The Magician's Nephew*. New York: The Macmillan Company, 1955.

LEWIS, CLIVE STAPLES. *The Silver Chair*. New York: The Macmillan Company, 1953.

LONDON, JACK. *The People of the Abyss*. Oakland: Star Rover House, 1982.

LUCRETIUS. *On the Nature of the Universe* (Ronald E. Lathan, tr.). Harmondsworth: Penguin Books, 1951.

MACAULAY, DAVID. *Underground*. Boston: Houghton Mifflin, 1976.

MACDONALD, GEORGE. *The Princess and the Goblin*. Harmondsworth: Penguin Books (Puffin edition), 1964.

MACDONALD, ROSS. *The Blue Hammer*. New York: Alfred A. Knopf, 1976.

MCBAIN, ED. *Killer's Choice*. New York: Random House, 1958.

MELVILLE, HERMAN. *Great Short Works* (Warner Berthoff, ed.). New York: Harper & Row, 1969.

MILLAR, KENNETH (aka ROSS MACDONALD). *The Dark Tunnel*. New York: Dodd, Mead, 1944.

MUMFORD, LEWIS. *The City in History*. New York: Harcourt Brace & World, 1961.

MURDOCH, IRIS. *A Word Child*. New York: The Viking Press, 1975.

MURRAY, LES. Interview in *American Poetry Review*, March/April 1986.

ORWELL, GEORGE. *A Collection of Essays*. New York: Harcourt Brace, 1946.

ORWELL, GEORGE. *The Road to Wigan Pier*. Harmondsworth: Penguin Books, 1962.

OVID. *The Metamorphoses* (A.E. Watts, tr.). San Francisco: North Point Press, 1980.

OWEN, DAVID. *The Government of Victorian London, 1855–1889*. Cambridge: Harvard University Press, 1982.

POE, EDGAR ALLAN. *Great Short Works* (G.R. Thompson, ed.). New York: Harper & Row, 1970.

POE, EDGAR ALLAN. *The Narrative of Arthur Gordon Pym*. New York: Hill and Wang, 1960.

POUND, EZRA. *Selected Poems*. New York: New Directions, 1957.

PROUST, MARCEL. *Remembrance of Things Past* (C.K. Scott Moncrieff and T. Kilmartin, trs.). New York: Random House, 1981.

RATHBONE, JULIAN. *A Spy of the Old School*. New York: Pantheon Books, 1982.

RILKE, RAINER MARIA. *The Selected Poetry* (Stephen Mitchell, tr.). New York: Random House, 1982.

RILKE, RAINER MARIA. *New Poems [1907]* (Edward Snow, tr.). San Francisco: North Point Press, 1984.

SACKS, OLIVER. *Awakenings*. London: Gerald Duckworth & Company, 1973. (Revised edition, New York: Dutton, 1983.)

SACKS, OLIVER. *A Leg To Stand On*. New York: Summit Books, 1984.

SENDAK, MAURICE. *In the Night Kitchen*. New York: Harper & Row, 1970.

"Sewer Cave Dwellers Move to a Hotel," in the *San Francisco Chronicle*, December 19, 1986.

SILVERBERG, ROBERT. *Lost Cities and Vanished Civilizations*. New York: Bantam Books, 1963.

SIMPSON, GEORGE GAYLORD. *The Meaning of Evolution*. New Haven: Yale University Press, 1967.

SJÖWALL, MAJ and PER WAHLÖÖ. *The Laughing Policeman*. New York: Random House, 1970.

SJÖWALL, MAJ and PER WAHLÖÖ. *The Terrorists*. New York: Random House, 1976.

SJÖWALL, MAJ and PER WAHLÖÖ. *The Locked Room*. New York: Random House, 1973.

SKENAZY, PAUL. "Bringing It All Back Home: Ross Macdonald's Lost Father," in *The Threepenny Review 12* (Winter 1983).

SONTAG, SUSAN. "The Aesthetics of Silence," in *Styles of Radical Will*. New York: Farrar, Straus & Giroux, 1969.

SWIFT, GRAHAM. *Shuttlecock*. Harmondsworth: Penguin Books, 1982.

The Third Man, a film directed by Carol Reed, 1949.

TWAIN, MARK (aka SAMUEL CLEMENS). *The Adventures of Tom Sawyer*. Berkeley: University of California Press, 1982.

VAN DE WETERING, JANWILLEM. *The Mind Murders*. New York: Ballantine Books, 1983.

VERNE, JULES. *Journey to the Center of the Earth* (Robert Baldick, tr.). Harmondsworth: Penguin Books, 1965.

VIRGIL. *The Aeneid* (C. Day Lewis, tr.). New York: Doubleday, 1953.

WELLS, H.G. *Three Prophetic Science Fiction Novels*. New York: Dover Publications, 1960.

WHEELER, MORTIMER. *Archaeology From the Earth*. Baltimore: Penguin Books, 1954.

WILSON, EDMUND. "The Boys in the Back Room," in *Classics and Commercials*. New York: Farrar, Straus & Giroux, 1950.

WOOLLEY, SIR LEONARD. "Digging Up the Past." In *Archaeology* (Samuel Rapport and Helen Wright, eds.). New York: Washington Square Press, 1963.

WRIGHT, RICHARD. *The Man Who Lived Underground*. In *Eleven Modern Short Novels* (Leo Hamalian and Edmond L. Volpe, eds.). New York: G.P. Putnam's Sons, 1970.